*A*dventure Guide

St. Lucia

Lynne M. Sullivan

HUNTER

HUNTER PUBLISHING, INC.
130 Campus Drive, Edison, NJ 08818-7816
☎ *732-225-1900 / 800-255-0343 / fax 732-417-1744*
www.hunterpublishing.com
E-mail comments@hunterpublishing.com

IN CANADA:
Ulysses Travel Publications
4176 Saint-Denis, Montréal, Québec, Canada H2W 2M5
☎ *514-843-9882 ext. 2232 / fax 514-843-9448*

IN THE UNITED KINGDOM:
Windsor Books International
5, Castle End Park, Castle End Rd, Ruscombe
Berkshire, RG10 9XQ England, ☎ *01189-346-367/fax 01189-346-368*

ISBN 978-1-58843-644-3

© 2007 Hunter Publishing, Inc.

Cover photo: © mediacolor's/Alamy

Maps © 2007 Hunter Publishing, Inc.

For complete information about the hundreds of other travel guides offered by Hunter Publishing, visit us at www.hunterpublishing.com.

Most of our guides are also available in digital form as e-books through NetLibrary.com, ebrary.com, Ebooks.com, Overdrive.com and other partners. For more information, e-mail comments@ hunterpublishing.com.

4   3   2   1

Contents

Adventures

Introduction

You've made a wonderful vacation choice. St. Lucia is one of the most beautiful and diverse islands in the Caribbean.

Picturesque fishing villages bump up against golden-sand beaches. Towering mountains loom over sprawling banana plantations in deep green valleys. The island's twin peaks, the **Pitons**, soar majestically out of clear turquoise waters that cover coral reefs teeming with tropical fish. World-class resorts, small inns, and private villas hide behind flowering shrubs tucked into rolling green hills.

Tourism is welcome and on the rise, but officials hold a tight reign on galloping growth and prohibit the uncontrolled development that has ripped through neighboring islands.

Much of the countryside is still untouched, natural resources are protected and the island moves at a relaxed pace.

As one of the larger Windward Islands of the Lesser Antilles, 238-square-mile pear-shaped St. Lucia measures 27 miles end-to-end and 14 miles across at its widest section. Its nearest neighbors include Martinique (to the north), St. Vincent (to the southwest), and Barbados (to the southeast).

A third of the 160,000 residents live in or near the capital city, **Castries**, on the north end of the island. Ninety percent trace their ancestors back to Africa, and the same percentage claims to practice the Roman Catholic religion.

Life on St. Lucia is low-key and informal, which is one of the biggest attractions for visitors. With few exceptions, locals are friendly, helpful and happy to include you in whatever's going on. Friday nights are for partying, and you'll be welcome at the "jump up" street party in **Gros Islet** or the similar "fish fry" in **Anse la Raye**.

Duty-free shopping is better on St. Thomas or St. Martin, but you'll find plenty of attractive buys at wharf-side malls, including unique works by local artists and craftsmen. The public market in Castries is especially lively on Saturdays. This colorful 100-year-old marketplace offers produce, fresh fish, West Indies spices and locally-made pepper sauces. Nearby, the craft market sells baskets, straw hats, wood carvings and pottery.

The Windward Islands. From bottom, Grenada, St. Vincent (Barbados to the east), St. Lucia, Martinique, Dominica, Guadeloupe

If you're a nature lover, scuba diver, hiker or off-road biker, St. Lucia offers spectacular adventures. Emerald green mountains will lure you onto trails that lead through lush forest to waterfalls and warm mineral springs. Soft beaches will beckon you with the promise of sheltered close-in reefs teeming with sea creatures.

Two distinct island chains run through the eastern Caribbean Sea. The Greater Antilles extend west-to-east just south of the Bahamas from Cuba to the Virgin Islands. The Lesser Antilles run north-to-south from the Virgins to Grenada, which sits just north of the Netherlands Antilles (Aruba, Bonaire, and Curacao) and Trinidad – off the coast of South America.

Top 10 Adventures

The Pitons

- Seeing, for the first time, the majestic 2,000-foot-tall twin peaks of the **Pitons** soaring dramatically out of the sea on the island's southwest side.
- Strolling along wide sandy beaches, washed by the gentle Caribbean Sea on the west coast and battered by the wild Atlantic Ocean along the eastern shore.
- Hiking the trails through **Pigeon Island National Park** to the historic hilltop ruins of **Fort Rodney**.
- Exploring the 19,000-acre **National Forest Reserve**, with its colorful orchids growing wild beside cascading waterfalls.

- Investigating the collapsed crater called **Mount Soufrière**, a dormant "drive-in volcano," where water seeps from the ground at a hotter-than-boiling 340°F.
- Taking a dip in the natural springs near the Soufrière volcano, which are high in iron oxide and reported to heal skin problems, arthritis, gout and sunburn.
- Biking **Tinker's Trail** on forested land of the former Mamin Plantation, which is named after world-champion biker Tinker Juarez.
- Enjoying the restaurants and nightlife at **Rodney Bay**, an 83-acre man-made harbor, the largest and best-equipped marina south of St. Thomas.
- Snorkeling or diving the coral gardens that shelter a throng of fish in the protected **Marine Reserve**.
- Trekking up (or gazing up at) **Mt. Gimie**, the island's highest point at 3,117 feet.

Map Key

1. Pigeon Island National Historic Park, Fort Rodney
   HOTELS: Le Sport, Club St. Lucia by Splash, Sandals Grande
   RESTAURANTS: The Great House, Jambe de Bois
2. See detailed Rodney Bay Village map
3. Choc Bay (Labrellotte Bay to Castries)
   HOTELS: Windjammer Landing & Villas, Rendezvous,
   Sandals Halcyon, Almond Morgan Bay, Ladera Resort
4. George F.L. Charles Airport;
   See detailed Castries Town map
5. Morne Fortuné & Marigot Bay Area
   HOTELS: Discovery, Marigot Beach Club, Oasis Marigot
   RESTAURANTS: Doolittle's, JJ's Paradise, Café Paradis, Rainforest Hideaway,
   The Shack, Chateau My'go
6. Sandals Regency (South of Marigot Bay)
7. Ti Kaye Village (South of Marigot Bay)
8. Anse Chastanet & Canaries
   HOTELS: Anse Chastanet, Jade Mountain
   RESTAURANTS: Trou au Diable, Piton, Treehouse
9. Soufrière Area
   HOTELS: Stonefield Estate Villa, Still Beach Resort
   RESTAURANTS: Camilla's, La Haut Plantation, Lifeline, Dasheene
10. Morne Coubaril Estate, La Dauphine
11. Petit Piton Area inland: Diamond Falls, Botanical Gardens
    HOTELS: Hummingbird Beach Resort, Ladera Resort
    RESTAURANTS: Lifeline, Dasheene
12. Anse des Pitons coastal: Jalousie Plantation
13. Fond St. Jacques, Sulfur Springs, Drive-in Volcano
    The Still Plantation & Restaurant
14. Fond Doux
15. Art & Craft Cooperative
16. Vieux Fort, Hewanorra International Airport, Anse des Sables, Maria Islands,
    HOTELS: Coconut Bay, Juliett's Lodge
17. Mamiku Gardens, Fox Grove Inn
18. Frégate Island Nature Reserve

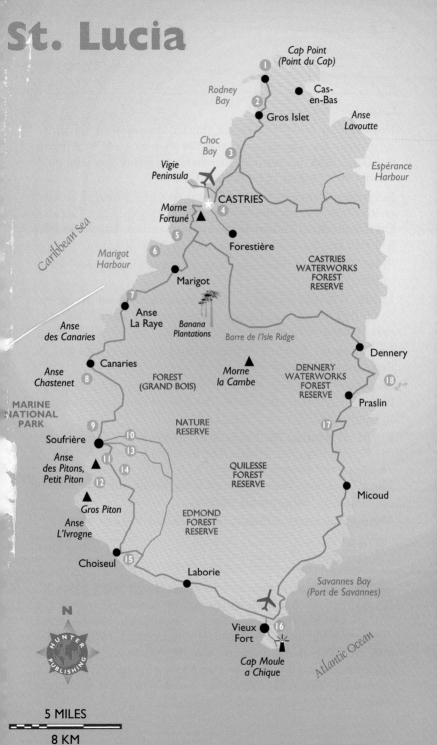

St. Lucia

Cap Point
(Point du Cap)

(1)

Rodney
Bay

(2)

Cas-
en-Bas

Gros Islet

Anse
Lavoutte

Choc
Bay

(3)

Espérance
Harbour

Vigie
Peninsula

CASTRIES

(4)

Morne
Fortuné

(5)

Forestière

Caribbean Sea

Marigot
Harbour

(6)

CASTRIES
WATERWORKS
FOREST
RESERVE

(7)

Marigot

Anse
La Raye

Banana
Plantations

Barre de l'Isle Ridge

Anse
des Canaries

Canaries

FOREST
(GRAND BOIS)

Morne
la Cambe

DENNERY
WATERWORKS
FOREST
RESERVE

Dennery

(8)

Anse
Chastenet

(18)

Praslin

MARINE
NATIONAL
PARK

(9)

Soufrière

(10)

NATURE
RESERVE

(17)

(11)

(13)

Anse
des Pitons,
Petit Piton

(14)

QUILESSE
FOREST
RESERVE

(12)

Micoud

Gros Piton

Anse
L'Ivrogne

EDMOND
FOREST
RESERVE

Choiseul

(15)

Laborie

Savannes Bay
(Port de Savannes)

N

Vieux
Fort

(16)

HUNTER
PUBLISHING

Cap Moule
a Chique

Atlantic Ocean

5 MILES

8 KM

© 2007 HUNTER PUBLISHING, INC.

Just the Facts

Capital: Castries.

Population: 160,000. About a third of the population resides in or near the capital city, and the majority are of African ancestry. The people call themselves Saint Lucians and almost 70% profess to be Roman Catholic.

Location: Between the Caribbean Sea and Atlantic Ocean, north of St. Vincent and south of Martinique in the Eastern Caribbean chain known as the Lesser Antilles. The geographical coordinates are approximately 13 N, 60 W.

Size: 238 square miles, about three times larger than Washington, DC.

Land: Volcanic in origin, with mountains reaching up to 3,000 feet, dense rainforests, fertile valleys, sandy beaches, and mineral-rich springs.

Languages: English (official) and Creole (Kréwyòl), a French-based patois

Weather: Average year-round daytime temperatures range from 23°C/75°F to 29°C/85°F. The driest months are January through April.

Political Status: St. Lucia is an independent state within the British Commonwealth. The monarchy is represented by an appointed governor general, who is official chief of state. The official head of government is the prime minister, who is appointed by the governor general.

Money: Eastern Caribbean dollar, EC$. US$1=EC$2.67.

A Brief History

The first people to live on St. Lucia were peaceful, artistic **Arawak Indians**, who populated most of the Caribbean Islands. They arrived around 200 AD and supported themselves by hunting, fishing and farming. About 800 AD, the more militant **Caribs** made an aggressive appearance, conquered the Arawaks, set up villages, and named the island **Hewanorra**, "Land Where the Iguana Is Found."

Discovery

 Many historians believe the island was first sighted by Europeans when Juan de la Cosa, one of Christopher Columbus's navigators, spotted land here in 1499. Others allege that Christopher Columbus himself landed on St. Lucia on December 13, 1502. Records show that the island is not within the routes known to have been explored by Columbus, and some scholars credit Spanish explorers with *discovering* the island later in the 16th century. For years, St. Lucians celebrated *Discovery Day* each year on December 13. However, the day has recently been renamed **National Day**.

French, Dutch & English Influences

By 1520, St. Lucia was marked on a Vatican globe, but at that time it was merely a hideout for pirates and other bad chaps who wreaked havoc on legitimate businessmen trading in the islands. The most infamous was **François Le Clerc**, whom the Spanish called *Pie de Palo* and the French *Jambe de Bois* (leg of wood) because of his prosthetic limb.

Old Peg-Leg Le Clerc and his cohorts were joined on the island in 1600 when the Dutch military arrived and built a bastion at **Vieux Fort** on the far southern tip. Europeans didn't try to actually colonize St. Lucia until a few years later, and even that was an accident. In 1605 a British ship called *Olive Blossom*, under the command of Captain Nicholas St. John, blew off course, and her 67 passengers came ashore to seek refuge. For some reason, the Caribs sold a parcel of land and a few huts to the English refugees, allowed them time to settle in. Then they turned inhospitable. Most of the new colonists were killed by their Indian hosts, and the rest were forced off the island in makeshift boats.

A larger British group, under the commission of Captain Judlee, came over from St. Kitts in 1638, but the 300 settlers didn't fare much better. All were killed or driven off St. Lucia within two years. Understandably, the English hesitated to attempt colonization again for more than 20 years.

Castries

In 1651, a group came over from the nearby island of Martinique, led by a Frenchmen named Rousselan. Aware of the trouble the English had experienced, they quickly constructed a fort on what is now known as the **Vigie Peninsula**, armed it with cannons, and surrounded it with a moat. To further guarantee their safety, Rousselan married a Carib woman.

This diplomacy worked well and French settlers spread south from the peninsula to a site across the natural harbor that they first called Petit Cul de Sac and later renamed **Castries**, in honor of an important French navy officer, Marquis de Castries. When Rousselan died in 1654, the Indians ended their unofficial peace treaty by killing the next three French governors of the island.

Learning of the renewed turmoil on St. Lucia, the British decided to try again to seize control. Battles between the French and English raged over the next 100 years, with the island's administration changing hands 14 times. During this period, most of the Caribs were killed or exiled. Finally, in 1763, the Treaty of Paris bestowed ownership on France.

With the indigenous people out of the way, St. Lucia settled into a stable, multi-cultural democracy, and colonists began to build roads and set up plantations. Soon, they were exporting sugar, cocoa, coffee, and spices to Europe. Warehouses sprung up along the wharf in Castries, and shops and homes were built along roads radiating inland from the bay.

Peace and prosperity were short-lived, and the English and French were battling again by 1778. This time, the English won control of the island through agreements outlined in the 1814 **Treaty of Paris**. However, language, religious preference, place names, and cultural traditions remained decidedly French for the first half of the 19th century. Even today, the citizens of this English island speak a French-based patois that flows like thick honey from the back of the throat, and they live in villages named Soufrière, Vieux Fort, and Gros Islet.

African Influences

St. Lucians today

A third culture also played a significant role in the island's character. That of Africa. Europeans brought African slaves onto the island by the boatload to work their plantations. While French and English customs were mingling in one segment of society, African traditions established a stronghold in another. Descendants of former slaves constitute the largest percentage of the island's present population, and their proud heritage has survived to become the basis of St. Lucian culture today.

When slavery ended in 1834, plantation owners brought East Indians to the island as indentured servants. Their numbers were small compared to other nationalities, and their culture has almost disappeared. However, a significant East Indian community still lives in the area around Vieux Fort, and their foods and cooking methods are a popular addition to the island's cuisine.

MOVING TOWARD EMANCIPATION

An 18th-century slave ship

■ In the early 1700s, African rulers set up trading posts on the west coast of Africa to exchange slaves for European goods. Individual tribes were forbidden from dealing directly with Europeans, and the trading posts collected their human cargo from groups of criminals, prisoners of tribal wars and kidnap victims.

■ Slaves transported from Africa to the West Indies often died during the crossing due to overcrowding, starvation and disease.

■ Elite plantation owners got first pick of newly arrived slaves. Those that remained were sold at auction.

■ On St. Lucia, the governor encouraged fair treatment of slaves, because it was to the owners' advantage to keep workers healthy so that they could work longer and harder. Priests preached the advantages and humanity of educating slaves.

■ In 1786, the "Code Noir" mandated that daily working hours be reduced to 12 and allowed no more than 50 lashes as punishment for misbehavior.

■ A famine in 1777 caused uprising among the slaves and escapees (maroons) hid in the interior forests on St. Lucia.

■ By 1789, slaves had grown bolder, and it was reported that they freely roamed the towns and countryside bearing arms and discussing their rights.

Slave ship cargo

■ The French-decreed abolition of slavery in 1794 was meant to gain support of the slaves in ousting the British from French territories in the Caribbean.

■ Brigands, as the freed slaves were called, fought fiercely when the British retook St. Lucia in 1796. Finally, the former slaves agreed to form the British West Indies Regiment and return to west Africa to defend the British in return for retaining their freedom. Blacks who remained on St. Lucia were returned to their masters as slaves.

■ In 1834, an apprentice system was introduced on the island, and children under six received free status. Field workers apprenticed for six years. House workers apprenticed for four years. The apprentices were paid for a fourth of their working hours and could buy their freedom as soon as they had sufficient money.

■ On August 1, 1838, slavery was forever abolished and declared unlawful throughout the British Colonies, plantations and possessions abroad.

Introduction

The Government Today

Since February 22, 1979, St. Lucia has been an independent state within the **British Commonwealth**. Currently, Queen Elizabeth II, as head of state, designates a resident governor-general to head the island's democratic government, foster national unity, and promote national economic, cultural, and social interests. At press time, the queen's representative is **Her Excellency Dame Pearlette Louisy**, and the elected prime minister is **Sir John Compton**. Seventeen members of the **House of Assembly** are elected for five-year terms, and 11 members of the **Senate** are appointed.

Land & Sea

St. Lucia is a volcanic island with steep mountains, deep river gorges, lush forests, tumbling waterfalls, and an astonishingly beautiful coastline. Natural resources are treasured and government officials recognize the value of promoting responsible tourism and conscientious development. Thus, tropical vegetation still covers much of the island, and spectacular underwater reefs are protected by environmental laws.

Except for the area around the capital city of Castries, St. Lucia is predominantly rural, and much of its rainforest has been preserved or restored. Developers have built exclusive resorts on small patches of prime land, and many more would like the opportunity to claim a prize piece of paradise. Nevertheless, conservation groups are doing a fine job of curtailing the rampant over development that has plagued some of their Caribbean neighbors.

DID YOU KNOW?

St. Lucia's highest point is 3,118-foot (950-m) **Mount Gimie**, but its most famous landmark is a pair of pyramid-shaped volcanic mountains called the **Pitons**. From a distance, they appear to sit side-by-side, but they're actually on opposite sides of a bay and linked by the **Piton Mitan Ridge**. **Gros Piton** is 2,619 feet (798 m) high; **Petit Piton** stretches to 2,461 feet (750 m).

In 2004, the Pitons were declared a **UNESCO World Heritage Site**, which includes a geothermal field with hot springs. More than half of the adjacent marine reserve is covered by coral reefs that are home to 168 species of fish. Hawksbill turtles come ashore, while pilot whales and whale sharks are regularly spotted offshore.

Climate

 As is typical of all the Caribbean, St. Lucia enjoys a year-round average temperature of 77°F. Daytime highs occasionally reach 90°F, and nighttime lows sporadically dip to 55°F, but thermometer readings usually range from 65°F to 85°F in non-mountainous areas. The surrounding waters, on both the Atlantic and Caribbean sides, maintain an average temperature of 80°F throughout the year.

Rainfall varies more dramatically. The driest months fall between mid-December and the end of March, and the rainy season runs from late May through November. Traditionally, the dry winter months are considered "high tourist season," but you should expect brief warm rainfall at any time in the tropics, especially at higher elevations. During the summer "off season," you can depend on frequent showers followed by long stretches of sunshine, with the resulting humidity tempered by northeasterly trade winds.

Don't be concerned when you see that the forecast calls, even during the dry season, for clouds and rain. The clouds are most likely the white fluffy type that move quickly across the sky and add to the beauty of the day. When rain does fall, it is usually for brief periods. This doesn't hold true for higher elevations in the rain forest, where a fine mist is expected most of the time, and light to heavy showers occur frequently.

At sea level, rain comes in short bursts during most of the year. But, if a tropical wave is passing through during hurricane season, low dark clouds can linger for days and rain falls in sheets for hours. The worst months for heavy rain are usually October, November and early December.

Hurricanes are always a possibility in the Atlantic and Caribbean during summer and early fall, but the odds of any one island suffering a serious hit in any given year are quite low. The advice from here is be informed, be prepared, and go anyway.

Several agencies maintain websites that make it easy to track tropical storms as they develop, including the National Weather Service's Tropical Prediction Center on the campus of Florida State University in Miami (www.nhc.noaa.gov) and The Caribbean Hurricane Network, which posts reports from correspondents living on the islands (www.stormcarib.com). Other reliable links are The Weather Channel (www.weather.com) and Intellicast (www.intellicast.com). If you plan to be boating, check the forecast frequently at The Caribbean Weather Station (www.caribwx.com).

Growing Wild

A wide assortment of tropical plants and trees flourish on St. Lucia due to dependable rainfall and fertile soil. Scrub vegetation along the coast gives way to dense forests harboring hundreds of species of ferns and flowering plants on inland mountainsides. At least 148 plant species have been recorded on the Pitons, including eight rare types of trees.

Ixora

Seagrape trees grow wild along sandy beaches. Some get as tall as 30 feet, and the female bares clusters of fruit that turn purple when they ripen. These "grapes" are edible, but most people prefer them sweetened in jams or desserts. Coconut palms also are common on the beaches, and they can grow in sandy areas where few other plant survive. Islanders drink the liquid from the shell before eating the soft meat inside.

The national plant of Saint Lucia is the strong-smelling pink cabbage rose. The national tree is the calabash.

Orchids, African tulip trees, ferns, hibiscus and bird-of-paradise are cultivated in gardens and grow wild throughout the island. Even drier land supports colorful bushes such as oleanders, and a variety of fruit trees grow along the roadways. Much of the local diet is based on the abundant supply of mangos, bananas, papayas, soursops, passionfruit, guavas and coconuts.

Huge gommier and chatagnier trees are the tallest and most impressive in the rainforests.

Pink cabbage rose

They tower over a tangle of vines, ferns, mosses, and more than 300 other types of trees. Drier areas support cactus and cedars. Throughout the island, gorgeous flamboyant trees (poinciana) put out a blast of red flowers every summer, and African tulip trees turn orange with blossoms each spring.

Calabash

THE MANCHINEEL TREE

This is one of the most poisonous trees in the world, and illness or death can result from eating the fruit. The name is from the Spanish word "manzanilla," which means "little apple," because its fruit is similar to that of an apple tree. The trees typically grow along the coast, and today most are identified by warning signs or a line of red paint on the trunk. The sap and small fruit of this tree are poisonous and cause intense stinging if they come in contact with the skin. Historians say the Caribs tied their captured enemies to these trees as a form of torture. They also used the sap and leaves to poison their darts and the enemy's water supply.

A large part of St. Lucia's economy depends on the exportation of bananas. While the industry has dropped behind tourism in importance, the recent worldwide interest in Fairtrade allows the island farmers to continue production with confidence. (Fairtrade is an international movement that promotes just labor laws and equitable prices for goods produced in developing countries for exportation to developed countries.) Some chain supermarkets, including Sainsbury in England, have converted entirely to Fairtrade, which guarantees producers a stable price to cover the full costs of production plus an extra US$1 per box of fruit, which is known as the Fairtrade premium. Also, during the past few years, organic production methods have increased interest and demand for bananas grown on St. Lucia.

Plantain

What this means to you, the tourist, is pleasant views of verdant banana tree fields and abundant delicious fruit whenever you need a snack. In addition, it gives employment to the locals, so they have less time and less need to bother you for a handout as you walk along the beach or stroll through town.

The large plantain banana is often peeled, sliced, fried and served as a side-dish in many St. Lucian restaurants. A smaller Malayan banana, the type normally seen in supermarkets throughout the US and Europe, is exported, but also sold in stores and by street vendors all over the island. You also may see red bananas, which are more rare and not exported. Only a few farmers grow the reds, but you may be able to buy some of the sweet fruit at a local market.

Red banana

Flying Free

You don't have to be a bird-watcher to get caught up by the vast number and variety of species that live on or migrate through the northern Windwards. They land on your table when you eat outdoors, tease you while you try to nap on the beach, and steal small items off your patio when you're not looking. The Pitons are home to at least 27 bird species, including five indigenous breeds.

The following will help you identify a few of the most common winged creatures:

- The **brown pelican** is grayish-brown with a long neck, long beak, and short legs – usually seen feeding along the shore.

■ The **magnificent frigate bird** (magnificent is part of its name) has a majestic wingspan that can reach more than six feet. All of them are jet-black, and the males have red throats, while the females have white throats. They are pirates and hunt everywhere on the island.

■ The small **green-backed heron** has a distinctive call and gray-green feathers. The **great heron** has long legs and a long black feather growing from its white head.

Magnificent frigate bird

■ The **snowy egret** is white with black legs, while the **cattle egret** (usually sitting on a cow) has white plumage and a tuft of orange feathers on its head.

Bananaquit

■ The **kingfisher** is blue with a white breast and a ruffled tuft on its head. It floats in the air looking for food, and dives into the surf to catch fish.

■ The **bananaquit** is a little bird with dark feathers on its back and a bright yellow throat and breast. It loves sugar and will make itself at home on your outdoor table.

■ **Broad-winged hawks** are frequently seen soaring in wooded areas.

■ Various species of **hummingbirds**, especially the purple-throated carib, green-throated carib, and the Antillean crested, are often seen feeding among flowers.

Antillean crested hummingbird

The **purple-throated carib** is one of the most beautiful hummingbirds. Both males and females are mostly black in color with emerald-green wings and an iridescent rosy-red patch on their throats. You probably won't see them land, but you can catch sight of their green flash as they speed through flowering foliage.

Native **parrots** nest high in the rainforest, and all species are rare and endangered. You probably won't see a parrot unless you hike with a guide who is experienced in spotting them. The **jacquot** is St. Lucia's national bird, and experts estimate that about 800 of them live on the island. If you don't run into one of them, visit the three that live at the mini-zoo run by the Forestry Department. Jerry was born on St. Lucia and brought to the zoo in 1997. His buddies, Lucy and Oswald, aren't native, but have lived at the zoo for almost 20 years.

The zoo is adjacent to the Union Nature Trail, on the road to Babonneau, inland from Rodney Bay. It's open Monday through Friday 8:30 am until 4 pm. ☎ 758-450-2231.

The **St. Lucian jacquot** is mostly geen in color, with cobalt blue forehead feathers that become turquoise to emerald green on the cheeks before turning red on the breast. The birds fly along the tops of trees in the forest and feed on fruit, nuts and berries. Females lay two or three eggs in the hollow of trees between March and June. A parrot is not fully mature until it is five years old.

Scuttling Among Us

Wildlife on St. Lucia is rather limited. The good news is, there's not much around to bite, sting, or attack you. The bad news is, there's not much around. Other than rats and mice – which you probably don't care to see – wild mammals are limited to opossums, mongooses (a ferret-like animal) and an occasional agouti (a rodent that looks somewhat like a rabbit).

Crapaud

Reptiles are more common, and you will have no trouble finding frogs and toads. The most interesting is the **tree frog**, which is tiny but puts on a loud symphony at night. You might run into a giant, squatty frog known as a **crapaud** who likes to hang out in forests and is hunted for its meaty legs.

*If you order **mountain chicken** in a restaurant, you'll be eating crapaud legs, which are considered a delicacy. Forget what it is and order it Creole-style. Delicious.*

Common geckos – small, plain lizards – scurry everywhere, along walkways, through window sills, and up walls (and usually run under something when you turn a light on at night). Be nice to them. They eat lots of mosquitoes. Native Carib Indians thought they carried evil spirits and spread rumors that they could only be removed from a person's skin with a scalding iron.

Pygmy geckos are just two inches long and found only on St. Lucia. Their color can change to various shades of brown to match their surroundings. **House geckos** hide in dark crevices until nightfall, when they scurry throughout dwellings. They grow to be five inches long, mostly tail. **Tree geckos** grow to about six inches long. They have an elongated body, stubby tail, and can change color to blend with the foliage.

Iguanas look scary with their spiny backs, but they are strict vegetarians and don't care to share space with humans. These large lizards are rare and becoming rarer, so you'll only see them in a few remote areas. The **green iguana** grows up to six feet long, with almost half of the length invested in a whip-like tail.

Green iguana

They are on the endangered species list of St. Lucia and you find them mainly along the remote northeast coast. Look for them in trees, where they live, and on the ground, where they search for food. If you don't run into one in the wild, the St. Lucia Forestry Department has a mini-zoo that houses five of the creatures. It's adjacent to the Union Nature Trail, on the road to Babonneau, inland from Rodney Bay, and open Monday through Friday, 8:30 am until 4 pm. ☎ 758-450-2231.

Female iguanas lay up to 17 eggs per season. The nests are on the ground, and eggs hatch after 14 days.

The island does have **snakes**, but not as many as you would expect, and most are harmless. Even the **boa constrictors** are non-venomous and shy away from people. However, the **fer de lance** snake that lives

Fer de lance

on St. Lucia is poisonous and extremely dangerous. You're not likely to run into this snake unless you're in tall brush along river beds, but take extra precautions when you hike, especially if you go off heavily-used trails.

Caution: Check with locals about recent snake sightings before you head into an unfamiliar area without a guide.

Sea Creatures

A variety of marine life lives in the clear waters surrounding St. Lucia. Shallow reefs have an amazing medley of colorful corals, sponges and tropical fish, and islanders are committed to preserving their stunning beauty. The marine park at Anse Chastanet has some of the best snorkeling in the Caribbean because of the abundant angel and parrot fish, turtles, nurse sharks, seahorses, and spotted eels living near the shore. Certified divers can see even more by exploring deeper waters where many wrecks and caves shelter huge barracudas, groupers, rays and squids.

Before you head into the water, visit the following websites to view pictures and get information about the species you're most likely to see:

- ■ **Reef Environmental Education Foundation** (REEF), www.reef.org (click "Fish Gallery and Quizzes", then "Caribbean/Florida/Bahamas").

■ **New World Publications**, **Marine Life Learning Center**, www.fishid.com.

Island Culture

Most of the residents of St. Lucia trace their ancestry back to African slaves, who were brought to the island to work on plantations. Today, islanders are free citizens of an independent nation within the British Commonwealth.

Census records show that the population of St. Lucia is just under 170,000, with approximately 67,000 living in the vicinity of Castries, the capital. These figures are more meaningful when you consider that St. Lucia, with 238 square miles, is about three times the size of Washington, DC, where the population is 572,000.

Language

 Officially, English is the language of St. Lucia. However, locals prefer a hybrid patois known to scholars as **Lesser Antillean Créole French** and to residents as Creole or Kwéyòl. It's a musical dialect, and you may be able to pick out a few recognizable French, English, and Spanish words. Don't expect to understand conversations between islanders, but you won't have any trouble communicating, since most people quickly switch to lilting British-accented English when they speak with tourists.

English is taught in schools, and the literacy rate is high and growing. Créole is the most used language, not only on the streets, but also on local radio and television programs. Don't confuse this hybrid with street slang. According to erudite publications, such as *Ethnologue, Languages of the World*, edited by Barbara F. Grimes, Kwéyòl has an established orthography (spelling) and grammar, and is used in literary works, newspapers, and by well-educated professionals during business transactions.

You don't need to know a word of Kwéyòl to blend in with locals, but if you want to give it a try, these useful phrases are easy to remember:

Thank you . . . . `Mesi.

No thank you . . . . Non mesi

Have a good day . . . . Bonn jounnen

Good day, Sir . . . . Bon jou, Misyéé

Good afternoon . . . . Bon apwee midi

Good night . . . . Bon swéé

Cuisine

 West Indies and Créole dishes make good use of locally available seafood, fresh produce, and island spices. **West Indies** cooking is influenced more by Africa, while **Créole** takes its cue from France. Many food items must be imported, so restaurant meals tend to be pricey. If you're on a budget, pick up breakfast at a bakery and make a picnic lunch from supermarket purchases. Some hotels offer all-inclusive plans, but signing on to them limits your chance for excellent cuisine at local cafés. Plan to enjoy at least some of your meals at colorful island establishments.

If you're stocking your condo kitchen or provisioning your boat, go to the **Central Market** in Castries to buy an assortment of delicious, and sometimes peculiar, fresh produce. Some of the most popular with locals are red bananas, which are good for eating right out of hand, and green bananas, which are also called "figs." **Figs** (green bananas) are peeled, boiled and served as a side-dish.

Other Caribbean favorites include:

Plantains are a relative of the common banana and are eaten peeled and fried, either as a side-dish or dusted with sugar and cinnamon and enjoyed as a dessert.

Breadfruit is a starchy fruit that looks like a green ball. It is often boiled whole or cut in half and grilled, then served peeled and sliced as a side-dish. Most people prefer it cooked, mashed, seasoned and rolled into little balls, then fried like hush puppies.

Christophine is a white, ridged pear-shaped fruit that grows on vines. It can be peeled and sliced, then served raw in salads or cooked as a side-dish. It is often served mashed and topped with melted cheese.

Provisions are commonplace on Caribbean menus. They are any type of root vegetable, such as dasheens, yams, sweet potatoes or white potatoes, served as a side-dish.

Pumpkin in the Caribbean is green on the outside and yellow-orange on the inside. It's served like potatoes as a side-dish or boiled and puréed into a creamy soup.

Cocoa sticks are made from dried and roasted cocoa beans that have been grated and pressed into a stick. Locals boil them like tea, then add milk and sugar to taste.

In restaurants, look for these common dishes:

Bakes – a fried dough patty filled with fish or meat.

Cabri – small bony goat, usually smoked or used in a curry.

Callaloo – a vegetable similar to spinach, usually made into a soup of the same name.

Casabe – bread made with cassava (tapioca), dates back to the Arawaks.

Christophine – a side-dish similar to potatoes. Try it au gratin style.

Colombo – curry. In the Caribbean, it is usually a mild green type that is not as hot as Indian curry. The most common colombo is made with goat meat, but occasionally it is chicken or pork.

Conch/lambi – large shellfish whose chewy meat is served in spicy sauces.

Dasheen – a potato–like vegetable. The leaves are called callaloo.

Johnnycake – pancake-like treat made of cornmeal and cooked on a griddle.

Lambi – conch, a large shellfish.

Langouste – Caribbean lobster, no claws.

Mountain chicken – frog legs that come from the large *crapaud*.

Ouassous – big freshwater crayfish.

Oursin – sea urchin.

Pepperpot – stew made of meat and hot peppers, usually cooked over coals in a clay pot.

Provisions – root vegetables such as dasheen, yams, sweet potatoes and white potatoes. Very popular side-dish.

Roti – curried meat and/or vegetables wrapped in flat bread like a burrito.

Ti-punch – drink made of rum, sugar cane syrup, and lime.

Festivals, Events & Holidays

 The St. Lucia Event Calendar is packed with festivals and holidays, so you can count on some type of celebration taking place during your visit. If you consider yourself a party animal, make early reservations for **Carnival**, which kicks off in July. Music lovers may prefer the **Jazz Festival**, an international event that draws big crowds each May. If you don't want to hassle with a major extravaganza, but still want to dance to some good Caribbean music, just show up in the little town of **Gros Islet** on any Friday night for the weekly street party known as **Jump Up**.

Get a current schedule of upcoming events from the **St. Lucia Tourist Office**, ☎ 800-456-3984 (US), 800-869-0377 (Canada), 0171-413-3675 (UK), 758-452 7577 (St. Lucia), www.stlucia.org.

Holiday Calendar

Banks and most businesses close on the following days (expect some type of celebration):

New Year's Day, January 1

New Year's Holiday, January 2

Independence Day, February 22

Labor Day, May 1

Emancipation Day, August (first Monday)

Thanksgiving Day, October 5

National Day, December 13

Christmas Day, December 25

Boxing Day, December 26

Variable religious holidays observed by public closings:

Good Friday, late March or early April

Easter, late March or early April
Whit Monday, Eighth Monday after Easter
Corpus Christi, Ninth Thursday after Easter

Major Annual Events

Carnival

Carnival

Traditionally, the Carnival Season begins in February and leads up to Mardi Gras on the Tuesday before Ash Wednesday, but in 1999 the St. Lucian Cultural Development Foundation decided to move the island's biggest blow-out celebration to late spring or early summer, so that it wouldn't conflict with pre-Lenten festivals held on other Caribbean Islands.

St. Lucia's Carnival is the ultimate multi-day bash. Most official activities take place in and around the capital city of Castries, but warm-up parties and concerts are held all over the island. Various camps are set up for the production of costumes for the many shows and street parades, and calypso tents boom with the traditional sounds of local musicians.

Each music tent has a team of dancers who organize a series of shows leading up to the main calypso challenge. It's meant to introduce the public to current songs, and the audience is encouraged to participate by showing their approval or rejection of the performance. In recent years the event's popularity has grown along with the prize winnings. Today, the **Calypso**

Monarch walks away with a new vehicle and a generous cash prize.

Carnival also names a **Soca Monarch** each year. Soca Music originated on Trinidad in the late 1970s and has a faster rhythm than calypso, with less social and political commentary. Another prize goes to the **Road March** song, which typically features a mix of English and Creole lyrics. Bands are judged as they march through the streets and scores are tallied from six locations along the route. The winning song is declared the official Carnival song for the current year.

For exact dates and more information about Carnival, contact the **St. Lucian Cultural Foundation**, ☎ 758-452-1859, www.luciancarnival.com.

At the Jazz Festival

Jazz Festival

St. Lucia's Jazz Festival in May is similar to Jamaica's Sunsplash, except that the music is jazz instead of reggae. Renowned musicians from all over the world perform during the exquisite festival, which has become an internationally-recognized event. Since 1999, free-of-charge performances known as **The Fringe** take place all over the island and include music other than jazz.

Main concerts take place in Castries, Rodney Bay, and on picturesque Pigeon Island, where performers are showcased on a sand stage with historic buildings and the ocean in the background. Smaller shows are held on open-air stages in Soufrière and Vieux Fort.

Acoustical/straight-ahead jazz highlights the main concerts, but you may also hear new age, fusion, and rhythm-and-blues performed by international stars. If you prefer steel drums, salsa, or reggae, just ask around. Bands playing all types of music show up to perform at mid-day picnics in the park and at late-night clubs.

Jazz Festival travel packages are put together by **Delta Vacations** (☎ 800-654-6559, www.deltavacations.com) and **Alken Tours** (800-327-9974, www.alkentours.com). For ticket information and a schedule of events contact the **Jazz Shop**, ☎ 758-451-8566, www.stluciajazz.org.

International Créole Day

Jounen Kwéyòl Entenasyonnal or International Créole Day is held on the closest Sunday to October 28. On this day, Creole-speaking people on many Caribbean Islands celebrate their language and culture. Small villages on St. Lucia host a series of parties featuring island foods, crafts, music, and cultural displays. Many of the women dress in traditional "jupe," a red-yellow-and-green madras plaid skirt worn with a white blouse embroidered with flowers and decorated with red ribbons. A "tête-en-l'air"

International Créole Day

bandana, also made of the traditional island madras, is tied in a number of ways to signify the woman's marital status or availability. It's a great day of partying, games and national pride – sometimes people are fined for not speaking Kwéyòl (Creole). Traffic all over the island is horrendous as everyone tries to hop from village to village to visit their friends and participate in all the activities. Roads become hopelessly grid-locked, but overlook this inconvenience and go out anyway. It may be your only opportunity to taste the "national dish," grenfig-and-saltfish.

National Day & The Feast of St. Lucy

December 13th is National Day as well as the Feast of St. Lucy. For many years, the islanders referred to this date as Discovery Day in the belief that Christopher Colombus landed on their island December 13, 1502. However, logs of the voyages show that Colombus was nowhere near the area on that date, and facts about the actual "discovery" by anyone other than Arawak Indians are vague. But a celebration is still appropriate, and the island's patron saint is celebrated in style. Lantern-lighted processions, traditional music, cultural activities, sporting events, and a bounteous feast of local food are dedicated to Saint Lucy and the nation.

Rum & Food Festival

St. Lucians enjoy good food and fine rum on a daily basis, and now they have a festival to celebrate their epicurean obsession. Scheduled for the last days of October, the annual event features rum sampling, cooking demonstrations and non-stop noshing along Rodney Bay's famed strand of eateries known as "restaurant alley." Award-winning chefs from around the world participate in the festivities, and the best Caribbean rums are in abundant supply. Many of the island's resorts offer special packages during the festival. If you plan to attend, get details online (www.foodandrumfestival.com) or from the **St. Lucia Hotel and Tourism Association** (☎ 758-452-5978), or the **St. Lucia Tourist Board** in Castries (☎ 758452 7577; www.stlucia.org).

Travel Information

When to Go

The Caribbean enjoys perpetual summer, but the islands do have seasons – high and low. Temperatures remain in the 80s year-round, but vacation costs vary significantly between winter and summer. udget-conscious travelers often choose to visit during low-season when more bargains are available.

Airfares and hotel rates are at their peak from December through mid-April, with Christmas, winter break, spring break, and Easter weeks topping out at about double summer prices. If you want to escape miserable weather in your hometown, consider scheduling your Caribbean holiday after New Years Day and before the start of school children's winter break. The crowds will be sparser and the prices a bit lower.

After Easter week, prices begin to drop, until they bottom out during hurricane season in late summer and early fall. You'll be able to find airline tickets, cruises, car rentals, and resort packages at bargain rates, but be aware that some businesses close during this down time. If you can live with the downside, or consider the possibility of a hurricane an exciting lure, by all means take advantage of the low-season bargains.

Planning the Trip
Get Help

A good travel agent can save you hours of work, endless frustration, and, with any luck at all, a sizeable sum of money.

Contact a couple of certified agents who specialize in the Caribbean, then check their quotes with a bit of Internet research. You may find cheaper rates online, but a good agent should be able to put together a total package that meets or beats Web prices.

Once you decide on the details, pay for your vacation by credit card. This allows you the right to dispute charges for services that were misrepresented or never delivered. Trip insurance offers further protection, and you can compare the costs and coverage of various policies online at **www.InsureMyTrip. com**.

Who's Qualified to Advise?

The **Travel Institute** (formerly ICTA) is an international, nonprofit organization that accredits qualified travel agents. To earn status as a **Certified Travel Agent** (CTA), professionals must work in the industry for at least a year and a half, and complete specified training. The **Certified Travel Counselor** (CTC) status is granted to those with at least five years of experience in the industry. The Travel Institute website, www.thetravelinstitute.com, allows you to search for a certified travel agent with an office near your home. Click on "Find a Travel Professional" in the top banner of the home page to get started. You may also call the Travel Institute for a referral, ☎ 800-542-4282. If you're planning a cruise, find a certified agent through the **Cruise Lines International Association** (CLIA, www.cruising.org). Enter your zip code in the space near the bottom of the website's home page to be guided to a CLIA associate near you.

Going It Alone

By reading this book, you're already on the fast track to planning a glitch-free vacation on St. Lucia. You can get additional help at the island's official website: www.stlucia.org.

The interactive map is particularly interesting and valuable. Other good websites are www.stluciatravelnet.com, www. geographia.com/st-lucia and www.stlucia.com.

Following page: Windjammer Landing (Paul Sullivan)

Documentation

Do I Need a Passport?

Yes. Congress continues to change the deadlines, but soon every American citizen will need a passport to leave and return to the United States. Since the passport office will be overwhelmed with applications for new and renewed documents, it seems reasonable to get yours now to avoid disappointment or additional fees later.

The Western Hemisphere Travel Initiative (WHTI) went into effect in January 2007, stating that passports would be required for all air travel to the Caribbean from the United States, Canada, Mexico and Bermuda. By January 1, 2008, a passport will be required of all travelers entering or re-entering the US by air, sea or land border crossings.

A passport is valid for 10 years and costs $97 for a new one and $67 for a renewal. You can apply at one of 6,000 offices across the country and get information by calling ☎ 877-487-2778 or from the government website, www.travel.state.gov. Click "passport" on the home page.

Canadians can get passport information by phoning ☎ 800-507-6868 or online at www.dfait-maeci.gc.ca/passport.

UK citizens can call ☎ 099-210-410 or go online to www.ukpa.gov.uk.

Australians can apply for a passport at any post office or make inquires by calling ☎ 131-232. Passport information is available online at www.passports.gov.au.

Other Forms & Requirements

St. Lucia is happy to see you, but also eager to know when you'll be departing and where you plan to go when you leave. Immigration officials will ask to see your return or on-going airline ticket before they welcome you onto the island. If you plan to do a little island-hopping, be aware that inter-island ferries and airlines may refuse to sell you a ticket or allow you onboard unless you present the return ticket that will get you home at the end of your trip.

You will receive an entry card when you clear Immigration that will be stamped with either the number of days you will be on the island or the date of your departure. If you later decide to extend your visit, apply for an extension at the Immigration office or police station. Also, you probably will be asked where you plan to stay, so be prepared to give some type of answer, even if you don't have a reservation at one of the hotels. Governments are understandably cautious these days about nonresidents who may have unscrupulous intentions, so be patient with procedures that seem unnecessary.

Citizens of countries other than the US or Canada, and anyone planning a long visit, should check with the island's embassy or consulate. In the US, contact the **Embassy of St. Lucia**, ☎ 202-364-6792.

TRAVELING WITH CHILDREN

 Child abduction and child smuggling have become an international concern, and the islands have set up procedures at entry and exit points to curtail such illegal activity. If you plan to travel with your own minor children, carry original documents that prove your relationship to the child, such as a passport, birth certificate or adoption papers. If you will be traveling with a child who is not your own, bring along a notarized document from the parents or legal guardians giving the child permission to travel with you. You also may be asked to present these documents when you return to your own country. Carrying proof of your relationship to a child while on vacation may prevent travel delays and inconveniences.

Lost Documents

What should you do if your passport, money, airline tickets, or other valuables are lost or stolen while you're on St. Lucia?

Immediately contact the local police and ask for a written report. Also, contact an official at the embassy or consulate of your home country. The United States, Canada, and Australia do not have embassies or consulate offices on St. Lucia, but visitors can get help by calling the following offices:

Citizens of the **US** can contact the US Embassy on Barbados, ☎ 246-436-4950 or the US Consular Agency on Martinique, ☎ 596-71-96-90.

Canadian citizens can call their embassy back in Canada collect, ☎ 613-996-8885, or the Canadian High Commission based on Barbados, ☎ 246-429-3550.

Australians can call the Australian High Commission based in Canada, ☎ 613-783-7665.

Citizens of the **UK** do have representation on St. Lucia and can call the British High Commission in Castries, ☎ 758-452-2584.

Citizens of other countries should check with their government representatives before leaving home for emergency contact information while on vacation in the Caribbean.

Clearing Customs

Arriving on the Islands

You don't want to spend your vacation in jail or be denied entrance to the islands, so don't try to slip illegal drugs or unlicenced firearms through customs. Keep prescription medicines in their original, labeled containers. If you have a legitimate need for an unusual or narcotic substance, carry a letter from your doctor giving the details.

Customs officials have the right to look through your luggage and ask about unusual articles or large quantities of items. A few possessions that may slow or prevent your clearance through customs include more than a liter of liquor, more than 200 cigarettes, items valued at more than $250, meat, birds (living or dead), or uncertified living plants.

Returning Home

Foreign-made personal items that are taken out of the US are subject to duty each time they are brought back into the country, unless you can prove you owned them prior to your trip. Other countries may have similar regulations, and you should check before leaving home. You can avoid the expense and inconvenience of paying duty on foreign-made products by registering watches, cameras and other valuables with the

Customs Office in advance. You can also carry a dated receipt, insurance policy, or jewelers' appraisal to prove prior possession.

Each country has its own regulations for taxing and exempting purchases made by residents while traveling to a foreign destination. If you think you may buy more than a T-shirt, request a copy of rules listed in *Know Before You Go* from the **US Customs Service**, ☎ 202-354-1000, www.customs.gov.

Citizens of the UK can obtain a copy of regulations by contacting the National Advice Service of the **UK Customs and Excise Center**, ☎ 0845-010-9000, www.hmce.gov.uk.

Australian residents can request a copy of *Know Before You Go* from **Australian Custom Services**, ☎ 1-300-363-263, or check Customs Information for Travelers on the Internet, www.customs.gov.au.

Canadians living in all provinces can get a summary of regulations by contacting the **Canada Customs and Revenue Agency**, ☎ 800-461-9999, www.ccra-adrc.gc.ca.

Citizens of other countries can find information and contact numbers on the Internet at www.taxmaninternational.tk.

DEPARTURE TIPS

■ Don't misplace the entry card that you receive when you clear immigrations on arrival in the islands. You will be asked to return it to officials when you depart.

■ Don't get caught at the airport without cash to pay your departure tax. Plan to have the exact amount in Eastern Caribbean dollars or US dollars to prevent delays and avoid receiving change in local currency.

■ St. Lucia's departure tax is US$25/EC$68. Children under 12 years of age are exempt.

Customs regulations are complicated and subject to change, so it's unwise to list specific rules, but the following generalities are offered as an unofficial guideline. Although the personal exemption for US citizens returning from most foreign destinations was recently raised to $800, the duty-free limit remains at $600 if you are returning from one of the 24 Caribbean Basin countries, including St. Lucia. (The limit is $1,200 when returning from the US Virgin Islands.) If you arrive back with new items worth more than the allowable credit, you will be charged a flat rate of 10% on the excess.

US citizens who are at least 21 years old may reenter the country with two liters of alcohol as part of their $600 personal exemption, providing one of the liters was produced on a Caribbean-Basin island. You may also bring back 200 cigarettes and 200 cigars, as long as they were not made in Cuba.

You may mail duty-free gifts to friends in the US, as long as the same person does not receive more than $100 worth of items in a single day. You do not have to declare these gifts as part of your personal exemption, but it is against federal law to send alcoholic beverages, tobacco products, and perfume containing alcohol and worth more than five dollars retail.

The bad news is, you cannot send yourself or someone traveling with you a duty-free gift. The good news is, you don't want to. You may mail yourself a duty-free package from abroad worth up to $200 – twice as much as the gift exemption, and it does not count as part of your personal exemption. If you plan to mail yourself a package or send gifts to friends while you're out of the country, check the labeling directions in *Know Before You Go*. Boxes marked with the proper wording get through Customs much more smoothly.

> *Tip:* Your trip through Customs will be quicker and more hassle-free if you pack all the items you buy on the islands together in the same bag. Organize your purchase receipts so that they are readily available for inspection by the officials, and remember to declare everything acquired while you were out of the country, even if it was given to you as a gift or you had it shipped home.

Practical Points

Going Metric

US citizens continue to have trouble with temperature, distance, and quantities measured in anything other than

"American" units. Commit the following to memory and avoid the shame.

Pounds vs. Kilos

At the market, if you want a pound of fruit, ask for half a kilo. Need more or less? You do the math.

1 kilogram = 2.2046 pounds

1 pound = 0.4536 kilograms

On the Road

When you buy gas, you'll need almost four liters to make a gallon. The distance from one town to the next may be 10 kilometers, but that's only a little over six miles. The numbers work out this way:

1 liter = 1.06 quarts or 0.264 gallons

3.8 liters = 4 quarts or one gallon

1.6 kilometers = 1 mile

Temperature

Temperature is converted from °C to °F by multiplying the Celsius temperature by nine, dividing the result by five and adding 32.

Too hard? Here's about all you need to know in the Caribbean:

15°C = 59°F

20°C = 68°F

25°C = 77°F

30°C = 86°F

35°C = 95°F

Electricity

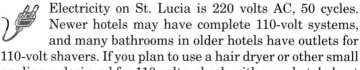 Electricity on St. Lucia is 220 volts AC, 50 cycles. Newer hotels may have complete 110-volt systems, and many bathrooms in older hotels have outlets for 110-volt shavers. If you plan to use a hair dryer or other small appliance designed for 110 volts, check with your hotel about the need for a converter or plug adapter. Even dual-voltage computers and appliances may need a plug adapter, depending on which country it was sold in. Conversion devices are

relatively inexpensive, so you may want to pick up a set at a travel store or electrical shop before you leave home.

Be cautious about using sensitive equipment, such as computers, while on the islands. You would be wise to use a surge protector and monitor equipment for overheating. Appliances with internal clocks may not keep the correct time, and dive equipment, such as strobes, should be charged at regulated outlets available in dive shops.

> *Tip:* See a picture of various international plugs and find voltage information by country online at www.franzus. com/voltage_guide.htm.

Time

 St. Lucia is on Atlantic Standard Time, which is one hour later than Eastern Standard Time in the US, and four hours earlier than Greenwich Mean Time. Since the islands do not observe daylight-saving time, they are on the same time as the eastern United States during the summer.

Health & Safety

 St. Lucia has a relatively low crime rate, but it has risen in recent years, especially in certain areas. Most offenses are perpetrated by islanders against fellow islanders.

The island is also relatively free of disease, but you can get updated Caribbean reports from the **US Centers for Disease Control and Prevention**, ☎ 404-639-3311, www.cdc. gov/travel/caribbean.htm, and **The World Health Organization**, www.who.int/ith (enter the country name in the *Search* box).

CHECK YOUR INSURANCE

Check the coverage of your existing health insurance and homeowner's policy before you consider buying additional protection for your vacation. Chances are, you're covered. If you do decide to purchase extra insurance, compare the costs and offerings of various policies online at www. InsureMyTrip.com. Package policies usually provide reimbursement for trip cancellation, lost baggage, medical and dental care, and emergency evacuation. You can also buy separate policies to cover specific needs. Find a list of international and US-based medical-emergency insurers at www. travel.state.gov/medical.html.

Take responsibility for your health and safety while you're on vacation by following these common-sense precautions:

■ Tap **water** is generally clean and safe to drink. However, you may want to drink bottled water, especially in remote areas. Bottled water is readily available, so why risk infection? Do not drink from outdoor faucets, which may be intended for irrigation only.

■ As a general rule, eat in clean **restaurants** with a heavy tourist trade, but keep in mind that some of the best meals are found in small family-run cafés in areas without many tourists. If the locals eat there, or recommend that you do, it's probably OK.

■ Avoid **raw fish**, **undercooked meats** and **eggs**, any prepared food sold by a **street vendor**, and foods that look as though they've been on the buffet table too long. If you drink milk, or add it to your cereal, be sure it's pasteurized. Wash all fresh fruits and vegetables before eating.

■ Bismuth subsalicylate, the active ingredient in products such as *Pepto-Bismol®,* isn't the best treatment for **diarrhea** (Immodium AD® is better), but it may help prevent the dreaded scourge. Research indicates that chewing a couple of the pink tablets before every meal may help deter hostile bacteria that hope to set up shop in your gastrointestinal tract. If you want to give this prophylactic strategy a try, get your doctor's OK before you leave home. Do not take products containing salicylate if you're allergic to aspirin or are already taking blood-thinning medication.

Travel Information

- You want to enjoy the warm sunshine, but Caribbean rays can burn quickly and severely. Bring along a high-SPF (sun protection factor) waterproof **sun block** that contains zinc oxide or titanium dioxide, and spread it liberally on all body parts that will be exposed to the sun. Add sunglasses and a hat or visor if you're going to be out longer than a few minutes. Sunshine along the equator is strong year-round, and you may not notice that you're burning if a cool wind is blowing or there's a cloud cover. If you do get sunburned, drink plenty of water to prevent dehydration and cover reddened skin with a lotion or gel containing aloe vera. Seek medical attention if you feel dizzy or develop a fever, headache, or nausea, since these conditions may indicate sunstroke.

- Don't touch anything in the ocean or on land unless you know for certain what it is. Some of the most beautiful sea creatures and wild vegetation cause nasty rashes and painful abrasions. **Manchineel trees** are particularly troublesome because the fruit, leaves, and sap are poisonous and cause severe skin blisters. Never stand under one during a rain storm, because sap can wash off the tree and onto you. These trees have round, shiny green leaves, and their fruit resembles a small, green apple. Those in public areas are usually marked with red paint, but be cautious in secluded spots.

- **Bugs** are a part of the Caribbean, especially in dense forests and around lakes. You probably won't be bothered when a breeze is blowing or in open areas during daytime, but remember that insects are drawn to sweet smells such as perfume. Wear lightweight long-sleeve tops and long pants when you hike into wooded areas. If you want extra protection, use a bug repellent containing DEET. Some people have good results with various natural repellents. Vitamin B-1 (thiamine) in 100 mg. tablets taken up to three times daily is said to cause an odor on the skin that humans can't detect and insects detest. Bugs also hate the smell of chlorine, so frequent dips in the hotel pool might be a good idea.

- Keep **valuables** locked in your hotel's safety deposit box or in your private room safe. Do not leave valuables in view in your rental car, even while driving. Thieves have been known to reach inside open windows while cars are stopped at intersections and make off with wallets, purses, and electronic equipment.

- Invest in a **waterproof pouch** that you can wear around your waist to keep your hotel key and a small amount of money safe and dry while you're at the beach or swimming pool.

- **After dark**, stay in well-lighted areas that are frequented by other tourists.

*Look for other helpful tips in **A Safe Trip Abroad**, published by the Bureau of Consular Affairs at the Department of State. Request a copy from the Communications Office in Washington, DC, ☎ 202-647-6575, or find it online at www.travel.state.gov/asafetripabroad.html.*

Travelers With Special Needs

 Several organizations offer information and assistance to older travelers and persons with health problems. If you have special needs, contact one of these groups:

- **AARP** offers 50-and-older members discounts on airfares, hotels, and rental cars. ☎ 800-424-3410, www.aarp.com.

- **Access-Able Travel Source** is an online publication that helps make travel easier for mature and disabled people by providing information about accessibility at hotels and attractions around the world. You won't find much specifically about the Caribbean, but look for details on cruise ships, travel agents, equipment rental and packing at www.access-able.com.

- **Society for Accessible Travel & Hospitality** is a clearinghouse for disability-access information. They also publish the magazine *Open World*. ☎ 212-447-7284; fax 212-725-8253, www.sath.org.

- **Emerging Horizons**, a travel magazine and newsletter, is geared toward people with mobility impairment, from wheelchair users to slow walkers. It has feature articles and a section with advice on accessible tours, lodging, transportation, and recreation. www.emerginghorizons. com.

- **The American Diabetes Association**, ☎ 800-DIABE-TES, www.diabetes.org, and **The Canadian Diabetes Association**, ☎ 800-BANTING, www.diabetes.ca, offer suggestions on how to prepare for a trip and manage while on vacation if you have diabetes. In the US alone, more than 15 million people have the disease, and almost 20% of senior citizens suffer from the condition.

Getting Married

 More and more couples are choosing destination weddings and walking tropical isles instead of church aisles. You can make all the arrangements before you leave home, then arrive a few days early to relax and finalize the plans. After the ceremony, you're already at your honeymoon destination.

In recent years, St. Lucia has become one of the most popular wedding and honeymoon spots in the Caribbean, partly because the tourist bureau promotes the island as the most romantic place on earth (for good reason), and partly because local resorts and businesses consider themselves marriage experts. Thirty hotels on the island have at least one person on staff who specializes in arranging wedding ceremonies, receptions and honeymoons. In addition, there are several independent planners who work with a variety of resorts and also coordinate ceremonies and receptions at local churches and public sites.

One of the most idyllic public sites is **Pigeon Point National Park**, a hilltop landmark with flowering gardens, historic ruins and panoramic views of the Caribbean Sea. The **St. Lucia National Trust** is charged with preserving this area, and they have people on staff who will handle all arrangements for weddings and receptions (☎ 758-452-5005, www.slunatrust.org).

Jalousie Plantation (Paul Sullivan)

Another prime outdoor choice is anywhere within photography range of the **Pitons**, the island's well-recognized trademark. These twin mountains are a breathtaking World Heritage site and an awesome setting for a wedding. (**Jalousie Plantation** and **Ladera** offer the best views.) **Marigot Bay** and **Anse Chastanet** are two of the many out-and-out gorgeous beach settings. (Check out the packages offered at **Oasis Marigot**, **Discovery Marigot Bay**, **Marigot Beach Club** and **Anse Chastanet Resort**). Many of the resorts have built gazebos and gardens with ocean views on their properties, and these make lovely locations for a wedding, especially at sunset.

Sandals reportedly performs the most resort weddings on St. Lucia, but they have three hotels on the island, so the numbers are skewed in their favor. Each property has its own wedding consultant who coordinates every detail of the ceremonies. Other large resorts, such as **Windjammer Landing**, **Coconut Bay** and **Jalousie Plantation**, are popular locations for a luxurious wedding.

If you're looking for something more intimate, investigate the packages offered by wedding planners at smaller hotels, such

Jade Mountain infinity pool

as **East Winds**, **Jade Mountain**, **Ladera** or **Ti Kaye Village**. The Rodney Bay area is a good choice if you want a wide range of activities, including nightlife, or have a lively group of friends along. **Bay Garden**, **Ginger Lily** and **Harmony Suites** are good choices among the boutique hotels with wedding packages. (See *Where to Stay* for hotel reviews and contact information.)

Traditional church ceremonies take more time to arrange, since you must reserve the church and secure a minister to officiate. A wedding consultant can walk you through the steps and make most of the plans. The island has several lovely churches, and most denominations are represented.

If you plan to be married in the Catholic Church, you will need to arrange for the parish priest of your home congregation to consult with the priest at the **Minor Basilica of the Immaculate Conception** in Castries, the capital of St. Lucia. This is standard procedure to insure that you have fulfilled the marriage requirements for a Catholic wedding. You or your local priest may contact the church directly. ☎ 758-452-2271.

Legal requirements for getting married on St. Lucia are relatively simple, but if you aren't a resident, you may find it difficult to cut through the red tape without professional help. The first major task is choosing a lawyer who will represent you in applying to the Attorney General for permission to marry. Since the request must be made seven business days before the ceremony, you must either arrive on the island a couple of weeks early to get the process started, or simply sign on with a consultant who will handle everything in your absence.

Island law requires you to do the following:

- Arrive on the island three business days (weekends do not count) prior to your wedding day.
- In addition to your passport, bring your birth certificate.
- If either the bride or groom is widowed or divorced, provide the divorce papers (*Decree Absolute*) or the death certificate for the deceased.
- If either the bride or groom has changed their name, provide the *Deed Poll* or court order.
- If either the bride or groom is under the age of 18, provide a sworn affidavit of parental consent stamped by a Notary Public.
- All documents must be in English or translated into English by a certified translator.

Fees include:

- Marriage License (obtained seven days before date of marriage), US$125/EC$335.
- Special Marriage License (obtained less than seven days before the marriage),US$200/EC$540.
- Registrar Fees, US$37/EC$100.
- Marriage Certificate, US$3/EC$8.00

A professional marriage officer, who is confirmed by the St. Lucian parliament, will preside at your wedding and follow government-approved vows, unless you opt for a religious ceremony preformed by an ordained minister. Most marriage officials also will add vows or readings that are chosen by the couple. Once your island wedding is over and all the papers are in order, your marriage will be recognized and considered a legal union by most countries worldwide, including the United States and the United Kingdom. (France and a few other countries require that citizens register the marriage with the local embassy.)

Once you've decided on an island wedding, get the preparations underway by choosing a hotel to handle all the arrangements (see reviews in *Where to Stay*) or checking with the independent services listed below.

Previous page: View from Ladera (Paul Sullivan)

Local Contacts for Wedding Services

Awesome Caribbean Weddings is run by three awesomely romantic women, Kayt, Fenella and Michele. They work in Castries and know all there is to know about getting happily married on St. Lucia. Contact them for help every step of the way. ☎ 758-450-0300, www.awesomecaribbeanweddings.com.

Elope To Paradise is the wedding site for Anse Chastanet and Jade Mountain Resorts. These two properties have been given over-the-top kudos for the island's most romantic setting. We think there are many romantic settings on St. Lucia, but we'll agree that the beach and lush hillside at Anse Chastanet is certainly one of the most spectacular. Check out the pictures on the website and, if you decide to get married there, contact the resorts' wedding planner, ☎ 800-223-1108 (US & Canada), 758-459-7000, www.elopetoparadise-weddings.com.

Dreamy Weddings and Tours has an office in the US and on St. Lucia to plan every detail of your island wedding. They can set things up at a beach or at the national park, even onboard a chartered boat. The website will give you some ideas on location, costs and honeymooning. ☎ 877-694-4565 (US), 758-452-6473, www.dreamyweddings.com.

Oasis Marigot has put together a five-page booklet about planning a wedding on the island. You can download the information, free, at the resort's website or call to speak with the wedding consultant. ☎ 800-263-4202 (US), 00-800-2785 8241 (UK), www.oasismarigot.com (resort site), www.oasismarigot.com/images/pdf/st-lucia-wedding-guide.pdf (wedding booklet).

St. Lucia Wedding Photographers

A Beach Dream Wedding is the romantic branch of Kirk Elliott Photography. View his photos online, then call him directly for more information. ☎ 877-499-8476, 758-450-2438, www.abeachdreamwedding.com.

Envision is owned by **Mikael Lamber**, who you may have seen credited with some of the famous photographs of St. Lucia and the island's top resorts. Weddings are one of his specialties, and you can look over his online portfolio for inspiration. If you like what you see, contact him about photo-graphing your big event. ☎ 758-450-0462, 758-488-7191, www.evisionstlucia.com.

Getting Here

Arriving by Air

 St. Lucia has two airports and good air links from North America, Europe and other Caribbean islands. International flights arrive at **Hewanorra Airport** (UVF ☎ 758-454-6355) in Vieux Fort on the remote south coast. Smaller inter-island planes land on the shorter runway at **George F. L. Charles Airport** (formerly called Vigie, SLU, ☎ 758-452-1156) near Castries. Both airports have tour-ist information counters where you can pick up maps and bro-chures. In addition, banks with ATMs, taxi stands and car-rental booths are at both locations.

> *Hewanorra Airport is on the far south end of the island, and most tourist areas are on the north end, more than an hour away by car. Expect your taxi fare from the airport to your hotel to run EC$140/US$52 to EC$180/US$67. Since a one-day car-rental fee is about the same or less, consider renting a car at the airport when you arrive.*

Visitors from North America have several choices for direct or nonstop jet service to St. Lucia's Hewanorra International Airport. **US Airways** arrives direct from Philadelphia twice a week, **Delta Air Lines** comes nonstop from Atlanta twice a week, and **Air Jamaica** flies direct from New York daily. Travelers from Canada have direct service on **Air Canada** from Toronto and Montreal on Saturdays. Visitors from Europe travel nonstop from London to Hewanorra on **Virgin Atlantic** and direct through Barbados on **British Airways** and **Air Jamaica**.

In addition, **American Eagle** and **BWIA/Caribbean Air-line** offer connecting flights into **George Charles Airport**. **LIAT**, **Air Caraibes** and **Caribbean Star** offer many options for flying to St. Lucia from within the Caribbean.

Flying Time to St. Lucia

- Four hours from New York
- Three hours from Miami
- Five hours from Toronto
- Eight hours from London

Airline Contact Information

The 800 numbers below are toll-free when calling within the area in parentheses. Use the 758 numbers when you're in the Caribbean, unless a specific toll-free number is listed. When you're on St. Lucia, dial only the seven-digit local number. Do not dial the 758 area code.

Air Canada, ☎ 888-247-2262 (US & Canada), 758-454-6038, www.aircanada.ca.

Air Caraibes, ☎ 877-772-1005(US), 758-452-2463 or 758-453-6660, www.air-caraibes-charter.com

Air Jamaica, ☎ 800-523-5585 (US), 0208-570-7999 (UK), 758-453-6611, www.airjamaica.com.

Air Martinique, ☎ 758-452-2463.

American, ☎ 800-433-7300 (US), 758-454-6777, www.aa.com.

American Eagle, ☎ 800-433-7300 (US), 758-454-6777, www.aa.com.

British Airways, ☎ 800-247-9297 (US), 0870-850-9850 (UK), 758-452-3951, www.britishairways.com.

Caribbean Airline (BWIA), ☎ 800-920-4225 (North America), 845-362-4225 (UK), 800-744-2225 (St Lucia), 758-452-3778, www.caribbean-airlines.com.

Continental, ☎ 800-525-0280 (US & Canada), www.continental.com.

Caribbean Star, ☎ 800-744-7827 (Caribbean), 268-461-7827 (Antigua base), 758-452-5898.

Delta Air Lines, ☎ 800-221-1212 (US & Canada), 758-452-9683.

Dominica Air Taxi, ☎ 800-744-2323, www.dominicaairtaxi.com.

LIAT, ☎ 888-844-5428 (Caribbean), 268-462-0700 (US), 758-456-9100, www.flyliat.com.

Northwest, ☎ 800-225-2525 (US & Canada), www.nwa.com.

SVG Air (St. Vincent & the Grenadines), ☎ 784-457-5124 (St. Vincent), 800-744-5777 (Caribbean), 800-624-1843 (North America).

United, ☎ 800-538-2929 (US & Canada), www.ual.com.

US Airways, ☎ 800-428-4322 (US & Canada), www.usairways.com.

Virgin Atlantic, ☎ 800-744-7477 (Caribbean), 800-821-5438 (US), 0870-380-2007 (UK), 758-454-3610, www.virgin-atlantic.com.

Arriving by Sea

Cruise News

Cruise ships dock almost daily at the terminals in Castries. **La Place Carenage** is near city-center on the south side of the seaport, and **Pointe Seraphine** is on the north side of the port, farther from town. Both terminals are air-conditioned, duty-free shopping centers with food and beverage service, an ATM and stores offering jewelry, international gifts, electronics, liquor and Caribbean art.

Castries Harbor

When ships are in port, you can take a water taxi between La Place Carenage and Pointe Seraphine for US$1 per person. Taxis and tour operators meet the ships at both areas with offers to drive you around the island and show you the major sights. If you decide to take a tour, be sure you're clear on the itinerary, cost, and what's included. You may agree that admission fees are an acceptable extra charge, but stopping along the roadside to take pictures is not. Also, be sure you know whether prices are quoted in US or East Caribbean dollars.

Ferry

L'Express des Iles operates a high-speed catamaran between Castries and the islands of Martinique, Guadeloupe and Dominica. You can buy one-way or round-trip tickets, sign up for an overnight package or take a guided day-trip. View your options on their website (www.express-des-iles.com) or call the office in Castries for information and reservations. ☎ 758-456-5022.

Private Boats

If you're arriving on your own private boat or charter, you can dock at **Rodney Bay**, **Castries**, **Marigot Bay**, **Soufrière** and **Vieux Fort**. Castries and Vieux Fort cater mainly to commercial shipping; Rodney Bay Marina, Marigot Bay and Soufrière are involved primarily with pleasure craft.

One of the most popular marinas is at **Rodney Bay**, which offers shower facilities, restaurants, grocery stores, a swimming pool and boat-maintenance shops. The marina has five docks with 232 berths that can accommodate boats of up to a 12-foot draft. Normal business hours for customs are Monday through Friday, 8 am to noon and 1 pm until 4:30 pm. Officers may be on duty at other times, but additional fees are charged for clearing customs outside regular hours. For information contact Customs and Immigration (☎ 758-452–0235) or the marina (☎ 758-452-0324).

Marigot Bay has recently undergone major construction that has made it one of the most exclusive Caribbean destinations. As part of the new **Discovery at Marigot Bay** complex, the original docks have been completely rebuilt and now have 40 berths with a minimum depth of 15 feet. Twenty new

Marigot Bay (Paul Sullivan)

moorings have been built on the inner bay, and older docks on the southeast corner of the bay have been extended to accommodate oversized yachts. These docks, with water, electricity and high-pressure refueling facilities, are managed by **The Moorings** and are adjacent to the new **Discovery Resort and Spa**, which is a marina village built around a courtyard, featuring a supermarket, bank, boutiques and other facilities. For information, contact The Moorings (☎ 758-451-4357) or Discovery at Marigot Bay (☎ 758-458 4767).

Soufriere Marine Management Authority (SMMA) handles the reception of yachts in Soufrière. The SMMA office is located in the same building as the customs department on the waterfront, and both are staffed daily from 8 am until noon and 1 pm until 4:30 pm. Immigration is housed at the police station, which is also on the waterfront and never closes. Rangers patrol the marine park area and collect mooring fees for use of the buoys. Anchoring is not allowed in the SMMA zone. For a complete list of regulations and mooring information, contact the customs office (☎ 758-459-5656), the immigration office (☎ 758-456-3620) or the SMMA (☎ 758-

Soufrière (Chensiyuan)

459-5500). For general information about Soufrière or St. Lucia, contact the Tourism Office (☎ 758-459-7419).

St. Lucia is also a popular place to begin a sailing charter, and both Rodney Bay and Marigot Bay have major charter centers that rent crewed and bare-boat motor and sail boats. If you want to charter for a week or more, contact on of the following:

Moorings Yacht Charters, based in Marigot Bay, ☎ 888-952-8420 (in the US) or 758-451-4357, www.moorings.com.

Destination St. Lucia, located in Rodney Bay, ☎ 758-452-8531, www.dsl-yachting.com.

Getting Around

Car Rentals

Driving is on the left in St. Lucia, and that can be a problem for visitors from non-British countries. If you want to give it a try, reserve a car before you leave home in order to guarantee availability and secure the best rate. You must be at least 25 years old, hold a valid license from your home country (or an international license), and purchase a local license for about EC$54/US$21 in order to rent a car. All car rental agencies issue local permits, and you may also apply for one at the immigration offices at both airports or at any police station on the island.

Roads are fairly well maintained, if you judge by Caribbean standards. However, most are narrow and you have to expect hairpin curves in the mountains and kidney-pounding ruts along the coast and in the forest. All the secondary roads are challenging, and even the nicest resorts and restaurants are often reached by unpaved lanes. If you plan to explore isolated areas, consider renting a four-wheel-drive vehicle.

You won't get lost if you stick to the main roads that connect the capital of Castries (northwest coast) to Vieux Fort (southern tip). One hugs the west coast, and another cuts through the center of the island via the town of Dennery, then runs south along the east coast until it connects to the west-coast road. Road signs are erratic, and some roads seem to have no name at all, but are known by locals as "the road to...." The main turnoffs are marked, usually, but sometimes with a homemade sign that's faded over the years. Just know that all roads lead eventually to the main coastal roads, and you can find your way north or south from there.

During high season, expect to pay around US$55 per day or US$330 per week to rent a typical compact car with manual transmission and no air-conditioning. From there, rates go up to about US$100 per day or US$580 per week for a fully-equipped four-wheel-drive vehicle. Low-season rates are US$10 to US$20 less per day.

If your regular car insurance doesn't cover you outside your home country or when driving a rental, plan to pay for your car with a credit card that guarantees coverage. Otherwise, expect to pay approximately US$15 per day for additional collision and liability insurance.

Car Rental Companies

Alto, ☎ 758-454-5311 (Hewanorra Airport), www.altorentacar.com

Avis, ☎ 758-454-3625 (Hewanorra Airport), 758-452-2046 (Charles Airport), www.avis.com.

Ben's West Coast Jeep & Taxi Service, ☎ 758-459-5457 (delivery island wide).

Budget, ☎ 758-452-3516 (Charles Airport) or 758-454-7470 (Hewanorra Airport), www.budgetstlucia.net.

Cool Breeze Jeep Rental, ☎ 758-458-2031 (Charles Airport), 758-454-7898 (Hewanorra Airport).

Cost Less Rent-a-Car, ☎ 758-450-3416 or 758-481-7376 (pager).

Drive-A-Matic, ☎ 758-452-0544 (delivery island wide), www. drivestlucia.com.

Economy, ☎ 758-451-7997 (delivery island-wide).

Guy's Car Rental, ☎ 758-451-7885 (Charles Airport).

Hertz, ☎ 758-451-7351 (Charles Airport), 758-454-9636 (Hewanorra Airport), www.hertz.com.

National Car Rental, ☎ 758-452-3050 (Charles Airport) or 758-454-6699 (Hewanorra Airport), www.nationalcar.com.

VC Rental, ☎ 758-452-9404, www.vcrental.com.

St. Lucia Car Rental deals with major car rental companies located on the island and claims to negotiate the best rate and service for their clients. Compare them with your favorite international or local agency online (www.stluciacar.com) or by phone ☎ 866-735-1715 (US), 0800-078-9054 (UK).

Buses

 You won't see any big public buses on St. Lucia, but colorful private minivans offer an inexpensive way to get around. They are usually crowded, especially during the morning and afternoon rush hours, and service stops entirely about 10 pm, except on Friday nights, when partygoers stay late in Gros Islet for "jump up."

If you want to give it a try, stands are located in **Castries** near the public market on **Jeremie Street**. All vans are marked with their route number and destination point, and have the letter "M" on their green license plate. Outside the city, look for signed stops or flag down a van along the main roads. Ask a local for help if you're unsure. Tell the driver or his assistant where you want to go so they can alert you when the bus arrives at a stop near your destination., and ask how often the van makes the return trip.

Have small bills so you can pay the exact fare (or close to it) either in US or EC dollars. Charges vary depending on distance, but the typical fare from Castries to Rodney Bay is about EC$2.50/US$1 and from Castries to Vieux Fort around EC$8/US$3.

Taxis

 Private taxis wait outside the airports, cruise-ship terminals and major hotels. Many are vans that carry six to eight passengers, which is convenient if you want to share a ride. Taxis don't have meters, but drivers are required to display or carry a tariff card with government-regulated fares. Rates are given in US dollars and based on three people traveling to the same destination, with a per-person charge for each additional passenger. Negotiate the fare and ask about charges for luggage before you get into the cab. Most drivers belong to a reputable cooperative that sets ideal standards and, with few exceptions, all are knowledgeable and polite.

Expect to pay about US$8 to go the short distance from Charles Airport to hotels in or near Castries, and approximately US$60 to go from Hewanorra Airport to Castries, a 40-mile, one-hour trip. Many drivers also conduct private tours of the island and charge about US$25 per hour for up to four people. This fee is set by the driver, not the government, so you may be able to negotiate a bargain price, especially during a tourist-season lull.

Tip: The license plate of a legitimate taxi is either blue or red, and bears the letters "TX."

Taxi Services

Courtesy Taxi Co-Op, ☎ 758-452-1733, www.courtesytaxi. com.

Holiday Taxi Co-Op, ☎ 758-452-6067.

Northern Club Taxi Association, ☎ 758-450-0431.

North Lime Taxi Association, ☎ 758-452-8562.

Soufrière Taxi Service, ☎ 758-459-5562.

Southern Taxi Association, ☎ 758-454-6136, www. southerntaxi.com.

Vigie Taxi Association, ☎ 758-452-1599.

Water Taxis

Water taxis are a great way to get around the coastal areas, and you can find small motor boats waiting beside the piers in Castries, Rodney Bay, Marigot Bay, and Soufrière. For a dollar or two per person, they will zip you from one side of the cove to another. For a bit more, they will drop you off at a nearby beach or take you to a seaside restaurant. Some also offer sightseeing tours along the coast, which is a marvelous way to see the island.

Water taxis may or may not belong to a regulatory association, and some aren't even a regular business, but rather just a guy with a boat who will take you some place. Rates vary widely, but expect short trips to run about US$10 per person round-trip. Sightseeing tours average US$100 per hour for up to six passengers. Some water taxi services sell weekly passes that allow passengers unlimited trips within a designated area and cost about US$35 per person.

Ask for information on water taxis at any marina office or business flanking the water. If you plan to have a meal at one of the seaside restaurants, call ahead to ask if they provide complimentary water taxi service or recommend a particular driver. In addition, you can check with the **Rodney Bay Ferry**, ☎ 758-452-8816, or **Soufrière Water Taxi Association**, ☎ 758-457-1351.

Helicopter

The fastest and most scenic way to get from the airport to your hotel is by helicopter. During the 10- to 15-minute trip you'll get a bird's-eye view of the lush island and, if you're flying into Hewanorra and staying in the northwest area, arrive at your destination without taking the long drive up the coast. The fare runs from US$120 to US$130 per person, depending on your destination, and some resorts can arrange to include the cost in your vacation package. If you're making your own

St Lucia Helicopter

arrangements, contact **Saint Lucia Helicopter Service**, ☎ 758-453-6952, www.stluciahelicopters.com.

Touring the Island

By Boat

S t. Lucia is most beautiful when seen from the water, and we suggest you allow one entire day for cruising on your own in a chartered boat or with a group on a scheduled excursion.

If you're lucky, you may have playful dolphins swimming alongside your boat as you glide past dozing fishing villages backed by the rolling hills of the fantastic rainforest. The highlight of any trip is spotting the magnificent green Pitons jutting dramatically out of the turquoise Caribbean.

Costs vary, depending on the length of the trip, the size and type of boat, whether food and drinks are included and the level of service. Shop around before you sign up. The concierge at your hotel should be able to tell you about the different boats and tours, but you'll get better feedback from other tourists who have actually taken the trip. Count on spending about US$100 per person for a full day of fun on the water. Half-day and sunset cruises range from US$40 to US$70.

Another option is to take a tour by water taxi. The drivers are usually natives who know the coastline well and enjoy entertaining with impromptu stories about island life. Water taxis are mostly small motorized boats that charge very reasonable rates, especially for a group of four to six sharing the hourly fee. Expect to pay about EC$270/US$100 per hour for a private water tour for two to six people. Some drivers supply drinks and snorkeling equipment, but others expect you to bring your own. Have your hotel arrange for a dependable guide or contact **Rodney Bay Ferry,** ☎ 758-452-8816 or **Soufrière Water Taxi Association,** ☎ 758-457-1351.

Scheduled Day-Cruises

Mystic Man 2

Mystic Man Tours is based in Soufrière and offers an impressive menu of tours. Their fleet includes sail-boats, motor-boats, fishing boats, even a glass-bottom boat. Their most inclusive all-day tour includes a water taxi to Castries for shopping, lunch at Marigot Bay, snorkeling at Anse Chastanet, and a visit to the Sulphur Springs drive-in volcano and waterfall. Look over the other choices online, or call the office for prices and reservations. ☎ 758-459-7783, 758-457-1360, www.mystic-mantours.com.

Sea Spray Cruises has a fleet of boats for regularly-scheduled cruises along the west coast. The 138-foot ***Brig Unicorn*** is a fantastic replica of an 18th-cen-

Mystic Man sailboat

tury ship and was used in the movies *Roots* and *Pirates of the Caribbean*. Kids especially enjoy the "Pirate Day" cruises that include face painting and treasure hunts. *Mango Tango, Jus Tango* and *Tango Too* are catamarans that accommodate 50-150 passengers on cruises called *Tout Bagay*, which is Creole for "a little bit of everything." For rates and schedules, contact Sea Spray, ☎ 758-452-8644, www.seaspraycruises.com.

Endless Summer has two 56-foot catamarans, *Endless Summer I* and *Sunkist*, which leave Rodney Bay for full-day sightseeing tours along the west coast, half-day snorkeling tours along the northwest coast, and sunset party cruises. ☎ 758-450-8651, www.stluciaboat-tours.com.

Brig Unicorn

Flying Ray is a 60-foot cata-maran that leaves Rodney Bay each morning at 7:30 to make a high-speed crossing to the French island of Martinique. Passengers spend the day shopping and sightseeing, then head back to St. Lucia, where the boat stops at a secluded cove for barbecue and swimming. This trip isn't the best for touring St. Lucia but, as long as you're in the neighborhood, you might as well do a bit of island-hopping. The views of both islands from the water are magnificent. Contact St. Lucian Wave Riders for more information. ☎ 758-452-0808 or 758-485-3527, www. stluciawaveriders.com.

Private Crewed Charters

Hacksaw Charters is a family business that started back in the 1940s with one boat. Today it is run by founder Bill Hackshaw's sons and grandchildren with a fleet of four cus-tom-outfitted boats. The new super-powered *Lady Hack* is the most suited for day cruising, and the crew takes her along the west coast from Castries to Soufriere, with stops along the way for swimming, snorkeling, picnicking or restaurant din-ing. Talk to Chris or David about joining a planned group trip or arranging a private charter. ☎ 758-453-0553 (office) or 758-453-0553 (home), www.hackshaws.com.

Following page: Smuggler's Cove (Paul Sullivan)

Dolphin- & Whale-Watching

Sighting a graceful dolphin or giant whale is a great thrill, no matter how many times you do it. Since the waters around St. Lucia are home to sperm, pilot and humpback whales

Dolphin

and bottle-nosed dolphin, you have a good chance of seeing them at play whenever you're cruising. From late October until January, you may spot huge male sperm whales who've journeyed all the way from New Zealand or Canada to mate. Female sperm whales and other species stay in the area year-round. If you want to better your chances of making a sighting, sign up for a whale-watching cruise with Chris or David Hackshaw (see listing above), who are well known for their successful spotting record. Before you leave the dock, you'll listen to recordings of whale and dolphin sounds and get a short briefing on what to look for out on the sea. Sonar equipment and a Global Positioning Satellite help the crew locate likely areas for viewing. Have your camera ready and be prepared to run

Hackshaw Charters

to the side of the boat as soon as someone announces a sighting. The giant mammals surface and dive quickly, then reappear in another area before they tire of all the attention and swim out of view.

Touring the Island

Crossfire is a 35-foot Chris Craft that accommodates up to eight passengers and can be chartered for a four- or eight-hour day-trip or a two-hour sunset cruise. The boat is moored at Rodney Bay Marina. Book by calling ☎ 758-450-6419 or reserve online at www.crossfiretours.com.

Free Spirit

Free Spirit is a 43-foot Sunseeker Tomahawk luxuriously outfitted and designed for 10 passengers. Captain Christian Richings takes private groups from Rodney Bay Marina along the west coast to Marigot Bay, Anse Chastanet or wherever they wish to stop, sightsee, snorkel or lunch. There's an open bar during day-trips and champagne during evening moonlight cruises, which dock for dinner at one of the open-air restaurants. ☎ 758-452-8491, 758-519-6860, www.freespirit-charters.com.

Un-Crewed Charters

If you know how to handle a boat, there's no better way to tour St. Lucia than from your own chartered boat. St. Lucia is a popular yachting destination and there are five official ports of entry: **Rodney Bay Marina**, **Marigot Bay**, **Castries Harbour**, **Vieux Fort** and **Soufrière**. Other bays along the west and south coast also offer protected anchorage.

Both Rodney Bay and Marigot Bay have full-facility marinas with restaurants, grocery stores and maintenance shops.

You may be satisfied traveling around St. Lucia, tying up in a different bay every night. But, if you want to go a bit farther, other Windward Islands offer exciting possibilities. During the winter, winds blow from the northeast, and in the summer, they come from the southeast, at an average speed of 10 to 25 knots year-round. You can make it to nearby islands in seven to 10 hours, depending on weather and wind conditions.

Rodney Bay Marina

Charter prices vary widely, depending on boat size, type of vessel and season. Plan on spending about US$1,500 per week for a small, basic sailboat and up to US$10,000 per week for a large luxury yacht. Add another US$200 or so per day for a captain or other crew members.

Contact these two reliable companies for information and assistance with planning your charter:

Moorings Yacht Charters is based in Marigot Bay, ☎ 888-952-8420 (in the US) or 758-451-4357, www.moorings.com.

Destination St. Lucia is in Rodney Bay, ☎ 758-452-8531, www.dsl-yachting.com.

Best Bays

Whether you're on your own or in a group, be sure your water tour includes **Marigot Bay**, one of the most beautiful coves in the Caribbean. This pristine blue-green lagoon lies at the end of a long, narrow inlet that cuts into the hilly coast south of Castries. It's completely sheltered and features a palm-

Marigot Bay Marina

shaded white-sand beach. From land it is gorgeous, but from the water, it is even more sensational.

You've probably seen movies or commercials that were filmed in this west coast bay when it was less developed. James Michener, the prolific writer of more than 40 novels set in scenic locations around the world, once said Marigot was "the most beautiful bay in the Caribbean." Moviegoers agreed when they saw the spectacular cove in *Doctor Dolittle,* starring Rex Harrison, in 1967. Today, restaurants, condos, homes and resorts hide among the trees on the steep hills surrounding the bay. It's still gorgeous, but you can more clearly see what Michener was talking about, if you look around with eyes squinted to block out all that is man made.

Many day-trip boats make a stop at **Anse Cochon**, three miles south of Marigot, near the rocky headland that marks the small community of Anse La Raye. Brightly-painted fishing boats and graceful sailboats glide past the shore. Snorkelers bob face-down in the water to view the coral and fish surrounding the offshore boulders. Divers favor this bay because of the sunken 165-foot freighter, ***Lesleen M***, that stands upright 60 feet below the surface. It was sunk by the Department of Fisheries in 1986 to provide an artificial reef,

Anse Cochon (Paul Sullivan)

and it now acts as a habitat for a variety of sea creatures. You can rent snorkeling and diving equipment from the dive shop, and get drinks and snacks from the colorful beach bar.

Touring the Island

Wooden stairs wind up the steep hill from the beach to the luxurious Ti Kaye Resort.

Anse Chastanet has one of the most beautiful beaches in the Caribbean. If you're a beach bum, photographer or snorkeler, you will be awed. The reef, in shallow water near shore, is famous among divers. It's protected by buoys, so snorkelers are safe from boat traffic. Scuba St. Lucia has a dive shop on the beach where you can rent equipment, take lessons or join a guided dive trip. Large schools of fish will swarm around you as soon as you get into the water. Look for parrot fish, sergeant majors, trumpet fish and many other species that feed among the coral.

South of Anse Chastanet, the waters are under the direction of the **Soufrière Marine Management Area** (SMMA, ☎ 758-459-5500, www.smma.org.lc). If you want to boat, fish or dive in that area, which includes the sea surrounding the Pitons, you must be with a licensed guide. Activity is highly restricted in order to preserve the coral reefs, fish stocks and beaches along the southwest coast.

Organized Tours By Helicopter

There's no more exciting way to tour the island than by helicopter. It's so popular, in fact, that **St. Lucia Helicopters** recently spent more than US$1.5 million for a third helicopter to handle the demand. About 250 people board the six-passenger air-conditioned choppers every day. Some hop on just to get quickly from the airport to their hotel, but most passengers are there for a high-adrenaline joy ride over the lush green island.

You can choose from three planned flightseeing tours, or charter a helicopter for a private tour designed just for you. The best standard tour is the North/South combo, a 30-minute flight that takes you over the national park at Pigeon Point, past the rainforests, amazingly close to the peaks of the twin Pitons and along the stunning coast. This full-island tour is priced at US$155. A 20-minute South Tour is US$120, and the 10-minute North Tour is US$70.

Each helicopter is outfitted with special insulation and seats to insure a smooth ride. You'll have fabulous visibility from the custom windows that allow trouble-free picture-taking, and you'll be able to hear the pilot's narration clearly through a headset. Make reservations early, especially during high season. ☎ 758-453-6950, www.stluciahelicopters.com.

On Land

We highly suggest that you spend at least one day touring the island with someone who knows it well. Some natural and historical sites are off-limits to anyone without a proper permit, so an official guide is a must. Other spots are hard to find on your own, and you may wreck the suspension system on your rental car getting there.

But the best reason for taking a guided tour is that you'll enjoy sightseeing more if you can actually see the sights rather than having to watch the road. Driving in St. Lucia is tricky, and many marvelous views are from hairpin curves with no guardrails. You can appreciate the dilemma of having to decide whether to sneak a peek or attend to the narrow passage around the upcoming hill.

The price range for tours varies, depending on length, type of transportation, entrance fees and inclusion of food and drinks. Expect to pay about US$20 per person for a half-day tour of a specific area, up to US$90 per person for a full-day van or Jeep tour including lunch. Many of the tour operators, independent guides and taxi drivers will customize a tour for you or your group. If you can get four people together, call the operators listed below about a group rate.

Author's tip: We were able to negotiate a US$160 full-day land tour for four, including snacks and entrance fees. That works out to a very reasonable US$40 per person, and we got the advantage of personal attention and a customized itinerary.

The St. Lucia National Trust is charged with protecting the island's natural and cultural heritage. You can take a tour with one of their official guides to the properties that they oversee, including **Pigeon Point National Park**, **Morne Fortuné** and the **Maria Islands**. If you're a nature lover or history buff, you'll want to sign up for all the tours offered by SLNT. But one that you can't do on your own is the tour to the tiny Maria Islands. The wide selection of unusual vegetation and wildlife is protected, and access is restricted to visitors accompanied by a guide who is trained and licensed by the National Trust. The most unusual species are the colorful ground lizards and rare, but harmless, kuowess snake. Find out about all of the scheduled tours and their prices by calling the National Trust at ☎ 758-453-76576 or 758-452-5005, www.slunatrust.org.

The Forestry Department manages short nature trails and longer hiking trails in the national forest reserves, where you are not allowed without permission. Get permission, pay your entrance fees and arrange for a trained guide by

The Maria Islands (Scott Sheridan)

calling the department's office at ☎ 758-450-2231 or 758-450-2078, www.geocities.com/sluforestrails/index.htm.

See *Hiking* in the *Adventures on Foot* section for more information on specific trails and tours.

Jungle Tours offers three rainforest adventures rated for beginning, intermediate, or advanced hikers. In addition, there are tours to the beach, waterfalls, and special outings for cruise-ship passengers with time restrictions. All include transportation in an open Land Rover, and most feature a buffet lunch. Check out the special rates offered on the Internet. ☎ 450-0434, www.jungletoursstlucia.com.

Trim's Tours is run by Tom Trim, a fun-loving professional who's crazy about his island and dedicated to making you fall in love with it, too. He has a selection of tours, but one of the most popular is the Maria Islands' Eco Tour, which he conducts in partnership with the St. Lucia Trust. Call to ask about other choices. ☎ 758-452-2502, www.trimtours.com.

Island Adventures is a large operator with a fleet of Land Rovers. They have a good selection of tours and will also customize a plan for individuals and groups. We highly recommend their bike-and-hike trips. They have their own mountain bikes, which are in top condition, so you'll enjoy the ride, and the hike takes you to a magnificent waterfall. The land-and-sea trips are also fun because you go out by Land Rover and come back by boat. ☎ 758-450-4001, 758-450-4491 or 758-484-4700 (cell), www.islandadventurestlucia.com.

Atlantic Coast Walk

Phillip Tours is run by a father-son team, Jackson and Martis. They use 12-passenger vans for their full-day tours to natural wonders such as the sulphur springs, the Pitons, waterfalls and Marigot Bay. The shorter tour is ideal for cruise-ship passengers who want to tour the capital, do some duty-free shopping and take in the hilltop views from Morne

Fortuné. The dad, Jackson, is a calypso musician and often breaks into song. You can't get more entertained than this. ☎ 758-712-0659 or 758-519-3931, www3.sympatico.ca/angeld/index.htm.

Sunlink Tours is in partnership with most vendors and hotels on the island, so if you don't know exactly what you want to do (or can't find a tour company to handle the arrangements), call the Sunlink office for assistance. ☎ 758-456-9100, www.sunlinktours.com.

Solar Tours specialize in Heritage Tours throughout the island. Look over their offerings online, or call for a schedule of tours to plantations, nature areas and other sites with historical or cultural significance. ☎ 758-452-5898, www.solartoursandtravel.com.

Self-Guided Tours
By Car

 If time is limited, it's quite possible to make a complete tour of St. Lucia by car in one long day. However, unless you're on a cruise with restricted shore time, we suggest you put yourself in island mode and take a relaxed approach to sightseeing. Allow time for a slow walking tour of **Castries**, the capital city, and drive up into the hills above the town to enjoy the historical sites and panoramic views on **Morne Fortuné**.

Devote one entire afternoon to the west coast with stops at **Pigeon Point National Park**, **Rodney Bay**, **Soufrière**, **Anse Chastenet**, **Marigot Bay** and the **Pitons**. On a third day, drive down to the southern tip of the island and watch from the **Anse de Sables** beach at **Vieux Fort** as windsurfers and kitesurfers perform amazing water feats, then head up the rugged and less developed eastern coast for stunning views of the Atlantic.

Warning: If you plan to make a driving tour in your own rental car, remember that vehicles travel on the left side of the road in St. Lucia. The main roads are paved and in reasonably good condition, but they are narrow, sparsely lighted and poorly signed. The coastal roads have hairpin curves and precipitous drop-offs, but few guardrails. Local drivers often travel at excessive speed, and accidents are common. Drive with extreme caution and give a short beep of your horn when approaching a blind curve. That said, confident drivers should not hesitate to rent a car on St. Lucia. It's by far the best way to explore the island.

Before you start your self-guided tour, pick up maps, brochures and visitors' magazines at one of the tourist offices. Kiosks are located at both airports and near both cruise-ship terminals. The best stock of free materials is available at the booths in the shopping complexes at Pointe Seraphine (☎ 758-452-4094) and La Place Carenage (☎ 758-452-2479), on the waterfront near the cruise-ship terminals in Castries. Staffing may be erratic, but the hours of operation are posted as Monday-Friday 8 am-4:30 pm, and anytime a cruise ship is in port.

Sightseeing with the Stars

Adventure Travel Guides cover all the sights and attractions, so you can decide what sparks your interest. But, vacation time is limited and precious, so we steer you to the best and the not-to-be-missed with a blatantly biased star system. Attractions that earn one star (★) are worth a visit. Two stars (★★) mean you should exert a bit of effort to go there. When you see three stars (★★★), just do it. You won't be sorry.

Touring the Island

Castries

- Morne Fortuné
- Derek Walcott Square
- Cathedral of the Immaculate Conception
- Pointe Seraphine and La Place
  Carenage Shopping Malls

Castries seen from Morne Fortuné

Many visitors skip a tour of the capital city because, to be honest, the capital is not pretty. The setting is gorgeous, between rolling green hills and the Caribbean Sea. But the main charm comes from the people, who are happy, energetic and friendly. Allow only an hour or two to glance at a few landmarks and shop at the duty-free mall and vendors' market.

Most of Castries' buildings date from after World War II and they are of utilitarian design. Fires ravaged the town four times between 1796 and 1948, so all of the original French and British commercial structures are gone. (If you're an architecture buff, you'll find the best French colonial buildings in Soufrière, the original capital and the island's oldest town.)

Castries

NOT TO SCALE

© 2007 HUNTER PUBLISHING, INC.

1. Tourist Office (two locations)
2. Cruise Ship & Ferry Dock
3. La Place CarenageDuty Free Shops
4. North Wharf; Police & Fire Stations; Cruise Ship Dock; Customs Office
5. Government House
6. Morne Fortuné Historic Area; Green Parrot & Bon Appetit Restaurants
7. Sir Arthur Lewis College
8. Police Headquarters
9. Derek Walcott Square; Library; Kimlan's Restaurant
10. Cathedral of the Immaculate Conception; Town Hall
11. Courthouse
12. Central Market; Constitution Park
13. King George V Gardens
14. Cara Suites; La Pensée
15. National Cultural Centre
16. To George F.L. Charles Airport
17. Auberge Seraphine
18. Coal Pot, Jacques Waterfront
19. To Almond Morgan Bay & Sandals Halcyon Resorts (Choc Bay)

For a panoramic view of the bustling downtown and harbor, take a drive to the top of 835-foot ★★**Morne Fortuné**, which rises over the south side of the city. This hilltop was coveted by French and English troops during the 18th and 19th centuries because of its high vantage point over the coast. At the top, you'll find the remains of **Fort Charlotte**, which was started by the French in 1768 and expanded by the British over years of back-and-forth rule by both countries. The name Morne Fortuné means "Good Luck Hill," and locals call it simply "The Morne."

Directions: From Castries, take Manoel Street south to Government House Road, which winds up the hill to the Morne. Coming from the south, watch for Government House Road on the right as you approach Castries on La Toc Road.

The most famous battle took place at Fort Charlotte on May 24, 1796, when, after a tremendous uphill struggle, the Royal Inniskilling Fusiliers captured the Morne from the French. If you visit the preserved historical site, which is now the **Sir Arthur Lewis College** (☎ 758-452-5507), you will see a monument that commemorates the gallantry of the British troops on that day. Some of the military buildings have been restored for use by the college, but the grounds still serve as a resting place for many ruins, gun emplacements and cannons. It's an interesting place for a stroll, and the views are stunning. On a clear day, you may be able to spot the island of Martinique far to the north.

SIR ARTHUR LEWIS

Arthur Lewis was born on St. Lucia January 23, 1915 to school teachers who had immigrated from the island of Antigua. His father died when he was seven years old, and Lewis completed high school by the time he was 14. This left him too young to apply for a college scholarship and too poor to pay for his own education. He went to work as a civil service clerk, but

won a government scholarship to study in England in 1932.

Lewis wanted to study engineering, but at that time, young blacks weren't being educated or hired as engineers. As an alternative, he signed up to study business administration at the London School of Economics (LSE) and planned to return to St. Lucia to work in government or private business. A quote from Lewis' autobiography says, "I had no idea in 1933 what economics was, but I did well in the subject from the start, and when I graduated in 1937 with first class honours, LSE gave me a scholarship to do a Ph.D. in Industrial Economics."

After graduation, Lewis took a job at the university of Manchester in England, taught economics, and was knighted for extraordinary service to the kingdom in 1963. That same year, he was offered a full professorship at Princeton University in the US. Many undergraduate students still read his history of world economics, *The Theory of Economic Growth*.

In 1979, Lewis shared the **Nobel Prize for Economics** with American Theodore Schultz. Not bad for a small-island orphan who didn't know the meaning of economics when he started college. He died in 1991, at the age of 76. He's buried on the grounds of **Sir Arthur Lewis College** on Morne Fortuné.

Once the British gained control of St. Lucia in 1814, the hill became a prestigious residential area. Many of the lovely mansions have been destroyed by a series of fires, but a few are still standing. Halfway up the hill, the Victorian-style **Government House** is the official residence of the governor general of the island, and you can peek through the iron gates at the grand old house and beautiful grounds.

When the residence was built in 1895, it was considered a "scandalous waste of money" and "a piece of costly extravagance, out of proportion with our means." Today, it seems an appropriate showplace for the island, and the Royal Guard patrolling the grounds couldn't look more at home.

Touring the Island

Government House

Inside the mansion, **Le Pavillon Royal Museum** holds documents and relics from the island's past. Tours are conducted by appointment only on Tuesdays and Thursdays, 10 am-noon and 2 pm-4 pm. ☎ 758-452-2481. The mansion itself isn't open to visitors, but you can take a virtual tour online, www.stluciagovernmenthouse.com/index2.html. If you don't want to bother with an appointment to tour the museum, a virtual look is possible at www.stluciagovernmenthouse.com/lepavillonroyalmuseum/tour.html.

A viewing area near the Government House offers a magnificent view of Castries' harbor. On most days, a rather aggressive group of vendors sell souvenirs in the paved lookout, which gives you no peace while admiring the view. Plan to come around mid-afternoon if you don't want to be bothered. The vendors tend to leave between 1 and 3 pm.

As you make your way back down the hill, consider a stop at one or more of the unique studios and workshops in the area. **Bagshaw's Studios** (☎ 758-452-6039), on the road down to La Toc, allows visitors to watch the creation of original silk-screen designs. At **Caribelle** on Old Victoria Road, (☎ 758-

Bagshaw's Studios (Paul Sullivan)

452-3785), you can observe local artists producing fine batiks on silk and cotton fabrics. **Eudovic Art Studio** (☎ 758-452-2747), at Goodlands, on the road leading down to the Cul-De-Sac valley, is the working studio of renowned sculptor Vincent Eudovic. You can visit the workshop where the artist and his students create art from the wood of the extinct *laurier canelle* tree. The studios are open Monday-Saturday 8:30 am-5 pm.

Back in **Castries** proper, seek out **Derek Walcott Square**

Eudovic sculpture (Paul Sullivan)

on Brazil Street. The park is named for one of St. Lucia's two Nobel Prize winners. Derek Walcott won the award for literature in 1992. Sir W. Arthur Lewis won the prize for Economics in 1979. Busts of both Laureates are displayed in the square. The square has been restored and is considered a national heritage treasure. Castries' oldest French-style wooden buildings surround the green park, and a 400-year-old samaan tree sits on the eastern side.

A samaan tree, also called a rain tree because its leaves are thick and hold rain water. After a shower, the tree continues to drip water long after the sky has cleared. On St. Lucia, it's known as the massav tree.

 Tip: Leave your car in the multi-level parking lot opposite the Castries Market on John Compton Highway for EC$1.50/US$.60 per hour, or park free on the edge of town and walk or taxi around the city. A water taxi will bring you to downtown Castries from Pointe Seraphine (a shopping complex on the Vigie peninsula with free parking) for about EC$2.60/US$1.

Who is Derek Walcott?

Derek Walcott is a poet and playwright who won the Nobel prize for literature in 1992, due in part to his 1990 masterpiece *Omeros*, an epic poem that put St. Lucia on the literary map. He is known in the United States as the founder and former artistic director of Boston Playwrights Theatre. His plays have been produced by many American groups, including the New York Shakespeare Festival, the Mark Taper Forum, the Negro Ensemble Company and the American Repertory Theatre. His stage adaptation of Homer's *The Odyssey* was performed by the Royal Shakespeare Company in London in 1993, where it received rave reviews and played to sold-out audiences.

Derek and his twin brother, Roderick, were born in Castries, St. Lucia in 1930. Their father, a watercolor artist, died when the boys were young, and their mother raised them while running the island's Methodist school. Derek studied at St. Mary's College on St. Lucia, and later at the University of the West Indies on Jamaica.

At the age of 18, Derek published *25 Poems*, but he is better known for poems and plays that he wrote later in life. Among his most recent works is the musical *The Capeman,* written with singer Paul Simon, and performed on Broadway in New York City.

In addition to winning the Nobel prize for literature, he has been honored with the 1971 Obie Award for *Dream on Monkey Mountain*, and the 1988 Queen's Medal for Poetry. Currently, the 77-year-old author teaches poetry and drama in the Creative Writing Department at Boston University and gives readings and lectures throughout the world. He divides his time between his homes on St. Lucia and New York City.

Touring the Island

Across Laborie Street from the east side of the square, you'll see the stone **Cathedral of the Immaculate Conception**, which was begun around 1894 and completed in 1931. This building is the largest Catholic church in the Caribbean and was elevated to the status of a Minor Basilica on May 11, 1999. The clock tower is particularly noteworthy. It is centered on Derek Walcott Square and is of a slightly different style than the Romanesque church itself.

Go inside to see Biblical scenes painted by internationally-renowned St. Lucian artist **Dunstan Saint-Omer**, who also designed the national flag. (Notice his trademark black Christ and Madonna.) Fresh flowers sit on side-alters and candles give off a lovely light. If you can arrange to attend mass on Sunday, you will be in the company of parishioners decked out in their multicolored best. Service times may change seasonally, so call the cathedral for current information. ☎ 758-452-2271.

Castries Market (Paul Sullivan)

Another colorful sight is the **Castries Market** and **Vendors' Arcade** on Jeremie and Peynier streets. A bright orange-red roof covers one area, but stalls spill out of the buildings and spread along both sides of the road. You can't help getting caught up in the vibrant excitement as countless merchants invite you to sample their wares. Vendors open their stalls Monday-Saturday 6 am-5 pm. Saturday mornings are the busiest time, but things get chaotic when a cruise ship is in port, too. Booths are stocked with fresh produce, straw baskets, wood carvings, T-shirts and local crafts. Follow the smoke and enticing aromas coming from behind the market to the restaurant stalls that serve up generous, but inexpensive, meals featuring fish, rice, and vegetables.

Architecture buffs will want to wander down **Brazil Street** to view the colonial West Indian buildings that have withstood hurricanes and fires over the years. One of the most attractive structures is a green-trimmed white house across from Walcott Square. It was built in 1885, about the same times as its gingerbread-embellished neighbors. These houses were once the homes of European aristocrats who colonized the island. Some are now shops, but most are private residences and closed to the public.

La Place Carenage

If you would like to do a little shopping before leaving town, stroll down Jeremie Street toward the bay to **La Place Carenage**. This waterfront shopping complex is a converted cargo shed. It has housed duty-free shops for years and was recently spruced up and expanded to include 27,000 square feet of new shops, art galleries, and restaurants. The top floor features an interactive historical display, and a new well-stocked tourist office is located on the ground floor. Shops and offices are open Monday-Friday 9 am to 4 pm and Saturday 9 am to 1 pm; if a cruise ship is in port, they're open on Sundays from 9 am to 4 pm.

Touring the Island

Take a water taxi from the downtown wharf to **Pointe Seraphine**, a Spanish-style shopping mall on the south shore of the Vigie Peninsula. It is not as large as La Place Carenage, but it still has about three

Pointe Seraphine

dozen upscale shops. It was built a decade ago on reclaimed land at the north end of Castries' inner harbor adjacent to two cruise-ship berths. It's laid out around a pleasant courtyard and houses the usual international duty-free stores, local boutiques, a bank, several restaurants, a tourist information office, and a car rental agency. Most businesses here are open Monday-Friday 9 am to 5 pm and Saturday 9 am to 2 pm; if a cruise ship is in port, Sundays 9 am to 5 pm.

Remember: You must show your passport and airline ticket to make duty-free purchases.

The Northwest

- Rodney Bay
- Gros Islet
- Pigeon Point National Park
- Pointe du Cap

The road north out of Castries is the well-maintained John Compton Highway, which intersects the Gros Islet Highway at the George F.L. Charles Airport on the **Vigie** peninsula, the northern arm of the Castries harbor. A left turn to the west and another left turn onto Peninsular Road will bring you parallel to **Vigie Beach**. The water here is calm, and the beach is popular with locals who often leave litter behind.

Rodney Bay Village & Marina

Gros Islet

Cemetery Street

Dauphin Street

Coral Avenue

Castries-Gros Islet Highway

Reduit Beach

Reduit Beach Avenue

Orchid Road

Flamboyant Drive

Cashew Drive

Orange Crescent

1. Yacht Club
2. Spinnakers; Rex Resorts
3. Tuxedo Villas, The Buzz, Memories of Hong Kong
4. The Lime Restaurant; Taxi Stand
5. Caribbean Jewel Resort
6. Pizza Pizza, Elena's Ice Cream
7. Ti Bananne, Dominos, Coco Palm, Coco Kreole
8. JQ Rodney Bay Mall, Burger King, KFC, Subway
9. Bay Gardens Hotel & Bay Gardens Inn
10. Key Largo
11. Endless Summer Cruises
12. Marina; Scuttlebutts. Bread Basket, Elena's Ice Cream
13. Boat Yard
14. To Pigeon Island National Park
15. Police Station (2 locations)
16. To Rendezvous, Windjammer, Sandals, Stonefield Estate Villa, Ladera Resort

N

NOT TO SCALE

© 2007 HUNTER PUBLISHING, INC.

Follow the road uphill to the far western tip, where you will see some government buildings (built in the late 1800s by the military) and a lighthouse, built in 1914. According to map dated 1746, the French used this area as their capital and had a fort here before they moved to higher ground on Morne Fortuné. Vigie means lookout or watchtower in French, and on a clear day, you may be able to spot the Pitons and Mount Gimi, the island's tallest peak.

The Coal Pot (Paul Sullivan)

The Coal Pot restaurant (☎ 758-452-5566) is right on the water and the food is excellent. You'll have to call ahead to get one of the few tables, especially during high season, and lunch is served for only two hours, noon to 2 pm, on weekdays.

Back on the Gros Islet Highway, heading north, you'll pass some unsightly commercial and industrial sites before you come to **Choc Bay** and its superb beach. Watch for turnoffs that lead to the water. Several beach bars and restaurants line the golden sand, and you can enjoy lunch or a snack while observing **Rat Island** a short distance offshore. Arawak Indians once lived on the outer island, and people with communicable diseases were banished there in the 1800s, but the place

Choc Bay

is uninhabited now. One of the Sandals hotels is nearby, and you can pick up supplies or souvenirs at Gablewoods Shopping Mall.

Union Nature Trail and Mini-Zoo is a short distance inland from Choc Bay, so you may want to stop there to see the exhibits and take a short stroll through the herb garden. Drive in the direction of Babonneau, then watch for signs to the Union Agriculture Center. If you're dressed and shoed for hiking on gravel, consider doing the one-mile **Hillside Trail** that loops through the woods and gains about 350 feet in elevation. The **Garden Trail** is only a one-mile walk along a garden path, and you can do that quickly, even wearing flip-flops. If you don't spot a parrot in the wild, there are three in the zoo.

★Rodney Bay

Rodney Bay is a short distance north, once you return to the Gros Islet Highway. This isn't a town, but rather a district of hotels, restaurants, nightclubs and shops around an 80-acre lagoon that opens to the sea through a man-made channel cut between Reduit Beach and the village of Gros Islet. The large, modern marina is a popular stop for yachtsmen. You can spend an enjoyable afternoon just strolling around the dock looking at all the magnificent boats.

Following pages: Rodney Bay

Touring the Island

Admiral George Rodney

George Brydges Rodney began his long career in the British navy in 1732 at the age of 14. He was an admiral in 1782 when he used the bay that bears his name as a base of operations for his memorable victory over the French in the "Battle of the Saints."

In the spring of that year, François de Grasse commanded the French fleet stationed on nearby Martinique. Rodney kept on eye on de Grasse from an observation point on Pigeon Island, so he saw the 33 French ships sail into the Caribbean to join forces with their Spanish allies on Haiti. Suspecting they intended to attack Britain's major stronghold on Jamaica, Rodney set out with 37 ships to intercept de Grasse.

The two admirals met head-on between Guadeloupe and Dominica near the Iles des Saintes. On the morning of April 12th, both fleets positioned themselves for battle, but Rodney ordered his captains to break formation from "line ahead" and burst through the middle of the French line. This ungainly move confused the French, who had no strategy for countering it.

The British fleet splintered the French ships into three unequal contingents, and De Grasse was unable to regroup the vessels into line. With the French fleet completely disorganized, de Grasse surrendered his flagship; Rodney and his men emerged the victors with seven French ships in captivity. The loss crippled the French campaign in the Caribbean, and secured Britain's power on key islands.

De Grasse was the first French naval commander ever to be taken in combat, making Rodney the first to capture a French fleet commander in a battle as well as the first commander to successfully challenge the orthodox British navy "Fighting Instructions." King George III of England honored Rodney by granting him the title of baron.

Before the channel was dug, the harbor that is now called Rodney Bay was a mangrove swamp. You will see the marina on your left just after you pass the JQ Charles Shopping Mall heading north on the Gros Islet Highway. To get onto **Reduit Beach**, turn left onto a signed road just before the shopping center.

The annual Atlantic Rally for Cruisers (ARC) ends at Rodney Bay Marina each year. Sailors start from Las Palmas de Gran Canaria (Canary Islands) in November and cross the Atlantic in the world's largest trans-ocean

The Atlantic Rally for Cruisers

sailing event. About 225 yachts from 25 nations make the 2,700-nautical-mile trip in 12 to 24 days. The race ends with a celebration at Rodney Bay, which spills over onto the entire island. For information about the upcoming event, see www. rodneybaymarina.com/Events.htm.

Spend some time at the marina and on the long, beautiful beach. You can book all types of watersports and cruises here, including a buccaneer adventure on the **Brig Unicorn** (☎ 758-452-8644, www.seaspraycruises.com), the tall ship that recently starred in the movie *Pirates of the Caribbean*. Kids especially like to climb aboard the *Unicorn* to sail down the west coast hunting for treasure and raiding villages.

Lunch break: Buzz (☎ 758-458-0450) is a favorite and always attracts a nice crowd. Have drinks at the bar or grab a table and order one of the Creole fish dishes. If you just need a snack, head for Elena's Italian Ice Cream and Coffee Shop (☎ 758-458-0576). Next door, you can order by the slice at Pizza Pizza, and there's a playground to keep the kids happy. (☎ 758-452-8282).

Gros Islet, on the north side of the harbor, is a charming little fishing village with a few narrow streets lined with brightly-painted wooden island-style houses and not much going on – until Friday night. On Friday night, you won't be able to get near the place. Streets are blocked off, rum shops expand out onto the sidewalks, grills on front lawns and street corners sizzle with enticing aromas, and *soca* blares from huge speakers on the main strip. Residents from all over the island join tourists for this weekly blowout, known as *jump-up*, which lasts long into Saturday morning. Do not miss this incredible transformation. It's a lot of fun even if you don't dance, hate current music trends, detest alcohol and never eat street-vendor food.

Author's tip: Take a cab to and from jump-up, because parking and traffic is a nightmare. Dress casually and conservatively in cool clothing. Bring just enough Eastern Caribbean cash to see you through the evening, and leave all other valuables locked up at your hotel. Stick to the main streets, and be sensible about what you eat and drink.

If you're driving to Gros Islet, turn off the highway from Castries onto Dauphine Street, just north of Rodney Bay Marina. Don't plan to spend much time in town, because there's little to see. The only interesting structure is the Catholic church on the north side of the village. **St. Joseph the Worker** (☎ 758-450-8325) was built in 1926 on the site of another church that was destroyed by an earthquake 20 years earlier.

Pigeon Island

★★★ Pigeon Point National Park

Just north of Gros Islet, the highway splits. Follow the road to the left (west) out to Pigeon Point National Park, which, along with its man-made connection to the mainland, forms the northern curve of Rodney Bay. Before this historic spit of land was connected to St. Lucia in 1972, it was known as **Pigeon Island**, and many residents still call it by that name. You can now drive out to the "island" along a lovely causeway.

Under the watchful eye of the St. Lucia National Trust, the 44-acre park has been landscaped with spectacular gardens spread across grassy hills that slope down to soft, sandy beaches and a calm sea. Ruins of **Fort Rodney** stand at the top of a rise, offering dramatic views in all directions.

Throughout history, Pigeon Island served as a lookout post. First for the Carib Indians, and later for pirates and other unsavory characters who had need of an observatory. One of the most infamous residents was the corrupt Frenchman François le Clerc, better known as *Jambe de Bois* because of his wooden leg. During the mid-1500s, he hid out on Pigeon Island with treasure he pilfered from Spanish ships.

Touring the Island

View from Fort Rodney

Two hundred years later, English troops attacked the French army stationed on St. Lucia and took possession of the island. Under the command of Admiral George Rodney, the British built a Naval Base at Gros Islet Bay and heavily fortified Pigeon Island so that they could safely spy on the French units based on nearby Martinique. After England and France settled their multi-year battle for control of the eastern Caribbean, Pigeon Island was deserted, and the fort slowly disintegrated into ruins.

Today, the park is a favored setting for weddings and serves as the main venue for the annual **St. Lucia Jazz Festival**, which draws more than 10,000 visitors each year. Allow plenty of time to wander along the garden paths, explore the ruins and relax on the beach. One of the historic military buildings near the entrance to the park has been converted into a **Museum and Interpretive Center** displaying Arawak artifacts found on Pigeon Island and a multi-media presentation of St. Lucia's history. A gift shop sells rum produced on the island and a variety of souvenirs and books.

Several marked walking trails run through the park and out to the ruins of Fort Rodney. Take the path that runs along the south shore to a shaded military cemetery, where you can wander among 18th-century monuments that mark the graves of British servicemen who died on the island. From there, a signed trail leads uphill to the fort, signal stations and lookout points. This is a fairly gentle hike, and you can get to the top in about 15 minutes.

Pigeon Island (Chensiyuan)

Most of the buildings are in fairly bad shape, but they still tell a fascinating story. You'll see the US signal station on one rise, where the American navy was stationed from 1941 through 1947. On the next rise, you'll find the remains of the signal station used by British troops under the leadership of Admiral Rodney during the conflict with the French in the 1780s. Other ruins on the hills include the 18th-century fort itself, barracks, a gun redoubt and an artillery depot.

Before you leave the park, spend some time on the **beach**, a half mile of soft sand sloping to warm, calm water with good snorkeling conditions. The house that sits on the shore, between the cemetery and far western point, is the former home of Josset Agnes Hutchinson, an actress who lived on Pigeon Island from 1937 until World War II, and again from the end of the war until the causeway work began in the 1970s. During her time on the island, she entertained lavishly and was a cordial hostess to visiting dignitaries who arrived by boat. She died in England in 1978 at the age of 90.

*Lunch break: Drop into the English-style **Captain's Cellar** for a pint of local beer (Piton) or a sandwich. Serving hours are Wednesday through Monday, 10 am to 11 pm, and Tuesday 10 am to 5 pm; ☎ 758-450-0918. More substantial snacks and lunch are available at the waterside **Jambe de Bois Restaurant**. Ask to sit outside on the deck. ☎ 758-450-8166.*

Pigeon Point National Park is open daily, 9 am to 5 pm. The National Trust (☎ 758-452-5005) offers tours, but you also can explore on your own. A day-pass costs US$5; it includes entrance to the park and admission to the museum and interpretive center. A 10-day pass is available for US$15, so you'll break even if you visit the park at least three times. (Children five-12 years old get in for US$2.)

Pigeon Island was named for the common wood pigeons (also called redneck pigeons) that once nested on the island. You can see them at the Mini-Zoo adjacent to the Union Nature Trail (see Hiking for more information).

Pointe du Cap

From Pigeon Point, take the main Gros Islet Highway north to Pointe du Cap and the elegant residential area known as **Cap Estate**. A vast section of this area was once owned by Monsieur de Longueville, the French military commandant of St. Lucia. He constructed a large house here in the 1740s, but the residence was completely destroyed 50 years later during a slave rebellion related to the French Revolution. Comte de Brette, a distant relation of Monsieur de Longueville, took over the land, planted sugar cane and built himself a lavish mansion to serve as the centerpiece of the island's largest plantation. In 1817, a hurricane demolished this house, too.

In the 1960s retired British Lt. Colonel E. Harrison reconstructed the de Brette home, and today the structure is the **Great House Restaurant** (☎ 758-450-0450. The 200-seat open-air **Derek Walcott Theatre** (☎ 758-450-0551) sits

Villa on Cap Estate

under towering trees adjacent to the exquisite colonial manor, and serves as the venue for dance, music and dramatic performances.

Some of the island's most beautiful homes are built in Cap Estate, and the rolling hills are also a lovely backdrop to exclusive resorts, vacation villas and an 18-hole golf course. Spend some time driving through this serene area, which seems far removed from the congestion of Castries and the high energy of Rodney Bay.

Art lovers will want to stop at the studio and gallery of internationally-known artist, **Llewellyn Xavier**. It's housed in a white building on your left just past the second traffic circle, as you drive in from the south (☎ 758-450-9155). Xavier's art is permanently displayed at the Museum of Modern Art in New York, the Smithsonian American Art Museum in Washington, DC and at Oxford University. His St. Lucia gallery also shows a selection of works by other well-known Caribbean artists, includ-

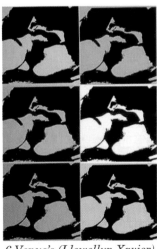

6 Venus's (Llewellyn Xavier)

Touring the Island

ing Derek Walcott (his Nobel Prize is for literature, but he is a man of many talents) and Roy Lawaetz.

Hikers and nature lovers should tackle the rugged roads that lead off into the wild hills of Pointe du Cap and around the northern tip to **Pointe Hardy** on the east coast. This portion of the island is arid and scrubby, quite unlike most of St. Lucia. Unmarked trails run through the craggy landscape, and you can explore on your own or contact the Forest Department to request a guide (☎ 758-450-2231).

A new development called **The Point at Cas en Bas** has tamed parts of this area somewhat. It covers 360 acres on the northeast tip of the island where the Caribbean meets the Atlantic. Once a sugar plantation, this parcel of land has been converted into a private residential area with a Jack Nicklaus signature golf course and luxury homes.

The Southern Loop

St. Lucia's main highway runs south from Castries, down the western coast, around the southern tip, and up the eastern coast to the village of Dennery. At Dennery, about mid-island on the Atlantic side, the main road turns inland, creating a shortcut back to the west coast. You can drive the entire southern end of the island in one day, even if you stop often to see the sites.

Top Sites

- Marigot Bay
- The Piton Mountains
- Diamond Falls and Botanical Gardens
- Sulphur Springs
- Qualibou – The Drive-In Volcano
- Cape Moule à Chique
- Anse la Raye Fish Fry

The loop road from Castries through the southern section of the island passes some of the most attractive scenery in the eastern Caribbean. Paved, but narrow and steep, the main highway spirals up into forested mountains and dips into river valleys thick with banana trees.

If you like military history and panoramic views, stop at **La Toc Battery**, a restored fort from the island's colonial period. You

La Toc Battery

can tour the grounds daily during the winter months from 9 am to 3 pm, but only by appointment from May through November (☎ 758-451-6300). Give special attention to the 19th-century high-tech cannons, which were the first to use a rifle-style barrel, and their advantageous positioning toward the capital. The hoist and lifts used to raise the ammunition were new technology in the late 1800s and worthy of a quick inspection, even if you care nothing about weapons. Troops stationed here must have felt quite superior with their state-of-the-art equipment and advantageous view of the southern entrance to the Castries Harbor.

★★Marigot Bay

Continuing south on the west-coast highway through the **Cul de Sac Valley**, watch for signs marking the right turn onto the steep road down to Marigot Bay, a gorgeous natural harbor and among the most outstanding anchorages in all of the Caribbean. When you see the secluded cove, you will understand why pirates considered it an ideal hideout. Boats passing by in open water often miss the narrow opening that leads to the bay, which is tucked deep into the mountainous coast. Several guesthouses and inns are set among the trees on both sides of the bay, and a palm-shaded beach stretches out at the foot of the green hills. Transportation from one side of the harbor to the other and from the marina jetty to the beach is provided by a water taxi.

Marigot Bay

The new **Discovery Resort** is at the end of the road, just before you reach the water, where the marina is crowded with boats belonging to Moorings Yacht Charters. A couple of good restaurants are set back from the shore. Across the bay, which is reached by water taxi, you will see a white-sand beach and the rooftops of restaurants and resorts scattered among the wooded hills.

Lunch break: Order pizza or a fish sandwich at **Chateau MyGo** (☎ 758-451-4772), an open-air restaurant surrounded by trees right at the water's edge, or call **Doolittles**, adjacent to the beach

Doolittles (Paul Sullivan)

across the bay (☎ 758-451-4974), where the chicken roti is a good choice. You can wait for the water taxi on the pier, or call the restaurant to request a pick up. Return for dinner at the **Rainforest Hideaway** (☎ 758-451-4485), a recently remodeled waterside restaurant that's considered one of the best on the island.

On Marigot Bay (Paul Sullivan)

Look for O'Neal Leubin carving bird houses from coconut shells on the waterfront. He can wrap his delicate creations for travel, and they make a wonderful souvenir from the island.

Just inland from Marigot Bay, the main highway winds through the banana plantations of **Roseau Valley**, and you'll see signs pointing the way to **St. Lucia Distillers**, the award-winning producer of 25 brands of Eastern Caribbean rums and rum liqueurs, including Bounty. The factory and showroom are open Monday through Friday between 9 am and 3 pm, but you'll need a reservation to take the tour and sample the products.

There's a US$5 charge for the 90-minute guided tour, which includes a presentation and video about the history of sugar cane production, the background of rum and the distillation process. At the end, you'll be invited to enjoy an all-you-care-to-sip tasting, followed by free time in the gift shop. If you just want to sample the products, the tasting charge is US$2 per person. Should you decide to buy, you'll find very friendly prices. Call the office on weekdays for a reservation, ☎ 758-451-4258, www.saintluciarums.com.

Touring the Island

East of the distillery, a string of handsome waterfalls cascades down an inland river and ends in a large pool that's ideal for swimming. Look for a sign for **River Rock Falls** on the left as you approach the small village of **Anse La Raye**. The falls themselves are hidden in a rugged area of the hilly community of **Millet**. The St. Lucia Heritage Tourism Programme has laid out a trail along the **Venus River** called **Circle the Centre River Trail**. It snakes though Millet and down into the Roseau Valley. Find a local guide by asking around as you drive through the tiny settlements of Roseau and Anse La Raye.

This is a fairly short hike, so you may want to make it part of an exploration of the nearby rainforest. Pick up maps and arrange for an official guide by calling the Forestry Department, ☎ 758-450-2078, or the Heritage Tourism Programme, ☎ 758-451-6967, www.stluciaheritage.com.

Bird Alert

If you're a bird lover, do not miss the **Millet Bird Sanctuary Trail**, a 1.75-mile path that climbs to an elevation of about 1,000 feet. You'll see a large number and varieties of birds, including the indigenous species of St. Lucia parrot, black finch, oriole, pewee (shown at left) and warbler. A guided two-hour tour costs US$30, or you can wander the trail on your own for US$10. The Forestry Department trail is open Monday through Friday, 8:30 am to 3 pm. ☎ 758-451-1691.

Anse La Raye

★★ Anse La Raye

After you visit the falls, return to the main highway and travel south to the little fishing village of Anse La Raye to see the colorful boats in the cove and colonial-style houses on the town square. Stop at the local Catholic church, which was built early in the 20th century over the remains of a colonial chapel that was destroyed by a hurricane in 1780 and again by fire during island uprisings that broke out during the French Revolution. Villagers raised money and provided labor for the present building, and the lovely alter is from France. On the outside, along the street, you'll recognize the art work of Dunstan St. Omer (designer of the national flag) and his sons on a large mural of village life.

The Friday Night Fish Fry

Every week, the little community hosts a **Friday Night Fish Fry**, an event you should not miss. Around dusk the main street that runs along the waterfront is closed off, and residents set up grills to cook and sell freshly-caught fish. Tables line the street and beach, the rum shops and bars are open, and island music mixes with the sounds of locals and visitors eating, drinking and dancing. Kids are welcome, and often a local band provides entertainment.

Look for a metal bridge spanning the Anse La Raye River, which empties into the bay at the southern end of the village. Just before you cross the bridge, you'll see a sign marking the road to **La Sikwi**, a restored sugar mill that was built by the

Boats at Anse La Raye

British in 1876 on the 400-acre **Invergoll Estate**. The property is included in several organized tours, but you can look around on your own on weekdays from 9 am until around 4 pm. Don't miss the impressive 40-foot waterwheel, part of the machinery that produced molasses in the 1800s and lime oil in the early 1900s. The gardens are lovely, with blooming flowers and towering trees. Ask about scheduled performances that take place in the small open-air theater.

Just down the road, the village of **Canaries** is tucked into a river-fed cove, and you'll be drawn to the aroma of freshly baked cassava bread floating from the open windows of a small wooden building. This is **La Place Cassave** (Plaz Kassan), where a generations-old recipe is used to make bread from cassava flour in wood-fired ovens. Master baker Joan Louis is aided by her daughters in preparing the popular breads and a few other baked goods, which are for sale to the public. ☎ 758-459-4050.

Cassava is a root plant which is often boiled and eaten as a side-dish instead of potatoes. The flour can replace wheat flour in recipes, and is popular with people who are allergic to wheat. Americans are familiar with the starchy root flour as tapioca, which is often made into a pudding.

Nearby, **Anse La Liberté**, the only campground on the island, features six miles of hiking trails and a small beach with watersports equipment on 133 acres of sloping coastal terrain. The St. Lucia National Trust oversees the rustic compound, which has tents, a communal bath house and cooking facilities. If you're interested in camping, hiking, kayaking or taking a tour of the nearby heritage sites, call the National Trust, ☎ 758-452-5005, www.stlunatrust.org.

The Pitons

Soon after leaving Anse La Liberté, the road heads up into the fringes of the rainforest, then breaks out with breathtaking views of the twin **Pitons** as you drive down to **Soufrière**, the second-most important town on St. Lucia. If the shocks on your car can take a beating, it's worth making a quick detour to see **Anse Chastanet**. Look for a sign pointing the way up

Anse Chastanet (Paul Sullivan)

an incredibly rough road to the bay and resort, which share the same name. The beach here is quite spectacular, one of the finest dark sand beaches in the Caribbean. The close-in reef is protected as a national marine park and is a favorite with snorkelers and divers. You can easily spend the day here, rent scuba equipment from the dive shop, and dine in the casual resort restaurant. ☎ 758-459-7000.

Soufrière

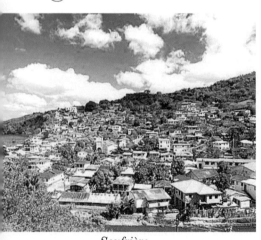

Soufrière

The town of Soufrière is older and, in many ways, more interesting than the capital. It was a spiritual place for the Arawak and Carib Indians because of its proximity to the inspiring Piton Mountains. French colonists set up a community here in 1746 and named it for the sulfurous springs that flow in the collapsed volcanic crater located a couple of miles away. In its prime, the city was an important port that bustled with businesses engaged in the export of coffee and cocoa. When the market for these products dwindled, Soufrière rapidly declined as well. Today, the village shows obvious signs of age and poverty, but the government is constantly encouraging improvements, especially around the waterfront.

> **Tip:** The **Soufrière Tourist Office** (☎ 758-459-7419) is on Maurice Mason Street across from the boat docks, near the police station. Stop in for brochures and advice about sightseeing in the town and surrounding area. The staff can suggest a guide, who will be more reliable than the fellows who approach you on the street. Office hours are Monday through Friday 8 am to 4 pm, and Saturday 8 am to noon.

Soufrière Bay

Plan to explore the town on foot, since the one-way streets are narrow and packed with slow-moving traffic, and parking spaces are scarce. Leave your car securely locked near the pier on the north end of the lively waterfront, then stroll around the jumble of crowded streets. Despite its lack of luster, Soufrière has an infectious spirit that makes it irre-

Touring the Island

sistible, especially on Saturday mornings, when the local market takes over the shaded walkway along the waterfront. A block inland, between Bridge and Church Streets off Sir Arthur Lewis Street (named for one of the island's two Nobel Prize winners), **Elizabeth Square** is the town's green centerpiece. Peek into the old stone **Lady of Assumption Church**, which overlooks the east side of the square. It was built in 1953, but stands on ground that housed older churches, which were destroyed by hurricanes, earthquakes, and fires. With so many disasters over the years, it's surprising that much is left of the original town, but you will see examples of French colonial architecture around the square and along the waterfront.

Plantations, Gardens & Waterfalls

★★ Diamond Botanical Gardens

Diamond Falls

Leaving Soufrière, follow Sir Arthur Lewis Street, on the south side of Elizabeth Square, about a mile inland to the **Soufrière Estate**. The plantation won a preservation award from American Express and is one of the historic sites targeted by the Nature Heritage Tourism Campaign, which seeks to increase tourism through environmental protection. The site encompasses the Diamond Botanical Gardens, a 30-foot **waterfall**, and thermal **mineral baths**.

King Louis XIV presented the 2,000-acre property to Philippe Devaux in 1713 as part of his landgrant program. The estate was developed into a thriving sugar plantation, and parts of it are still privately owned by the original family. You can visit the estate and gardens Monday through Saturday from 10 am to 5 pm. Tickets are US$4, ☎ 758-459-7155.

A marked path leads up a gentle slope through the shaded garden planted with flowering bird-of-paradise, hibiscus, and ginger lily. Signs below the plants explain what you're seeing, and it's interesting to trace the intoxicating fragrances of familiar spices to their source. At the end of the trail, you come to a steep gorge and **Diamond Waterfall** pouring from a fissure into a rocky pool. The cascade starts high up the cliff and comes down the rock face in six stages. Sulphur from underground springs colors the water shades of bright green, blue, and purple, and stains the rocks a deep, rusty orange.

In 1784, King Louis XVI ordered the construction of stone baths over the estate's sulphur-laden springs so that his troops could benefit from the curative powers of the water. The springs emerge from the ground at 106°F, with a mineral composition similar to the famous healing baths at Aix-les-Bains, France. Today, you can soak in the warm mineral baths that have been built next to the waterfall among the ruins of the original French structures. Admission to the communal pool is US$2.50, and a private soaking costs US$3.75.

Fact or Fiction?

Islanders claim that **Joséphine Bonaparte**, wife of Napoleon, bathed in the mineral baths built by Louis XVI. There's no proof, but no one can disprove it, either. Joséphine was born on June 23, 1763 in Les Trois-Îlets on the nearby French island of Martinique. Christened Marie-Rose de Tascher de la Pagerie, she was raised on a Martinique plantation, so it is very likely that she did come to the springs for an occasional beauty bath.

Touring the Island

Toraille Waterfall

When you leave the Soufrière Estate, take time to drive east, toward the village of Fond St. Jacques, until you come to the lush gardens that surround the Toraille Waterfall. A nature trail twists through the dense green foliage splattered with brilliant tropical flowers to the falls, which plunge 50 feet over a cliff and tumble into a natural pool. You can slip into your swim suit in the changing room, then stand under the falls for an

Toraille Waterfall

energizing massage. Tour groups show up at midday, so arrive early morning or late afternoon, when you'll have only the singing birds and scampering lizards for company. The grounds are open daily, 9 am to 5 pm, and admission is US$3.

En Bas Saut

Farther east, about six miles inland from Soufrière, is a nature trail within the rainforest that leads to two waterfalls at the foot of Mt. Gimie. The name is En Bas Saut, which translates as "below the falls," and refers to the natural swimming pools under the spectacular falls along the 2½-mile trail. The water is clean, so bring your swim suit and a snack and plan to spend the afternoon. Check in at the trail office Monday through Saturday 8:30 am to 2 pm to pay the access fee of US$10. ☎ 758-468-5645.

Morne Coubaril

Your next stop is one of the island's first major estates, which has been opened to the public as a re-creation of pre-mechanized plantation life. Visit the magnificent Morne Coubaril, if just for the glorious views of the Pitons. It's located east of the main west-coast highway, across from the entrance road to the Jalousie Plantation Resort. King Louis XIV granted this land to three brothers

Morne Coubaril

in 1713, one of the earliest allotments of Crown land on St. Lucia. The plantation originally covered 2,000 acres and grew cocoa, coconuts and manioc (tapioca), but today the estate is only 250 acres of lushly landscaped land and refurbished buildings.

If you opt for the 90-minute guided tour, you will walk along the original mule-carriage pathway to the restored slave quarters, then see how crops were processed in the days before mechanization. The renovated great house is lovely and furnished just as it was in the 1700s. Visit daily from 9 am to 4:30 pm for US$6, ☎ 758-459-7340.

Fond Doux Estate

Three miles from Soufrière is the working cocoa plantation on the Fond Doux Estate, which was established in the mid-1700s on land granted to French settlers. Recently, the estate began welcoming overnight visitors with accommodations in stand-alone cottages or refurbished bedrooms in the main house. But the primary purpose of Fond Doux is growing cacao beans and turning them into chocolate for the Hershey Company. If you visit for the day, you'll get a tour of the lavishly landscaped grounds that include thriving cocoa, banana and coconut trees, military ruins and other historical structures. In the work area, you'll be able to see how chocolate is produced, and then have the opportunity to buy some tasty

Touring the Island

Fond Doux

estate-made souvenirs in the gift shop. If you're up for a strenuous hike, take the steep trail up to **Chateaubelair** hill for an outstanding view of the Pitons and Caribbean Sea. Then, enjoy refreshments or a buffet lunch in the little restaurant. The estate is open daily 9 am to 4 pm. Admission is US$6. Call ahead to verify tour times and make a reservation for lunch, ☎ 759-7545, www.fonddouxestate.com.

★Qualibou – The Drive-In Volcano

This gurgling attraction on Mount Soufrière is a must-see, simply because it cannot be described with words. First, realize that it is no longer an actual volcano, and you can drive only as far as the parking lot. The Carib Indians called this spot *Qualibou*, a word that means "place of death." You'll understand why when you see the vast field of steaming jets and pools of boiling mud. To complete the scene, a hellish rotten-egg stench hangs in the air.

Nonetheless, Qualibou is a tourist magnet and today's residents flock to the warm sulfur springs to bathe in the mineral-laden water. The volcano that produced this devastated site collapsed about 39,000 years ago. Many years later, the Arawaks and Caribs worshiped their fire god in this awe-inspiring place.

The chemistry-lab odor is overwhelming at first, but you quickly become accustomed to it as you cross a footbridge that straddles a small stream and make your way uphill to a viewing point overlooking steaming craters and churning vats of black sludge. At one time, you would have been allowed to roam around freely, but some years ago a guide fell through the thin-crusted caldera into scalding water. He survived, but now the Soufrière Development Foundation restricts access, oversees safety and maintains the geological site. As part of an ongoing enhancement plan, the area now has landscaped sections, an interpretive center, vendor space (buy some soap made from the iron-rich mud to take home) and a restaurant.

★ Sulphur Springs

Sulphur Springs

Look for a sign pointing the way to the Sulphur Springs baths near the entrance from the parking lot. Take the path on your left to the natural hot springs pools, where you can stand under a waterfall that pours into a mud-bottom pool. This mud is loaded with minerals that are said to be therapeutic, and many sunburned tourists claim instant relief.

More modern baths are located a short distance upstream, where hot springs flow into a concrete pool. This water, which also is laced with minerals and will stain your swimsuit, is hotter and said to soothe arthritis and muscle pain. Try it after a strenuous hike up the Pitons. The admission fee is US$7 and includes a guided tour. The springs are open daily 9 am to 5 pm.

Touring the Island

The Pitons & Beyond

The Pitons

Back on the Soufrière-Vieux Fort highway, you will have a dazzling view of the Pitons as you drive south. These twin volcanic peaks were declared a **UNESCO World Heritage Site** in 2004 and are extraordinary in the way they soar almost 3,000 feet straight up out of the Caribbean Sea and dominate the island's entire western coast.

It's possible to hike **Gros Piton**, which is shorter and wider than its twin, **Petit Piton**, but you must have permission and be accompanied by a guide from the Gros Piton Tour Guides Association. Contact the office in the village of **Fond Gens Libre**, which is open daily from 8 am to 3 pm, to make arrangements and pay the US$25 access fee. ☎ 758-459-9748.

Even if you don't plan to make the difficult hike to the top, stop at the visitor center in Fond Gens Libre to see the exhibits and walk a bit of the nature trail. The first part of the path is an easy stroll up a gentle slope that opens onto panoramic views of the sea. About halfway up, the ascent becomes steeper and more rugged. You will need to be an experienced hiker in excellent shape to make it to the summit and back. Find the little village of Fond Gens Libre on a rough dirt road off the main highway, then watch for a sign directing you to the visitor center.

The Pitons with Soufrière below

In English, Fond Gens Libre means "village of the free people," which refers to the community of slaves who hid out in this area during their fight for freedom in the rebellion of 1748. Your guide up Gros Piton may well be a descendent of these revolutionaries.

Choiseul

The pleasant fishing village of Choiseul is a short distance south of the Pitons on the west-coast highway. Named for a duke who served under King Louis XV, the settlement is now home base for the **Art & Craft Center**. You can wander around the workshop to watch the artisans making pottery, baskets, and wood carvings. The store offers good prices, and there's a large selection of traditional Caribbean handicrafts. The center is open Monday through Saturday, 9 am to 5 pm. ☎ 459-3226.

Balenbouche Estate

Leaving Choiseul, watch for a sign signaling your approach to Balenbouche Estate, a working farm and heritage site. This lovely 80-acre plantation is open to visitors and features a fine garden surrounding a home built in the 1800s and furnished in West Indies antiques. Overnight guests stay in eco-friendly villas as well as bedrooms in the main house, and the estate often hosts groups for workshops or retreats. Don't hesitate

Bal en Bouche villa

to stop in just to wander the grounds or visit the sugar mill and unrestored ruins. If you would like a guided tour or want to have lunch on the verandah, call for a reservation. ☎ 758-455-1244, www.balenbouche.com.

Change is in the Wind

As this book goes to press, St. Lucia's southern coast is undergoing drastic changes. From the quaint fishing village of **Laborie** (just south of Choiseul on the west coast), where Ritz-Carlton is building a mega resort and residential area, around the south tip to **Micoud** (on the east coast), where Westin is managing the newly constructed Le Paradis Golf Resort, rural island scenery is being converted to luxury. Expect the unexpected as you travel east and west from the southernmost town of Vieux Fort.

Laborie & Morne Le Blanc

Nearby Laborie is a quaint little fishing village and a giant step back to the past. But, it won't be for long. The Ritz-Carlton plans to open a 275-room oceanfront resort on Black Bay, which will displace farmers and fishermen. Drive the rocky potholed road up Morne Le Blanc to view the waterfront progress and admire the still-undeveloped southern plains.

Vieux Fort

Vieux Fort, at the southern tip of the island, sits on a flat plain that extends out into the water where the clear-turquoise Caribbean meets the deep-blue Atlantic. It's a traffic-jammed large port city and site of Hewanorra International Airport, where the runway stretches across the narrow width of the island from the east coast to the west coast. You'll see some quaint wooden buildings in town, and a fleet of fishing boats anchored in the bay. But, for the most part, the town is just a crowded commercial center.

Cap Moule à Chique

The lighthouse at Moule à Chique

The real attraction is the lighthouse view from Moule à Chique Peninsula, which juts out into the ocean at the south end of town. From the traffic circle, exit left onto New Dock Road and stay to the left as the road goes up into the hills. Leave your car and take a moderate hike to the top of the 730-foot hill, where you'll be able to see the Maria Islands to the east, all of St. Lucia's interior mountains to the north, and, on a clear day, St. Vincent, 20 miles to the south.

Anse de Sables

The beach at Anse de Sables is popular with windsurfers because of the steady wind and rolling surf. Swimmers enjoy the relatively uncrowded sand, but there's little shade. A few

Touring the Island

snack bars serve drinks and sandwiches. **The Maria Islands Interpretive Center** is on the waterfront, directly across from the islands, which are about a half-mile offshore. A small museum has an interesting natural history exhibit, which highlights Amerindian culture and explains the island's delicate ecosystems. You can arrange for a tour of the islands during business hours Monday through Friday, 9 am to 4:30 pm, ☎ 758-454-5014.

Maria Islands

It's worthwhile going out to the two uninhabited Maria Islands, Maria Major and Maria Minor. They are the protected home of nesting seabirds and two rare reptiles, the extremely scarce and harmless *kouwés* snake and the colorful *zandoli te* lizard (or Maria Islands ground lizard). You won't be allowed to visit during the nesting season from May 15 to July 31. At other times, you can go by boat with a guide and spend the day hiking through the scrubby forest, swimming from the beach on Maria Major, and exploring the underwater coral reefs. Day-trips cost around US$35 for a private guide and US$30 per person for group.

> Did you know? The **zandoli tè ground lizard** lives only on the two Maria Islands and nearby Preslin Island. Males have a bright blue tail and yellow belly. Females are brown with dark stripes. The **kouwés snake** lives only on Maria Major. It is green and brown and grows up to three feet long.

The East Coast

Top Sites
- Mankote Mangrove
- Mamiku Gardens
- Fregate Islands

Mankote Mangrove

Soon after you leave Vieux Fort, driving north up the east coast, you'll come to Mankote Mangrove Swamp, which serves as a source of nutrients for the fish nursery protected by a living reef in **Savannes Bay**. The shallow bay is an active fishing area and excellent breeding ground for conch and other sea creatures. From the observation tower you'll have great views of the bay and mangrove. If you want to tour Mankote Mangrove or visit the nature reserves on the offshore Maria Islands or Frégate Islands, you must arrange a guided tour through the St. Lucia National Trust, ☎ 452-5005.

Frégate Islands

Another nature reserve is located on the Frégate Islands. These two rocky chunks of land are named Frégate Major and Frégate Minor for the thieving, fork-tailed, jet-black frigate birds that live there. Boa constrictors (light brown and locally known as *tête chien*) and fer-de-lance snakes (tan with orange, diamond-shaped markings) live in the tall grass on the islands, but they are quite shy and rarely seen.

Banana fields in the Roseau Valley

East Coast Trail

You can't visit the Frégates themselves, but you should hike the East Coast Trail, a one-mile path that begins north of the

Touring the Island

community of Praslin and loops through a lush nature preserve. Environmentalist Peter Ernest guides hikers through
arid vegetation growing along the cliffs that overlook stony
beaches and points out the most interesting species of birds
and plants among the hundreds that are protected in the preserve. Tours are offered Monday through Saturday, and you
can make arrangements by calling Eastern Tours, ☎ 758-455-
3163 or 758-384-7056 (cell).

*You'll see acres and acres of banana fields on St. Lucia.
They, and tourists, are the core of the island's economy.
Bananas are actually an herb, not a fruit, and they grow
year-round in the tropics. Each plant can produce fruit
only once before it dies.*

Praslin Bay

Praslin Bay has been taken over by a stunning new 18-hole
championship golf course designed by Greg Norman. It's on
the grounds of the 554-acre Le Paradis Resort, which may be
complete by the time you visit the island. The development
features a marina and private homes, as well as the resort
and its beach facilities, spa, shops and restaurants. Like the
Ritz on the west coast, this Westin-managed property on the
east coast has drastically changed the look of the island.

★★ Mamiku Gardens

History lives on, however, at the nearby Mamiku Gardens, an
18th-century estate that has been fabulously restored and
opened to visitors. Look for signs on the main east-coast highway marking the turnoff inland to the gardens. You can walk
along flagstone paths through 12 acres of wild woodlands to
manicured areas with names such as Secret Garden and Mystic Garden. There are benches made of tree branches where
you can sit and look out on fabulous views of the Atlantic and
the Frégate Islands. The Brigand's Bar serves refreshments.

The Shingleton-Smith family has owned the property since
1906, but the main estate house was built in 1766 by Baron de
Micoud, a French aristocrat and former governor of St. Lucia.
The word Mamiku is actually the creole pronunciation of

House at Mamiku Gardens

Madame de Micoud, the Baron's wife, who ran the household until the island was taken over by the British in 1796.

Archaeologists have uncovered amazing relics on the grounds, and the estate has a rough and fascinating history, which includes being burned to the ground during the slave rebellion. Learn the entire story and see the artifacts during a tour of the estate, which is open daily 9 am to 5 pm. Admission is US$15 for adults and US$7.50 for children 16 and younger. ☎ 455-3729, www.mamiku.com.

Mamiku Gardens

Gift shop at Mamiku Gardens

*Lunch break: The best meals on this side of the island are served in the **Whispering Palms Restaurant at Fox Grove Inn**. Owner/chef Franz Louis-Fernand and his wife, Esther, are in charge of the kitchen, which turns out excellent dishes prepared with locally-caught fish and island-grown produce. Sit at a table on the shaded terrace so you can enjoy the wonderful view. ☎ 758 455-3271.*

Dennery

The handsome town of Dennery is on a protected bay about mid-way along the east coast. Stop here to admire the colorful, hand-crafted and creatively-named fishing boats. If you have time, follow the road at the south end of town inland along the Dennery River until you run out of pavement for some interesting scenery. Across the bay, you'll see the rather large Dennery Island. Hardly anything grows out there on the steep cliffs, and it is inhabited only by some sheep and goats.

As far as sightseeing in the town, only **St. Peter's Catholic Church**, overlooking the seaside, is of much interest. It was built at the end of the 18th century and is one of the oldest churches on St. Lucia. On Saturday nights, residents get together for a community fish fry, and visitors are welcome to drop by for a delicious and inexpensive dinner. Don't expect a big street party, like the one in Gros Islet or Anse La Raye on Fridays. This is a much more laid-back event.

Dennery

Fond d'Or Bay is just north of Dennery, and you will want to stop there to admire the picturesque shoreline. A wide white-sand beach is surrounded by tall cliffs and the Atlantic pounds relentlessly against the shore. A new nature and historic park is nearby in the adjacent **Mabouya Valley**, which is dotted with the ruins of sugar plantations and ancient Amerindian settlements.

Plan to spend some time at the park's interpretive center, then hike along the trails to see the natural and man-made sights. The valley has a mystical past laced with tales of snakes and spirits and lizards that fly. Within the park, you'll find a mix of ecosystems and a variety of interesting relics from the island's earliest days. This is a favorite venue for fringe activities during the annual Jazz Festival because of the combination of forest and beach. Fond d'Or Nature and Historic Park is open daily 9 am until 5 pm, and admission is US$10 per person. ☎ 758-453-3242.

Barre de l'Isle Ridge

The main high-way out of Dennery turns inland and snakes its way over the steep Barre de l'Isle Ridge that runs through the center of the island. You'll have good views of the interior forest reserves and the Roseau Valley as you drive back toward Castries. If time permits,

The falls at Errand Plantation

turn into the **Errand Plantation** (☎ 758-453-4554), which is a private working farm with a nice waterfall. Ask permission to drive up the dirt road, which is best traveled in a four-wheel-drive vehicle, to the trail leading to the falls. Organized bike and jeep tours come here, and you may want to sign up for one of them rather than strike out on your own. One to contact is **Cycle St. Lucia**, Palm Services, ☎ 758-458-0908, www.cyclestlucia.com.

Adventures

On Water

St. Lucia's west coast has long stretches of soft sand, natural harbors, and gentle Caribbean waves. The rugged east coast offers spectacular views from cliffs that shelter picturesque coves and fantastic Atlantic surf suitable for riding. Several tour operators run popular fishing, snorkeling, diving, and boating excursions to sites that cannot be reached by land.

Best Beaches

St. Lucia's best beaches are along the western coast where warm Caribbean waters and soft sand provide perfect conditions for swimming and sunning. On the northern end, around Castries and Rodney Bay, you'll find white or golden sand. To the south, where there are numerous isolated coves at the foot of steep mountains, you find black volcanic sand. The wilder Atlantic coast has marvelous isolated beaches with heavy surf that makes them too dangerous for swimming, but perfect for getting away from the main tourist areas. Water off the southern tip has become popular with kite-, board- and windsurfers.

All beaches on St. Lucia are public, but tables, chairs, umbrellas and watersports equipment may be reserved for guests of nearby hotels or restaurants. Total nudity and topless sunning are illegal, and residents are offended by tourists who walk around town or into shops wearing only swimsuits.

West Coast Beaches

Smuggler's Cove is on the far north end of the island in an elite residential area called Cap Estate. You must park on the highway just north of LeSport Resort and take steps down a steep incline to the sand-lined bay. While the beach is public, all equipment and refreshments are for guests of the all-inclusive LeSport Resort, so you may feel like an unwanted misfit. Get over it, and enjoy the cliff-sheltered white sand, calm sea, and good snorkeling.

Vigie Beach

Vigie Beach is at the southern end of popular Choc Bay, located between Castries and Gros Islet. While its golden sand is shaded by palms, it's often shunned by tourist because it sits near the runway at George Charles Airport and the beach is often littered. However, locals gather here, and families come on weekends to swim in the calm water. Follow the road uphill to the far western tip, where you will see some government buildings (built by the military in the late 1800s) and a lighthouse dating from 1914. You can't get into the lighthouse without permission from the St. Lucia National Trust (☎ 758-452-5005), but even the view from the ground is excellent. In fact, the peninsula has been used as a signal station as far back as 1722 (in French, *vigie* means "lookout").

Reduit Beach (say *red-wee*) forms the eastern arm of sheltered Rodney Bay lagoon. It's a spectacular beach with soft, deep, beige sand and tranquil water that draws tourists from the ultra-chic Papillon, and Royal St. Lucian resorts. You can get a drink at the resorts' waterside bars or rent equipment from their sports centers.

Reduit Beach

Parasailing and windsurfing instruction is available from a couple of beach vendors. The waterway into Rodney Bay Harbour is cut through the north end of the beach, separating it from the town of Gros Islet.

Labrelotte Bay is just south of Reduit and stretches between Windjammer Landing Resort and East Winds Inn. It is public, of course, but most of the people on the beach are guests of the hotels. The atmosphere here is quieter than at Reduit, but there are plenty of eating and watersports options.

Pigeon Island

Pigeon Island National Park has a pleasant sand beach near the pier, as well as several rocky waterfront areas for relaxing and enjoying the views. You'll have to pay an entrance fee to get into the park, so plan to visit this beach after touring the grounds or hiking along the trails.

Adventures

La Toc Bay, just south of Castries, is the crescent-shaped home of Sandals St. Lucia Resort. The beach is lovely, but strong currents sometimes make swimming a chore.

Marigot Bay

Marigot Bay, which is simply stunning, has a white-sand beach shaded by palm trees. A water taxi will take you across the bay to the beach, which is next to Doolittles Restaurant

Anse Couchon

Anse Chastanet

and the Marigot Beach Club. You can get drinks and lunch at several restaurants on both sides of the bay.

Anse La Raye is a shady beach that's popular with village residents. Bring a picnic and snorkeling equipment, because there are no facilities on the beach. The water is clear and ideal for snorkeling. The community throws a fish fry on Friday nights, and all visitors are welcome.

Anse Couchon's magnificent silver-sand beach is most easily reached by boat, and you can ask around in Anse La Raye or Marigot Bay for a water taxi or fisherman who will take you there for a reasonable fee. You can also get to the cove by walking down the steep stairs from Ti Kaye Resort, which is at the end of a long, rugged dirt road. Many of the scuba outfitters conduct dive and snorkeling trips to the bay because of the many colorful tropical fish that live below the crystal clear water.

Anse Chastanet (*ahns-SHAS-tin-ay*) isn't for everyone, and that's what makes it so incredibly fabulous for some. From its gritty black-sand beach you have a breathtaking view of the Pitons. A sudden steep drop-off close to shore leads to an underwater world that's protected as a marine reserve, so snorkeling and diving are excellent directly from the beach. Children and weak swimmers may feel uncomfortable here, but anyone who enjoys the ocean and its remarkable creatures will be captivated by the raw beauty. The Anse Chastanet resort is here, along with Scuba St. Lucia Dive Center, so you can have meals, rent equipment, and schedule boat excursions right on the beach. Tall palms and thatched-roof huts provide shade. The road down to the bay is brutally rugged, but worth it.

Jalousie Beach

Anse des Pitons is a crescent-shaped bay set between Petit Piton and Gros Piton, south of Soufrière. Glamourous Jalousie Plantation Resort is here, and you'll be stopped at the front gate before you reach the beach. Tell the guard that you wish to have lunch and visit the beach, and a shuttle will come to transport you. You also can arrive by water taxi from Soufrière, which may be simpler in the long run. The sand here is naturally volcanic and black, but the resort has imported tons of white sand to create a more desirable beach for guests. The water current is sometimes strong at Anse des Pitons, but snorkeling and diving are excellent below both the Piton mountains. Try to sign on for a dive trip or day cruise that stops here.

East Coast Beaches

Anse de Sables, (Sandy Beach) in the eastern curve of the peninsula near Vieux Fort and Hewanorra Airport, is the hot spot for wave riders. The Reef Kite & Surf rents equipment, gives lessons and has a Beach Café. This wide open stretch of sand meets warm, breezy seas and provides just the right conditions for wind-

Anse de Sables

powered water sports. Even if you don't want to participate, watching the wave acrobatics is terrific entertainment. The Maria Islands are visible about a thousand yards off shore. Beach huts and wireless Internet access are available at the beach bar and café. ☎ 758-454-3418, www.slucia.com/windsurf/.

Grande Anse is off a dirt road north of Dennery in the community of Des Barras. You'll need a four-wheel drive vehicle to get there unscathed, but the journey's well worth it. Leatherback turtles, the largest marine turtles in the world, come ashore on this white sand beach to lay their eggs. Guides patrol the beach during the nesting season to ensure that the turtles are not disturbed, but you can sign up for a turtle-

Grande Anse

watch expedition with **Desbarras Turtle Watch Tours** (☎ 758-450-6910 or 758-715-2237), if you are visiting from March through July. Eggs must be left undisturbed for about 60 days, then tiny turtles emerge and waddle instinctively into the ocean. This is an all-night affair, so if you decide to take part, be prepared to stay up until dawn.

Grande Anse is also a nature reserve for rare birds and the endangered fer-de-lance snake. This is not a swimming beach, because of the brisk winds and hazardous surf but, outside of turtle-nesting season, it's a lovely spot for walking, exploring and picnicking.

Cas en Bas is a reef-protected bay on the far northeast coast with excellent windsurfing conditions and a beach bar. You get there by hiking (one hour) or driving in a four-wheel-drive vehicle (45 minutes) along the crater-riddled dirt road that turns inland near the gas station north of Gros Islet. A somewhat easier route, if you can find it and get past security, is the road behind the new residential area and

Cas en Bas

golf course known as The Pointe at Cap Estate. When you finally get to the water by either route, you'll be glad you made the trip. Walk north a bit along a trail to secluded **Secret Beach** where you'll have the sand to yourself. **Donkey Beach** is even farther north along a narrow path. Here you'll find a pretty, rocky inlet with golden sand. You will probably have the entire coast to yourself, but occasionally a group will ride by on horseback.

Snorkeling

Best Beaches for Snorkeling

- Anse Pillowie (access only by boat)
- Anse Chastanet
- Anse Cochon

Carry a pair of fins and a mask everywhere you go. You'll find plenty of opportunity to snorkel in pretty bays all along the coast of St. Lucia, especially on the western Caribbean side. The **Soufrière Marine Management Area** (SMMA) protects a large portion of the coast and sea on the southwest shore, including Anse Chastanet, Soufrière Bay, and Anse l'Ivrogne. Fishing and anchoring are restricted in this area, so reefs and marine life flourish.

Look for various brightly colored fish that live among the rocks and coral. You'll recognize the cherub faces of blue-

green **French angelfish**, the stunning posterior of the **yellowtail damselfish**, the skinny **pipefish**, the long-nosed **trumpet fish**, and the chubby **puffer fish**. Pick up a fish identification guide at any of the dive shops for photos and descriptions of Caribbean sea life. You'll enjoy snorkeling and diving more if you're able to identify some of the tropical species.

Surprisingly, there are relatively few dangerous critters in the sea, and humans are almost never attacked. Nevertheless, it doesn't hurt to be on the lookout for the less friendly among them. You know about **sharks**, of course. If you see their trademark dorsal fin coming your way, be careful and never try to feed them or attract their attention. Most will swim by without any trouble. A grouchy sort may attack, though, and even nurse sharks deliver a nasty bite, so be prepared to move slowly out of their way.

Angelfish

Barracudas look fierce but are fairly shy. They're curious about humans and will hang around divers and snorkelers, but if you ignore them, they will soon swim away. **Stingrays** and electric rays can hurt you, but the sting or shock is usually mild, and most injuries occur when people disturb them from their naps.

Moray eels scare most people, but they won't use their sharp teeth unless you stick your hand into their private residence. Even then, they may not want to hurt you, but they can't see well and tend to treat every moving object as food. Never try to coax them out of their holes with a treat.

Moray eel

You'll also see gorgeous living coral and other invertebrates in the St. Lucian waters. **Elkhorn** (tan), **finger** (pale yellow or white), and **brain** (looks just like its namesake) are the most common corals. One to look out for is the dingy-brown **fire coral**. You may mistake it for a dead coral, but you'll know immediately that you're mistaken if you touch it. The hair-like polyps that

stick out of its branches deliver a powerful sting that results in painful welts on the skin. If you come in contact with fire coral, resist the impulse to rub your injury, which will spread the stingers. Treat the welts with cortisone cream as soon as possible.

You can snorkel off the beach in many places, and dive centers will take you out with a scuba group if there's room on the boat. Day-cruises often include snorkeling, also. If you want to go out on your own, ask at your hotel about the conditions in nearby bays. You may need a boat to get to some of the best secluded spots, and your hotel can suggest a reliable water taxi. **Anse Chastanet** is probably the most popular snorkeling spot, but conditions are also good at **Anse Cochon** (at Ti Kaye Resort), **Anse des Pitons** (at Jalousie Plantation) and **Anse Pillowie** (take a water taxi from Marigot Bay).

Cruise & Snorkel Trips

Get out on the sea and see what happens. You may be content to view the sights from above water, or maybe you prefer taking a peek at all the wonders just below the surface. The following operators conduct water tours that make stops in

Mystic Man tour

remote bays to allow you to snorkel, swim and relax on the beach.

Mystic Man Tours is based in Soufrière and offers an impressive menu of tours. Their fleet includes sailboats, motorboats, fishing boats, even a glass-bottom boat. Their most inclusive all-day tour includes a water taxi to Castries for shopping, lunch at Marigot Bay, snorkeling at Anse Chastanet, and a visit to the Sulphur Springs drive-in volcano and waterfall. Look over the other choices online, or call the office for prices and reservations. ☎ 758-459-7783, 758-457-1360, www.mysticmantours.com.

Sea Spray Cruises has a fleet of boats for regularly scheduled cruises along the west coast. The 138-foot *Brig Unicorn* is a fantastic replica of an 18th-century ship and was used in the movies *Roots* and *Pirates of the Caribbean*. Kids especially enjoy the "Pirate Day" cruises that include face painting and treasure hunts. *Mango Tango*, *Jus Tango* and *Tango Too* are catamarans that accommodate 50-150 passengers on cruises called *Tout Bagay*, which is Creole for "a little bit of everything." For rates and schedules, contact Sea Spray, ☎ 758-452-8644, www.seaspraycruises.com.

The Brig Unicorn

Endless Summer has two 56-foot catamarans, *Endless Summer I* and *Sunkist*, which leave Rodney Bay for full-day sightseeing tours along the west coast, half-day snorkeling tours along the northwest coast, and sunset party cruises. ☎ 758-450-8651, www.stluciaboattours.com.

Free Spirit, captained by Christian Richings, is a lovely 43-foot Sun Seeker. You can book a day at sea or arrange a sunset dinner cruise. No more than eight, and usually only six, passengers are aboard, which allows everyone plenty of room to move about. ☎ 758-452-8491, 758-519-6860, www.freespirit-charters.com.

Scuba Diving

Veteran divers say St. Lucia's underwater world equals or surpasses other Caribbean sites, and new environmental regulations insure that the pristine coral reefs and abundant sea life thrive and remain as undisturbed as possible.

Soaring mountains that captivate visitors on land continue below the sea and provide shelter for a tremendous variety of creatures and plants. One of the most popular dives in the West Indies is off the beach at **Anse Chastanet**, which is part of the Soufrière Marine Management Area, where an underwater plateau starts near shore. This shallow dive, from five to 25 feet deep, is great for novice divers and snorkelers. Brightly colored sponges, soft corals, and large brain corals are found here, along with goatfish, parrotfish, chromis and wrasse. Frogfish live in a cave at the base of the reef. Night divers have reported sighting a Loch Ness-like monster in the area, and locals joke about *The Thing* favoring Anse Chastanet as a vacation spot.

As you move farther from shore, the reef drops quickly from 20 to 140 feet in a solid wall of mixed corals, surrounded by schools of fish, crabs, lobsters, eels and an occasional hawksbill turtle. At around 100 feet, layers of porcelain-like plate coral are stacked one on top of another. The massive coral reef continues all the way to the bay at Soufrière in water that habitually offers 80 to 100 feet of visibility.

Marine photographers often capture shots of **Fairy Land**, a current-cleaned coral plateau off the Anse Chastanet Point. Because of the swift current, you must be an experienced diver accompanied by a knowledgeable dive master to explore here. Nearby, **Trou Diable**, the "Devil's Hole," is a mass of swim-through coral-covered boulders teeming with fish.

If you like drift diving, an excellent choice is along **The Wall** off **Anse La Raye**. A

The Wall

strong current moves you along a formidable vertical wall at depths of 40 to 80 feet, and you will see a colorful display of sponges and corals. Watch for sea turtles as you drift through thick schools of fish. A reef slopes gradually down from Anse La Raye beach, and is a habitat for many species of fish, such as groupers, spotted drums, scorpion fish, chameleon flounders and needle fish, which hide and swim among the iridescent vase sponges, barrel sponges and soft corals. Brightly colored fire coral is found at shallow depths, and huge boulders cluster on a slope below the wall.

Nearby, you can explore *Lesleen M*, a 165-foot freighter that was deliberately sunk at Anse La Raye in 1986 to create an artificial reef. Soft corals, sponges and hydroids (plant-like organisms related to jellyfish) harbor juvenile fish at depths of 30 to 65 feet. The freighter sits on an even keel in sand, and the hold and engine room are accessible. Both dives in this area are good for intermediate divers.

Virgin's Cove is close to the wreck. It is a semi-circular reef wall that drops to a sandy bottom in about 50 feet of water.

Adventures

Here you'll see spotted eels and sea slugs around a rich growth of barrel sponges and plate coral.

The Japanese dredge, **Daini Koyo Maru**, was sunk at the south end of Anse Cochon in 1996, about a mile farther offshore than the *Lesleen M*. Experienced divers can go through the interior of the 16,000-ton, 244-foot vessel, which is mostly intact, but upside-down, in 55 to 100 feet of water. The fun here is swimming through the access holes in the upturned decks, and divers who don't get disoriented in the topsy-turvy interior can navigate the full length of the dredge.

Superman's Flight

Other favored areas include waters below **Petit Piton**, where there are incredible clusters of sponge and coral. This is the location of **Superman's Flight**, a wall that drops gently to 1,600 feet and was featured in a scene from the movie *Superman II*. The strong current clears debris and provides good visibility. Nearby, around the base of **Gros Piton**, five-finger coral grows solidly from a depth of 15 feet to 50 feet in a site known as **Coral Gardens**. Rare sargassum-trigger fish live at greater depths. The slope here continues for hundreds of feet, so divers must monitor their gauges to avoid going too deep.

At the far southern tip of the island, where currents are very strong, the **Wawinet Wreck** is popular with highly experienced divers because it is rarely visited. The 400-foot-long freighter was sunk in 1980 to create an artificial reef for marine life. She is still in good condition, lying on her starboard side at a depth of 105 feet, and fully loaded with all her original equipment.

Perhaps the most talked about dive area is the **Key Hole Pinnacles**, which have been voted one of the *Ten Best Dive Sites* by *Caribbean Travel & Life Magazine*. It's a remarkable site where four volcanic peaks rise sharply from the ocean floor to within a few feet of the surface. Black and orange gorgonian coral grows on

the peaks, providing shelter for filefish, trumpet fish, large groupers, and a few seahorses. The location gets its name from a keyhole-like cutout through the cliff above the dive site.

Can you see the fish?

If you've never tried scuba diving, sign up for a resort course offered by most dive shops. After you practice with the equipment in shallow water or a swimming pool, an instructor will take you down 25 to 40 feet for a supervised tour of a reef or sunken boat swarming with marine life. This one-day course costs about US$80, including equipment.

Some vacationers spend a week on St. Lucia earning their open-water certification card. This intensive training includes book work, water exercises, and a series of dives. Costs average US$450 for the full five-day course to US$250 for the two-day open-water certification (classroom instruction is completed before you leave home).

Seahorse

Experienced divers must present a certification card when they sign in at the dive shop. Expect to pay about US$40 for a one-tank dive and US$70 for a two-tank dive, plus equipment rental. Multi-day packages bring the per-tank dive price down to as little as US$25. Off-season rates may be somewhat lower, but most dive shops stay busy year-round and don't discount much.

If you intend to dive several days during your vacation, check into special packages offered by some of the resorts with on-site dive shops. Often, the package price includes daily diving for the standard price of a room. Anse Chastanet Resort, Ti Kaye Village, Marigot Beach Club, Sandals, and Oasis Marigot are a few of the many hotels, villas, and all-inclusive resorts that offer package deals. Check the accommodation listings in this book for contact information.

Dive Operators

Island Divers is a full-service PADI facility with an adjacent bar and restaurant near Anse Cochon, on the light-sand beach below Ti Kaye Resort. Master scuba trainer Terroll Compton is the manager who oversees an enthusiastic staff. They offer a long list of morning and afternoon dives for all experience levels. ☎ 758-456-8110, www.islanddiversstlucia.com.

The beach bar at Island Divers

SCUBA St. Lucia is on the beach next to the Anse Chastanet Resort, just over a mile from the Soufrière Marine Management Area, and within view of the Piton Peaks. A pristine coral reef is in shallow water 10 yards from the beach, and the dive shop offers equipment rentals and guides for certified divers who wish to dive from shore. In addition, the full-service facility is a DAN partner and PADI Gold Palm Resort. Managed by Paul and Kelly German, the shop organizes daily dive trips in three high-powered boats, and offers guided snorkel tours. ☎ 758-459-7755, www.scubastlucia.com.

Frog's Diving is run by Tommy de Nobrega, an ex-military master diver with world-wide experience. The shop is at Harmony Suites in Rodney Bay and offers small group trips to sites all around the island with friendly PADI-trained guides. ☎ 758-458-0798 or 758-715-7794 (cell), www.frogsdiving.com.

Dive Fair Helen has shops at Marigot Bay and Vieux Fort with a flexible schedule of dives and a range of options for snorkelers and kayakers. As DAN partners and committed environmentalists, the PADI staff is vigilant about protecting the reefs and marine life. They have two customized dive boats with bathrooms, show facilities, shade and easy on-off access. You'll learn something interesting every time you go out with this company. ☎ 888-855-2206 or 758-451-7716, www.divefairhelen.com.

Buddies Scuba is a dive shop and fully-outfitted store at Waterside Landing Marina in Rodney Bay. Ian Drysdale is the ex-Royal Navy owner who operates the shop with his son, Lawrence, and two PADI dive masters, Elton and Cyril. They keep up a varied schedule of trips to sites around the island using their 30-foot oxygen-equipped customized dive boat. ☎ 758-450-8406, www.buddiesscuba.com.

International Billfish Tournament

Game fishing is fun, even for those who think sitting on a dock with a pole is a waste of the day. It's also addictive, and true big-game anglers are fiercely competitive. With that in mind, St. Lucia hosts the **International Billfish Tournament** each September, and winners are qualified to move on to the annual Rolex/IGFA (International Game Fishing Association) Offshore Championships in Mexico, the World Cup of game fishing. Such recognition makes the island one of the most popular fishing destinations in the Caribbean.

The four-day international event emphasizes conservation to safeguard the ocean's stock for future generations. Anglers catch, weigh, measure, tag and release their monster-sized creatures to gather points, which earn trophies and prizes at the tournaments final awards ceremony.

For information about the upcoming tournament, contact Milton McKenzie, ☎ 758-484-0707, Annie Hamu, ☎ 758-584-7990, or Bruce Hackshaw, ☎ 758-452-7044, or any of the game-fishing charter companies listed in the *Fishing* section of this book.

Adventures

Fishing

Yellowfin tuna

St. Lucia has outstanding sports fishing, and even novices get hooked on the sport, often after catching a whopper. More than 160 types of fish live in the surrounding ocean, and you'll see the local professionals out fishing every morning. It's a fascinating process to watch. Five men stand confidently, single-file in a long, narrow, brightly-painted skiff. Each is perfectly balanced as they glide through the water. Then, two men dive in and swim underwater looking for a school of fish. The other three fishermen wait for the scouts to signal a "find," then cast their net into the sea to scoop up an abundant catch.

Sailfish

You'll do your sports fishing a bit differently, farther from shore and in deeper water. Big game fish congregate about two miles offshore, where the water depth drops dramatically, so you don't have to travel for hours to get to the best fishing spots. Several veteran pros run excellent sportfishing operations on the island. They know where the trophy-sized creatures live, and have the custom-outfitted boats to get you out there to land one. All those listed below are staunch conservationists, who practice tag-and-release of all billfish. If you catch one, a tag certificate is issued to you from the International Gamefishing Association.

Tradition in Action

When you visit small coastal villages, notice the distinctive fishing boats pulled up on the beach. These traditional canoes still are being made by local craftsmen from the trunks of the *gommier* tree. Each canoe is carved from a single tree trunk. Gommier trees grow abundantly in the rainforest and secrete a resin that protects it from saltwater. Each tree is cut at the time of the new moon, because locals believe that harvesting at any other time will make the trunk susceptible to insects. The trees are partially hollowed in the forest to lighten their weight, then moved manually to the coast, where skilled workers painstakingly chip away with an axe to carve the trunk into a canoe. One careless cut will split the wood and make it worthless. When the trunk is hollowed enough, wooden bars force the opening wider and prevent the newly-sliced wood from shrinking. Eventually, wet sand is dumped into the hull to make the cutout wider and more permanent. After about a month, the bottom-heavy canoe is stabilized along the sides with cedar strips. Then the boats are ready to be painted and labeled with a clever name. Religious and cultural names are popular, such as *African Man* and *Jesus Is Love.*

Adventures

Dorado

Certain fish are more plentiful in various seasons, but you can catch wahoo, dorado, blue marlin, sail fish and yellow fin tuna throughout the year. Expect to pay about US$75 per person to join a scheduled half-day-trip. Private charters for up to four people run around US$800 per full day, and half of that for a morning or afternoon outing.

CELEBRATION TIME

In late June, the fishing communities of Vieux Fort, Dennery, Choiseul, and Anse La Raye celebrate **Fisherman's Feast** or, in Creole, Fet Peche. It's an event similar to the one held annually in Boston, Massachusetts, and its roots go back to a tradition started during the 16th century in Italy. Sicilian fishermen were devoted to the Madonna del Soccorso (Our Lady of Help), and dedicated a day each year to thanking her for her protection and abundant gifts from the sea. On St. Lucia, the tradition continues with a joyous celebration and special activities that begin in the morning with services at the Catholic churches. Priests then come out to the beaches to bless decorated boats and seaside sheds. Afternoon events include land games, boat races, and fishing competitions, and the day wraps up with live music, cookouts, and street dances. Contact the tourist office for exact dates and the location of planned activities, ☎ 758-452-7577.

Deep-Sea Charter Operators

Hackshaws Boat Charters and Sportfishing is a family business started more than 60 years ago by the late "Big Bill" Hackshaw. Today his sons David and Paul run things from Vigie Marina in Castries with the help of their own children. They have four customized boats for fishing, touring and whale-watching. Each is fully

Blue marlin

licensed and insured, outfitted with good fishing equipment and diesel powered. ☎ 758-453-0553 or 758-452-7044, www. hackshaws.com.

Wahoo

Mystic Man Tours is based in Soufrière, near many of the most popular fishing spots. Captain Mark and Captain Jack have more than 13 years experience tracking the big ones, and they're eager to take you out for the day on one of the two Mystic Man high-powered fishing vessels. Call the office for prices and reservations. ☎ 758-459-7783, 758-457-1360, www. mysticmantours.com.

Adventures

Mako Water-Sports at Rodney Bay Marina is home to *Annie Baby*, a six-passenger customized fishing boat outfitted with all the latest equipment. ☎ 758-452-0412.

Capt. Mike's Sportfishing Cruises out of Vigie Marina in Castries is run by Captain Mike's sons, Andrew and Bruce, with help from Mother Pat and Andrew's wife Penny. Each is an avid fisherman and fish lover, and each aims to give clients the best possible sportfishing experience. They have four sportfishing boats and a whale-watching boat, all designed and outfitted for comfort and performance. ☎ 758-452-0922 or 758-450-1216, www.captmikes.com.

Trivial Pursuit Fishing Charters is run by Captain Francis, a passionate fisherman and founding member of the St. Lucia Game Fishing Association. He'll teach you things you would never learn on your own about fishing the deep Caribbean Seas. When you call, ask about his vacation rentals at Casa Del Vega. ☎ 758-720-4001 or 758-720-0799 (cell), www.trivialpursuitfishingcharters.com.

BOATING COMPETITION

Every year in December, participants in the **Atlantic Rally for Cruisers** (ARC) cross the finish line at the **Rodney Bay Marina**, latitude north 14.2 and longitude west 60.58. This annual transatlantic rally was founded in 1986 by journalist Jimmy Cornell and, in 1990, the St. Lucia Tourist Board and Rodney Bay Marina became official sponsors, as well as the official finish line.

The Atlantic Rally for Cruisers

Each November, more than 200 yachts from many nations leave Las Palmas de Gran Canaria to begin the largest trans-ocean sailing event in the world.

The 2,700-nautical-mile trip along the northeast tradewind route takes between 12 and 24 days. Participants include monohulls from 27 to 85 feet in length and catamarans from 27 to 60 feet, each carrying at least two crew members. Motor yachts also participate in a separate division.

The rally successfully mixes racers with cruisers and old-timers with young-bloods, providing tremendous fun for both the participants and spectators. A wide range of entertainment takes place both before the yachts leave Gran Canaria and when they arrive in Rodney Bay.

If you want to be on hand for the festivities that take place on St. Lucia when the international yachts and crews come ashore, get a schedule of this year's events from the St. Lucia Tourist Board, ☎ 758-452-4094, www.stlucia.org, or click on ARC at the World Cruising Club website, www.worldcruising.com.

Surfing – Board, Wind & Kite

Most of the large resorts have beach-side watersports centers where you can rent surfboards and windsurfers. Kitesurfing is the newest trend in water sports, and a new company has opened on the south end of the island to give instructions and rent equipment.

Windsurfing

If you're a beginner, stick to the west coast beaches. The waves are calmer and the wind blows more gently than on the Atlantic side. Experienced surfers will want to meet the trade winds head-on at Anse de Sable, near Vieux Fort. This large bay has onshore and cross-shore winds blowing straight off the Atlantic at an average speed of 15 to

Kiteboarder

20 knots. Real daredevils tackle the wild waters, strong currents, and mighty winds farther up the northeast coast at Cas-en-Bas.

Wind sports require a lot of water and air space, and Anse de Sable provides it. Windsurfers tend to take the upwind side of the bay, while kitesurfers go for the downwind side. Instruction for both activities is available through the centers listed below. Beginners need four or five lessons to catch on to the basics and feel confident handling the equipment. Another four or five lessons will put you into action. By the end of your vacation, you may be trying a few tricks.

StLuciaKiteBoarding.com is a web-based business with good general information on board-, wind-, and kitesurfing in St. Lucia. The site coordinates activities with **The Reef Beach Café** (☎ 758-454-3418, www.slucia.com/reef) to host happy-hour gatherings and parties for vacationing surfers, and the staff can arrange all or part of your surfing-based vacation. ☎ 758-454-3418, www.stluciakiteboarding.com.

Caribbean Wind puts together vacation packages for surfers and offers information about competitions in several international locations, including St. Lucia. ☎ 866-787-9463, www.caribbeanwinds.com.

Equipment Rental & Lessons

The cost of equipment rental and lessons varies, and prices go down the longer you rent or take classes. Expect to pay about US$50 per day for boards and US$75 per session for lessons. Package deals are the best bargain, and the following shops can hook you up with accommodations, instruction, equipment and more.

Tornado Kite and Surf is in Cas En Bas on the northeast coast. Its slogan is "built by surfers for surfers" and aims to serve demanding and experienced surfing fanatics. ☎ 758-486-0545 or 758-454-7579, www.tornado-surf.com.

The Reef Kite & Surf is in Vieux Fort at the southern end of the island. The adjacent Reef Beach Café is the hangout for surfers and beach bums who enjoy surfing as a spectator sport. Everyone is welcome to watch the big-screen videos of the day's action while enjoying one of the café's famous frozen drinks. ☎ 758-454-3418, www.slucia.com/reef.

Sea Kayaking

If you haven't tried it, this is the place to give it a go. Sea kayaking has become tremendously popular in the last few years, and St. Lucia has excellent conditions for learning and enjoying the sport. Outfitters provide Prijon sea kayaks with rudders, ergonomic seats, knee braces and carbon fiber paddles. Certified instructors take you through the basics dur-

Toraille Waterfall

ing the first part of the day, and you'll become comfortable getting into and out of the kayak on both open water and dry land, and you'll get a feel for paddling while staying balanced and upright.

St. Lucia's coast is lined with interesting coves, caves, cliffs and beaches to explore. Some guided trips go out to the base of the Pitons, where you can snorkel or go ashore to hike. You won't find a better place in the Caribbean for this type of adventure. Guided tours are priced from US$65 to US$90 per person. Be sure to wear a high SPF sun screen, a wide-

Adventures

brimmed hat, sunglasses secured by a strap and water shoes. A life jacket will be provided by the outfitter.

Kayak St Lucia is affiliated with Anse Chastanet Resorts. ☎ 800-223-1108 or 758-459-7000, www.ansechastanet.com/scuba.html.

Jungle Reef Adventures, near Soufrière, has both single and double Prijon sea kayaks. ☎ 758-459-7755 or 758-457-1400, www.junglereefadventures.com.

Island ATV Tours kayaks the Savannes Bay Nature Reserve on the far south end of the east coast. ☎ 758-454-3777, www.islandatvtours.com/kayaktours.php.

Waterskiing & Parasailing

Waterskiing

Many large resorts offer waterskiing and parasailing through their watersports center. If your hotel does not, head to Reduit Beach at Rodney Bay, where equipment is available at several beachfront huts. One to try is **Joy Tide Water Sports** on the beach at the Rex St. Lucia Hotel, ☎ 758-458-0085.

Jet skis are available during the winter season from **Reef Kite and Surf**, in Vieux Fort, ☎ 758-454-3418, www.slucia.com/reef.

Adventures on Land

Hiking

You can see a lot of St. Lucia as it passes by your car window, but the only way to fully experience the island's vast beauty is to explore it on foot. Even inexperienced hikers can manage the gentle paths through many areas, but seasoned hikers will want to tackle steeper climbs and longer distances over more remote terrain.

Two agencies manage most trails on St. Lucia. The **National Trust** (☎ 758-453-7656 or 758-452-5005, www.slunatrust.org.) oversees those in areas with historical, environmental or cultural significance, such as Pigeon Island, Marigot Bay, and the Frégate and Maria Islands; the **Forestry Department** (☎ 758-450-2231, www.slumaffe.org) controls the protected interior woodlands. Both agencies are committed to designing, constructing, and maintaining trails that provide optimum hiking experiences with the least impact on the environment.

Expect to pay an access fee of US$10 to use nature trails and US$25 to use the longer and more challenging hiking trails. The fee includes a guide trained by the Forestry Department, who will get you through difficult terrain and ecologically sensitive zones. Trails controlled by the National Trust are sometimes free of charge, but most require an entrance fee into the managed area, and some can be visited only on a guided tour. Get details about fees and tour schedules from the tourist board (☎ 758-458-7101) or the National Trust (☎ 758-453-7656).

Short & Easy

The Union Nature Reserve is adjacent to the nursery of the Union Agricultural and Research Station, where baby trees are nurtured until they're ready to go out into the reforestation world. An **Interpretive Center** and **Mini-Zoo** are near the parking lot. Don't

Start of the Union Nature Trail

Adventures

underestimate the zoo because of its size or outward appearance. Inside, you're guaranteed a sighting of the redneck pigeon (for which Pigeon Island was named), the Jacquot or St. Lucian parrot (the national bird), the indigenous agouti, boa constrictors, iguanas, and other elusive critters.

The Mini-Zoo

Spend a few minutes in the Interpretive Center to gather information about the forests, endangered species, and ecological concerns of the island. Rangers are usually available to answer questions and give tours, but you can get a good idea of the island's wildlife and vegetation by just looking over the displays. Next, head out to the two trails that begin behind the zoo.

The **Nature Trail** loops through about a mile of rugged terrain in what is known as a *dry forest* (as opposed to a rainforest). The path is a mile long and climbs to heights of 350 feet. If you amble along, watch for birds, and stop to read all the identification signs posted on many of the trees and plants, expect to spend about two hours on the trail.

The gentler **Garden Trail** is a pleasant half-mile walk along a gravel path with stops at a **medicinal herb patch**. Again, you don't need a guide, since pamphlets and placards identify the plants and their traditional use. However, the rangers tend the garden themselves and know a lot about herbal cures for everything from bug bites to the common cold. You may find their stories and experiences quite captivating.

Get to the Union Nature Reserve by driving north from Castries on the Gros Islet Highway, past the turn-off to George Charles Airport, to the signed Allan Bousquet Highway, which turns inland near the Sandals Resort on Choc Bay and leads to the village of Babonneau. The Union Nature Reserve is on the right, about 2½ km/1½ miles from the

Castries-Gros Islet Highway. The Interpretive Center and trails are open Monday through Friday 8 am to 4 pm, and the fee is a bargain at US$2 for the trail and zoo. ☎ 758-468-5645.

Pigeon Point National Park has several short, gentle paths connecting each area of the historic former island (a causeway now connects Pigeon Point to the mainland). The National Trust manages the park and the well-designed trails that lead you to significant sites, such as **Fort Rodney** and **Signal Peak**. Pick up a map when you pay your entrance fee.

Start in the **museum** and **interpretive center** that are set up in restored British officers' quarters, which are on your right as you enter the park. There you will get an overview of the park and its military importance. Afterwards, you have a choice of easy walks and moderate hikes through grasslands, gardens, and dry forest, along the coast, and up a couple of hills that offer fantastic views (Signal Hill is the tallest at 110 m/360 feet). Pigeon Point National Park is open daily 9 am to 5 pm. The entrance fee is US$5 for adults and US$2 for kids five-12, ☎ 758-452-5005.

The Barre de l'Isle Trail is one of the best paths through the rainforest. If you aren't in shape for the rigorous climb up to the *barre* (ridge) that runs north-south through the center of the island, you can take an easy stroll along the loop path near the ranger hut at the beginning of the main trail. Look for a viewing point at the trail sign on the main cross-island highway that connects west-coast Castries with east-coast Dennery. The

Barre de l'Isle Trail

quarter-mile-long loop begins there and does not require a guide, but one is included in the trail fee of US$10, so you may want to take one along to point out interesting stuff. Pay your fee at the ranger hut, which is up a short path from the parking area. (See details about the more difficult ridge hike in *Longer and Harder*, which follows.) The trail is open Monday through Friday, 8:30 am to 2 pm, ☎ 758-453-3242.

Anse la Liberté is a new campground run by the National Trust, which is just south of the small west-coast town of Canaries. More development is planned, but for now the grounds have a dozen tents, a few teepees, some basic bathing facilities, and four miles of nature trails. The 133-acre camp slopes down to a lovely bay, which you can reach on a 15-minute hike along a narrow path cut through thick vegetation. You must be accompanied by a Trust-trained guide, who will point out some of the 80 species of plants and 17 species of birds that inhabit the area. Arrange for a campsite (US$25-US$75) or a guide by calling the National Trust, ☎ 758-452-5005.

The **Frégate Island Nature Reserve** and the **East Coast Trail** has been disturbed by new development near the village of Praslin. Plans are in the works for additional trails as soon as construction is complete on a the new Le Paradis golf resort but, as this book goes to press, only a mile-long section of the northern trail is open. Environmentalist and scholar **Peter Ernest** is overseeing preservation in the area, and he conducts hikes along the available section of the trail, which offers breathtaking views of the Atlantic from high cliffs and winds through dense vegetation that draws a vast number of domestic and migratory birds. The Frégate Islands are still a nature preserve and bird sanctuary, but the adjacent peninsula has become part of the resort development. Arrange a tour with Peter, a fascinating conservationist, through Eastern Tours, ☎ 758-455-3163 or 758-384-7056 (cell).

Longer & Harder

Cas-en-Bas and the surrounding area is captivating and mostly undeveloped. You can drive along the rough crater-pitted dirt roads in a four-wheel-drive vehicle, but walking it is better. Get there from the north by taking the secondary road off the highway north of Gros Islet and south of the turnoff to Pigeon Point. When you reach the end of the road, you'll be in Cas-en-Bas, where the mighty Atlantic rolls onto a pleasant beach. This is not a swimming beach; the current is too strong. But, wave riders hang out here, and the Tornado Kite and Surf watersports shop is nearby.

The length and difficulty of your hike will depend on which direction you choose. South of the beach, a rocky path hugs the coast and takes you to **Anse Lavoutte** (allow about a half-hour each way), where leatherback turtles lay eggs from March until July. North of the Cas-en-Bas beach, another rocky path will take you to a secluded cove called **Secret Beach**, then on to **Donkey Beach** (allow 10-15 minutes to reach Secret and another 10-15 to reach Donkey). Wear sunscreen and good walking shoes, and carry plenty of water.

The Barre de l'Isle Trail is a moderate to rigorous hike along the *barre*, or ridge, that divides the eastern and western parts of the Central Forest Reserve, which covers the middle of the island. Expect to spend an hour on the two-km/1.2-mile (one-way) trail and another couple of hours, if you choose to climb 438-m/1,437-foot **Morne La Combe**. It's a good use of a full morning. There are fantastic views at four observation points along the ridge, and you have a fair chance of spotting a St. Lucian parrot. From the top of La Combe, you can see 950-m/3,116-foot Mount Gimie, Cul-de-Sac valley, the Caribbean Sea and Fond d'Or beach on the Atlantic coast.

The **Des Cartiers Trail** is a four-km/2½-mile loop that begins six miles inland from the east coast settlement of Micoud and crosses the **Quilesse Forest Reserve**. This is a strenuous hike, but if you're up to the challenge, you have a good chance of seeing a rare St. Lucian (Jacquot) parrot flying among the high tree tops deep in the rainforest. Some of the gommier trees grow to heights of more than 130 feet, and it's easy to understand how native craftsmen still carve boats from a single trunk. The trail is 300 m/984 feet above the sea,

The Des Cartiers Trail

well-marked, and relatively flat. Allow at least two hours to explore this part of the rainforest, and continue on to the Edmund Forest Reserve Trail (at the north end of the loop), if you have enough time and energy. Look for a sign marking the ranger hut and interpretive center on the secondary road leading inland from Micoud. The trail fee is US$10, and you may enter daily 8 am until 4 pm. ☎ 758-468-5645.

The Edmund Forest Reserve Trail begins seven miles inland from the west-coast highway off the secondary road connecting Soufrière and Fond St. Jacques. Only the fit and tenacious should attempt this 10-km/6.2-mile hike that requires a guide (to prevent you from getting lost on side-trails) and about six to eight hours of your day. The trail is demanding, but the rewards are great. You'll have incomparable views of the Pitons and Mount Gimie, see huge ferns and incredibly

Start of the Edmund Trail

beautiful wild orchids and bromelaids growing among the trees, and spot hummingbirds, parrots, and orioles. Expect to get wet, since the Edmund Forest is one of the rainiest parts of the island. Reach the trail head by driving about five km/three miles on a dirt road that branches off the main road and turns inland from the center of the village of Fond St. Jacques, going toward Mount Gimie. The ranger hut usually has guides avail-

Along the Edmund Forest Reserve Trail

able, but you may want to call the Forestry Department (☎ 758-468-5645) a day or two in advance to make arrangements. The trail isn't a loop, so you'll have to retrace your steps, or arrange to be picked up at the trail's end (north of Micoud on the Mahaut road). The trail is open daily 8 am until 4 pm; the entrance fee is US$25.

Jungle Jaunts

Jungle Tours has scheduled trips into the rainforest for beginner, intermediate, and advanced hikers. Each trail through the rainforest features something special, such as visiting a hidden waterfall or the ruins of a sugar mill built in the 1700s. After the tour, you'll be fed a tasty buffet lunch on a secluded beach, then have time for a swim. Tours are priced at US$75 per person and include entrance fees, drinks and lunch. ☎ 758-450-0434, www.jungletoursstlucia.com.

Adventures

On the En Bas Saut Falls Trail

The En Bas Saut Falls Trail (which means *below the falls*) is a moderate to strenuous hike that starts near the ranger station at the beginning of the Edmund Trail (see above). The four-km/2½-mile track winds through incredibly scenic terrain near the foot of Mount Gimie in the Central Rainforest Reserve, six miles inland from Soufrière. Two waterfalls cascade into clean, clear pools at the head of the Troumasse River. This remote trail is especially scenic and cuts through elfin woodlands and cloud forest, as well as the rainforest. Check in at the ranger station daily between 8 am and 4 pm. The fee is US$10.

The Forestière Rainforest Trail

The Forestière Rainforest Trail begins near the village of Forestière, about 30 minutes inland by car from Castries. Start at the ranger hut, on the main road just east of the town's school. The five-km/three-mile loop slopes down through dense ferns and trees into the central forest reserve and back up to the road. Allow a couple of hours to cover the entire route, which is classified easy to moderate, and another hour if you want to climb the steps up Piton Flore, located about midway along the trail and topped by a TV tower. The ranger hut is open Monday through Friday, 8 am until 2 pm, and you will be charged an entrance fee of US$10. ☎ 758-451-6168.

Looking down on Roseau Dam from the Millet Trail

Bird Watching

The Millet Bird Sanctuary

If the main purpose of your hike is to spot some of the island's endemic birds, you'll want to break away from the crowd and strike out along the **Millet Trail**. More than 30 species live or migrate through this area, and you have a good chance of seeing the unique St. Lucia parrot, pewee, black finch, warbler and oriole. You won't see these island natives anywhere else in the world. Set aside about four hours to follow a trained guide through the dense trees and lush greenery. This allows plenty of time to spot a variety of birds. Call a day ahead to reserve your time. ☎ 758-451-1691.

Adventures

More Rainforest Adventures

On a recent visit to the island, the Adventure Guide team tried a canopy ride through the Barre de l'Isle mountain range, which runs through the middle of St. Lucia, separating the east and west coasts. This dense green forest is stunning when seen from ground level and even more spectacular when seen from the tree tops.

Our first outing started just inland from the village of Dennery at the welcome station for the **Rainforest Canopy Adventure**. The guides there helped us into a harness system, heavy gloves and helmets, then led us to a platform

Canopy adventure

where pulleys attached to each of us were clipped to overhead cables. After a bit of easy instruction, we leaned back into a semi-seated position and the guide released us to go speeding along the cable, soaring above the tree tops. What an adrenalin rush!

We stopped on nine landing platforms along the descent to catch our breath, admire the views and hike a bit to explore the forest. Then, we were hitched to the zip line again and sent flying to the next landing area. By our final ride, we felt like experts and really let the speed build. You don't have to be in super-athletic shape to do this, but don't try it if you have a major health condition or can't hike short distances up steep paths. You must be at least eight years of age. Wear closed-toe shoes so you won't hit your toes on the landing platforms, and it's best to wear knee-length shorts or long pants to avoid discomfort from the rigging straps. Advance reservations are essential through Palm Services, ☎ 758-458-0908, www. adventuretourstlucia.com.

On another day, we opted for a **tram ride** through the forest. Honestly, it was not as exciting as the Canopy Adventure, but it was fun and we recommend it, especially if you don't want to take the zip-line ride. This attraction is suitable for all ages and is wheelchair-accessible.

The trams are located near the village of Babonneau at Ravine Chassin on a secondary road east of Castries. Before we boarded our gondola, we walked around the loop trail just inside the entrance and got an idea of the vast variety of plants and trees that grow in the forest. Then we hopped aboard our eight-passenger, open-sided cable car and headed up through the trees.

Nature lovers have questioned how we could approve of something this commercial cutting through the rainforest, but after seeing it for ourselves, we have to say that the tram probably protects far more than it destroys. The companies that construct these attractions take pride in following strict "green" policies set by environmental agencies, and very little of the forest is disturbed either during the building phase or after tourists begin to visit the area. In fact, the rides protect fragile growth from careless visitors who might otherwise tromp through the foliage unsupervised and unaware of what may be struggling to grow underfoot.

As we rose above the forest floor in the gondola, our clever guide pointed out hidden treasures that we would have missed on our own and entertained us with island myths. On our downward return trip, he pointed out an almost completed platform that was being built for wedding ceremonies. A bit farther on, we had a glimpse of both the Caribbean and

Atlantic coasts and neighboring islands in the distance. For information and reservations, call the Sky Ride office ☎ 758-458-5151.

Biking

St. Lucia is a hilly island, and biking here is not for the weak or timid. However, if you're in good shape and brave enough to tackle narrow roads (some no more than dirt paths pitted with potholes large enough to swallow a bike and rider whole), you'll have a fabulous two-wheel adventure.

A favorite route is at **Anse Mamin**, an isolated bay adjacent to Anse Chastanet, with 12 miles of trails on a densely wooded former plantation within the property owned by Anse Chastanet Resort. You get there by boat from the beach at Anse Chastanet. A large stone archway with heavy wooden doors marks the entrance to the former Mamin Estate and, once inside, you'll think more of prehistoric creatures than sugar cane. But, during the 1700s, this land was a thriving sugar and cocoa plantation, and as you ride through the clearing, you'll spot the ruins of a long-abandoned stone mill.

If you consider yourself an advanced rider, try the championship course named **Tinker's Trail** after Tinker Juarez of the Siemens-Cannondale racing team, who is a five-time world champion, two-time Olympian and four-time US National Champion. As would be expected, this is one demanding ride, but if you feel comfortable on a bike and have plenty of strength and stamina, you can quickly get the hang of maneuvering the extremely tight switchbacks and pre-

cipitous hills. At the top, you ring a bell to declare your triumph. The downhill ride promises a heart-pumping adrenalin rush that true champions crave.

Of course, you don't have to do the dare-devil stuff to have fun. Most people just take their bike for a comfortable cruise along the eco-friendly compost trails that lead along a river to historic ruins, fantastic hilltop vistas, a natural swimming pool and the beach. If you sign on with one of the tour companies, everything will be planned for you and you won't have to deal with transporting your bike to the trail.

Universal Cycle Center has shops in Castries and Vieux Fort. They rent bikes for independent touring and will give you directions to good cycling spots based on your level of experience and daring. Call the Castries shop at ☎ 758-453-6976, or the Vieux Fort shop at ☎ 758-451-8524.

The three companies listed below offer biking and biking-hiking tours of various intensity designed for novice to experienced riders. Most of the excursions include stops to explore, swim or picnic in off-the-beaten-path locations. Prices range from US$60 to US$100 per person and include equipment, transportation and bottled water.

Bike St. Lucia at Anse Chastanet conducts rides in the forest near Soufrière with stops to smell the flowers, wander through the ruins of a plantation and swim, snorkel or nap at a beach. ☎ 758-451-2453, www.bikestlucia.com.

Island Bike Hikes is affiliated with Palm Services in Castries and caters to all fitness levels. Tours start with a Jeep ride to the east coast, near Dennery, where everyone sets out on bikes to the rainforest. After hiking along the wooded trails, the group enjoys a picnic and swim at a waterfall pool. ☎ 758-458-0908, www.cyclestlucia.com.

Jungle Biking Adventures leads rides along 12 miles of trails through the jungle with speed and degree of difficulty dictated by the riders' experience and comfort on a mountain bike, which will be a top-of-the-line Cannondale with hydraulic disc brakes. ☎ 758-459-7755, www.junglereefadventures.com.

Fitness Clubs & Gyms

Most large resorts have fitness rooms with free use for their guests. The largest public facility is **Sportivo**, at Rodney Bay, above Key Largo Restaurant. It's open Monday through Saturday and offers a full range of equipment plus a variety of classes. Call for hours, class schedules and fees, ☎ 758-452-8899, www.sportivonow.com.

Horseback Riding

Riding the beach

Some parts of the island are best seen on horseback, and St. Lucia has several facilities that offer hourly rental and specialty-riding tours. You'll see the island from a whole new perspective on a horse. Some outfitters allow you to take your equine buddy into the ocean for a swim. Others stick to forest paths or cliff trails along the coast. Expect to pay US$20-40 per hour for guided tours, or about

US$56 for packages that may include transportation to the stables, drinks, or a meal.

Créole horses are available at some stables. They are an indigenous breed that is rather small, but strong and good-natured, which makes them especially good for beginning riders.

Trim's Stables, near Cas-en-Bas, has rides designed for beginners or experienced horsemen. One of their most popular trips is the picnic ride along the Atlantic coast. If you're getting married or engaged or celebrating a special occasion, ask  about a carriage ride along the beach at sunset. ☎ 758-450-8273.

Country Saddles give you the chance to tour the island's largest working plantation on horseback. The Marquis Estate covers 600 acres on the east coast and produces bananas, coconut oil and a variety of other fruit. You'll be assigned a horse appropriate for your skill level. ☎ 758-450-5467.

International Pony Club, on the Beauséjour Estate near Gros Islet, offers both English- and western-style riding. Riders have a choice of three tours geared to various skill levels. You can even take a bareback swim with your horse. Talk to Floria or Alvin about the type of horse and experience you want. ☎ 452-8139 or 758-715-5689 (Floria's cell).

Atlantic Shores Riding Stables, at Savannes Bay near Vieux Fort, has a four-hour beach ride that ends with a calypso-rhythm dance party. Other rides go up into the hills and along the cliffs overlooking the ocean. Call for information and scheduled outings. ☎ 758-454-8668 or 758-285-1090.

Belle Cheval Stables is a unique operation under the direction of Lynne DuPlooy, who rescues and rehabilitates injured and abandoned horses. When the horses are healthy, happy and serene, they are used for trail rides. If you're interested in

Adventures

riding with this group, contact Lynne for directions to the stables near Rodney Bay, ☎ 758-518-1118.

Horses from Belle Cheval Stables

All-Terrain-Vehicle Tours

Get off-road and into the wilds of St. Lucia on an all-terrain-vehicle. Exploring the outback on an ATV is thrilling, and you can go places where a Jeep or horse can't go.

These four-wheel motorized vehicles provide almost as much maneuverability as a motorcycle, with the stability and ruggedness of a Jeep. You can quickly learn to handle one because most are fully automatic, with few controls. After you take a spin or two around the parking lot to get a feel for the vehicle, you'll be off to unspoiled areas of the island that will stun you with beauty. The ATV can go over boulders, climb steep hills and forge through muddy water without getting stuck or tipping over. The driving experience itself is a thrill.

Wear clothes that you don't mind getting dirty, sun screen and closed-toe shoes. Helmets and goggles are provided. Most important: your camera. You'll be able to stop as often as you like to take pictures of flowing plants, panoramic vistas, colorful birds and miles of open water. Most tours include stops to swim or rest in scenic spots and cost about US$90.

ATV Paradise Tours is near the village of Micoud, on the Atlantic coast. Tours visit plantations, the rainforest and beaches. ☎ 758-455-3245, www.atvstlucia.com.

Island ATV Tours, on Honeymoon Beach near Vieux Fort. Guides take riders through private estates, mangrove forests and along the Atlantic coast. ☎ 758-454-3777, www.islandatvtours.com.

ATV Paradise Tour

Golf

St. Lucia is the ideal vacation spot for golfers. Several courses are operational now and more are under construction. The **St. Lucia Golf and Country Club** is public and open year-round at Cap Estate on the northernmost part of the island. The challenging 18-hole, par-71 course stretches across acres of rolling hills with incredible views. Facilities include a practice driving range, putting green, clubhouse with restaurant, and a pro shop where guests can rent clubs and motorized carts.

Winter fees are US$110 for 18 holes, including a cart and clubs. For off-season specials and tee times, call ☎ 450-8522, www.stluciagolf.com.

Guests of the all-inclusive **Sandals Regency Golf Resort and Spa at La Toc** can play golf free of charge at the private nine-hole, three-par course laid out on the rolling hills above La Toc Bay. Non-guests can play an 18-hole round for a fee of US$75, which includes the green fee, cart, clubs, balls and caddy fee. This is a short (3,141 yards) but challenging course, with spectacular views of the Caribbean. A beginners' clinic is held Wednesday mornings at 9, and you can arrange for private lessons with the pro. Get details and schedule tee times by calling the resort, ☎ 758-452-3081.

Jalousie Plantation has a nine-hole, three-par course for guest use, and a Resort Day Pass is available for US$75, which allows you to use of all the resort's facilities, including golf. A set of clubs can be rented for US$10 extra. Call the pro shop front desk for information, ☎ 758-456-8000, www. jalousieplantation.com.

Golfing legends **Greg Norman** and **Jack Nicklaus** have designed signature courses that are now under construction and will turn the island into the top golfing destination in the Caribbean. Soon, if not by the time that you visit, experienced golfers can look forward to testing their skills on Norman's award-winning course at the **Westin Le Paradis Beach & Golf Resort** in Praslin Bay. It's located on the rocky cliffs overlooking the Atlantic on the southeastern side of the island. Norman has designed the 18-hole course as the centerpiece to a huge development that includes a resort, marina, yacht club, restaurants and shops set amid flourishing tropical foliage.

The Pointe at Cas en Bas is a private club and residential resort owned by Point Hardy Development that will feature a members-only, 18-hole championship Jack Nicklaus Signature Golf Course. The legendary pro golfer designed the course to stretch across the isolated northern tip of the island as part of a US$100-million project that includes private homes and an upscale resort.

For updated information about these two new properties, contact the St. Lucia Tourism Board, ☎ 758-452-7577, www.stlucia.org.

Tennis

Most visitors play tennis on courts at their resort, but if you're staying at a hotel without a court, you can play at **St. Lucia Racquet Club**, ☎ 450-0551. This first-class facility is praised as the best in the Antilles and features nine lighted courts and a well-outfitted pro shop. Court fees are US$20 per day, and rackets are available for an additional US$8.

Among the resorts, the **Jalousie Plantation** has four courts, three lighted, which are free for guest use and available to outside visitors for US$20 per hour. If you're interested in lessons or a high-skill match, book with Vernon Lewis, the Eastern Caribbean men's champion and British Virgin Islands Open singles and doubles champion. ☎ 758-456-8000, www.jalousieplantation.com. The **Sandals Regency Golf Resort and Spa at La Toc** has five lighted courts, ☎ 758-452-3081.

If you want to play a lot of tennis during your vacation, plan to stay at a resort with at least two courts, to increase your chances of getting a match early or late in the day, when temperatures are cooler. Consider one of the following: **Windjammer Landing**, ☎ 758-456-9000; **Rex St. Lucian**, ☎ 758-452-8351; **Papillon**, ☎ 758-452-0984; **Royal St. Lucian**, ☎ 758-452-9999; **Sandals Grand**, ☎ 758-455-2000.

Squash courts are open to the public for a fee of US$4 per hour at **St. Lucia Yacht Club**, ☎ 452-8350. You can rent racquets and take a few lessons from the Eastern Caribbean men's champion, Charlie Sonson.

Adventures

Shopping

Visitors will find St. Lucia's shops full of good buys. Look for handcrafted items such as batik, pottery, wood carvings, shell jewelry, and straw products. Also, electronics, crystal, leather items, and luxury jewelry often are bargains, especially at the duty-free shops.

Shoppers typically look for jewelry when they come to the Caribbean because retailers are known to offer significantly lower prices than in the US or Europe. Often these shops purchase merchandise directly from the manufacturers and pay small import fees, or none at all, so they can pass the savings on to you. Large stores with branches on multiple islands usually offer the best discounts due to the savings they derive from high-volume buying. Expect to find a good selection of diamonds and other precious stones, gold chains, watches, and high-fashion jewelry.

If you think you may want to buy jewelry, watches, crystal, or other luxury items while you're on vacation, visit a few stores before you leave home and write down prices of pieces that interest you. When you get to St. Lucia, you'll be able to make informed decisions about prices and standards of quality.

To guarantee that you buy only high quality merchandise, shop in well-established stores with a good reputation. If you aren't sure, ask for advice from the staff at your hotel or on your cruise ship. You also can judge by the appearance of the store, its sales staff, and brochures. If it's a company with outlets on several islands, it's probably a reputable store. However, many local businesses with only one store are equally reliable, so keep an open mind. If the shop offers a guarantee and a certified appraisal on its merchandise, you can buy with confidence. Be sure to ask if the store has an office or contact near your home for after-sale services. A wide variety of stores are located in **La Place Carenage**, **Gablewoods Mall**, **JQ Charles Mall**, and **Pointe**

Pointe Seraphine

Seraphine. In addition, many of the large resorts feature boutiques and gift shops. The best places to find local arts, crafts and products is at the traditional outdoor markets held in Castries and Soufrière, and the **Craft Center** in the coastal village of Choiseul.

Most stores in Castries and Soufrière are open Monday through Friday from 8:30 am until 4:30 pm and many close during the 12:30 to 1:30 pm lunch hour. On Saturdays, shops in both towns open at 8:30 am and close for the day at 12:30 pm. If a cruise ship is in port on a Sunday, some stores in Castries open for a few hours in the morning. Shopping centers such as Pointe Seraphine, La Place Carenage, JQ Charles Mall, and Gablewoods Mall are open weekdays from 8:30 am to 5 pm and Saturdays 8:30 am until 2 pm. Marina stores keep later hours and open on Sundays. Most merchants accept major credit cards, but take cash with you when you shop at Castries Central Market and small shops, especially outside of the main towns.

Tip: You must show your passport and airline ticket or cruise-ship boarding papers to qualify for duty-free prices.

Big Name Duty-Free Shops

Diamonds International
Pointe Seraphine, Castries
La Place Carenage, Castries
Windjammer Landing Resort, Gros Islet
☎ 800-51-JEWEL or 758-457-4207, www.shopdi.com

Colombian Emeralds
Pointe Seraphine
Hewanorra Airport
Sandals Regency Golf Resort
Sandals Grande Resort
Almond Morgan Bay Resort
☎ 800-6-NO-DUTY or 758-453-7721, www.duty-free.com

Little Switzerland
Pointe Seraphine, Castries ☎ 758-451-6785
La Place Carenage, Castries ☎ 758-453-7587

Images Duty Free
4 Bridge Street, Castries ☎ 758-451-6111
Pointe Seraphine ☎ 758-452-6883

Shops & Markets

Castries

Castries' Central Market

At Castries Central Market

This has been an outlet for local vendors for more than 100 years. It occupies several buildings and adjacent outdoor spaces near the intersection of Jeremie and Peynier streets. The old iron structure is still visible in some of the walls, and you can't miss the original cement fountain near the craft vendors. Saturday morning is the best time to visit, but the market is also alive with activity during Carnival and the St. Lucia Jazz Festival. Most vendors open their stalls by 8:30 am each morning, and begin to close in early afternoon. If they don't run out of products, most stalls stay open as long as customers are looking, especially when cruise ships are docked in the nearby port. Look for good buys on coal pots, hot-pepper sauces, T-shirts, straw baskets and hats, West Indies herbs, island spices, cocoa sticks, and fresh produce for picnics.

La Place Carenage Mall

La Place Carenage Duty Free Shopping Mall recently was expanded to provide about 27,000 square feet of additional shopping space to what was once a waterfront cargo shed. Now there are dozens of retail stores, a roof-top restaurant, coffee shops, an ice cream parlor and a branch of the St. Lucia Tourist Board. Look for the shopping complex on Jeremie Street at the North Wharf in Castries, ☎ 758-452-7318.

One of the newest attractions is the **Desmond Skeete Animation Centre**, a state-of-the-art techno museum where you can see a 20-minute light and sound show and other exhibits highlighting St. Lucia's history and culture. Don't miss the skeleton of an Arawak woman that dates back to 400AD. The center is named after the late Desmond Skeete, who served as the chairman of the St. Lucia Tourist Board. He died in April, 2004. ☎ 758-453-2451.

The mall's contemporary two-story design spotlights duty-free shops with huge glass-panel fronts. A few of the most interesting shops are:

Modern Art Gallery displays a superb collection of Caribbean avant-garde art, ☎ 758-452-9079.

Noah's Arkade offers a large variety of Caribbean-made items, many created by St. Lucians, ☎ 758-452-2523.

Bagshaw Studios is a local operation that creates clothes and household items with silk-screen designs, ☎ 758-451-6565.

Bagshaw Studios (Paul Sullivan)

Little Switzerland has a large selection of famous-name Swiss watches, crystal, china, and jewelry. Their shops are well-known throughout the Caribbean Islands and they give guarantees and certified appraisals. ☎ 758-452-7587.

Hippo's Duty Free Liquor Shop is the place to pick up Caribbean rum and Piton beer. ☎ 758-452-4062.

Pointe Seraphine Mall

Pointe Seraphine is a large Spanish-style duty-free mall near the main cruise ship dock on the north side of Castries Bay. A ferry runs back and forth across the bay so, if you have a car, you can park on either side and avoid driving through town. A tourist information office is located in the courtyard and some of the best shopping is available at the following stores:

Little Switzerland has a large selection of famous-name Swiss watches, crystal, china, and jewelry. Their shops are well-known throughout the Caribbean Islands and they give guarantees and certified appraisals. ☎ 758-451-6785.

Colombian Emeralds features emerald jewelry, other fine gemstones and international watches. They're known for significant savings, full guarantees, certified appraisals and US after-sales service. ☎ 758-453-7721.

Jewellers Warehouse claims to save you 50% on all merchandise. ☎ 800-661-jewel or 758-453-7281, www.jewelerswarehouse.com.

Diamonds in Paradise specializes in romantic diamond pieces. ☎ 758-452-7223.

Essence highlights designer clothing and accessories from around the world. ☎ 758-452-3028.

Benetton sells the familiar Italian fashions. You'll find a selection of unique stripes, prints and colors in the latest styles with duty-free prices. ☎ 758-452-7685.

Banana Beach Shop stocks T-shirts, swimsuits, snorkeling gear, suntan lotion, and other beach necessities. In addition, they carry cookbooks, place mats, and other household items featuring the charming watercolor prints of Caribbean artist Jill Walker. ☎ 758-452-6909.

Natur Pur Designer Clothing is made from all natural fibers and designed by Sylvie Calderbank. You can choose from linen or cotton. ☎ 758-452-4252.

PEER has co-ordinated cotton clothes with colorful prints and embroidery designs. Adult and children's sizes are available in T-shirts, shorts, caps, and more. ☎ 758-453-0815.

Noah's Arkade has several shops around the island. All carry a good selection of imaginative handcrafted items such as straw hats, steel pans, hammocks, and jams, along with books, maps, film, and suntan products. Other stores are at the Hewanorra Airport and on Jeremie Street in Castries. ☎ 758-452-7488.

Bagshaw Studios is an internationally-known family-run silkscreen business that makes colorful cotton and linen fabrics and gifts. If you have time, visit the working studio at La Toc Bay. ☎ 758-452-7570.

Studio Images promises a 30-50% discount on fragrances by Calvin Klein, Oscar de la Renta, Ralph Lauren, Christian Dior and many other well-known international designers. They also offer good buys on designer sunglasses, watches, leather goods, and gifts. ☎ 758-452-3687.

Oasis has sports gear, men's casual wear, sandals, and shoes. They also carry ladies' fashions, swim wear, fashion handbags, and T-shirts. ☎ 758-452-1185.

St. Lucia Fine Art displays a large selection of fine local, Caribbean, and international art. Be sure to look for works by internationally renowned St. Lucian artist Llewellyn Xavier. ☎ 758-459-0891.

Harry Edwards Jewelers is the place to go for that Rolex watch you've always wanted. ☎ 758-451-6799.

Pickwick & Co. imports most of their lovely things from England. Look for brand names such as Wimbledon, Pringle, Portmeirion, Wedgewood and Edinburgh Crystal. ☎ 758-459-0992.

Other Shops in or near Castries

You can call for an appointment to see **Llewellyn Xavier's** collection at his studio in Cap Estate, ☎ 758-450-9155.

Artsibit Gallery, at the corner of Brazil and Mongiraud Streets, exhibits a large collection of well-priced art by local artists. In addition, you'll find pottery, sculpture, even postcards. Among the featured artists, don't miss the fantastic works of Derek Walcott, Arnold Toulon, and Ron Savory. A smaller exhibit is displayed at the Artsibit Gallery on Rodney Bay. ☎ 758-452-7865.

Caribelle Batik

Caribelle Batik, 37 Old Victoria Road on Morne Fortune, designs batik-art clothes and wall hangings. Visitors are welcome at the working studio and shop, located in the charming old two-story Victorian-style Howelton House that's been beautifully renovated. You can watch the artisans at work on this ancient art technique, which is a multi-step process that involves creating an original design on fabric with melted wax, then dipping the cloth in a dye bath. The finished cotton, silk and rayon fashions are for sale in the boutique, tax- and duty-free. Be sure to stop at the **Dyehouse**

Bar and Terrace for refreshments, and visit the tropical plant nursery before you leave. Caribelle is open Monday through Friday 8:30 am until 4 pm and Saturday 8:30 am until 12:30 pm. ☎ 758-452-3785.

Bagshaw Studios, overlooking the sea at La Toc, welcomes visitors to their workshop where they turn out popular silk-screened creations. Shops are scattered around the Castries area, but watching the designs emerge from the studio is especially worthwhile. Drop in Monday through Friday 8:30 am until 4:30 pm, Saturday 8:30 am until 4 pm, or Sunday 10 am until 1 pm. ☎ 758-452-7921 or 758-452-6039.

Bryden House of Wine and Spirits, on Jeremie Street in Castries, stocks a well-priced assortment of Piton beer, Caribbean rums, and other liquors. ☎ 758-458-8640. Their other shops are at Rodney Bay Marina, ☎ 758-458-8645, Gablewoods Mall, ☎ 758-458-8643, and J.Q. Mall, ☎ 758-458-8647.

Eudovic Art Studio, south of the city in Goodlands, is the working studio of St. Lucian artist Vincent Joseph Eudovic. He has been creating contemporary sculptures from the stumps and buried roots of a now-extinct native tree, laurier canelle, since he won a national award at the age of 11. Over the years, he has won additional international awards, and his studio has expanded to include a restaurant, guest house gallery, and

Vincent Joseph Eudovic (Paul Sullivan)

souvenir store. His son Jallim joins him in the workshop and has earned many awards for his own works. Visitors are welcome at the outdoor workshop and indoor gallery and shop that feature art and crafts by Eudovic and other local artisans. Since each piece of wood is unique, every sculpture is one of a kind. In addition to using the laurier canelle, Eudovic carves modern pieces from mahogany, teak and cedar. ☎ 758-452-2747, www.eudovicart.net.

North of Castries

Caribbean Perfumes is located in a cozy chattel house nestled into the flowering garden of Jacques Waterside Restaurant. Jack's wife, Cathy Rioux, loves perfume and has an innate talent for recognizing scents. She combines island-grown flowers and plants to make delicious fragrances such as Ile d'Or, Frangipani, Le Bleu and Marigot – all packaged in lovely frosted bottles. Men like the fresh scent of Tropique or Periquito, which come as aftershave or cologne. You can find Caribbean Perfumes at many resort gift shops, or visit the cottage in the bistro garden at Vigie Cove, north of Castries. ☎ 758-453-7249.

Gablewoods Mall

Gablewoods Mall (☎ 758-453-7752), on the Gros Islet Highway north of town, has an assortment of shops that sell everything from local crafts to groceries and household products. Some of the shops that are of interest to tourists include:

Sunshine Bookshop features work by the island's Nobel Laureate, Derek Walcott, as well as international newspapers, magazines, novels, and travel books. ☎ 758-452-3222.

Sea Island Cotton Shop features beach wear, T-shirts, fashion clothing, and original handicrafts. ☎ 758-452-1185.

Cards & Things, in the food court, carries a good selection of greeting cards, gift items, and other things. ☎ 758-452-6977.

JQ Charles Mall

JQ Charles Mall, near the entrance to Rodney Bay Village and Reduit Beach, is a multi-level air-conditioned complex with a well-stocked supermarket, a food court, and dozens of up-scale shops. You can also find services such as a post office, beauty salon, Internet café and pharmacy. Top shops include the following:

Island Craft Plus stocks arts and crafts made by locals. ☎ 758-458-4859.

Sunshine Bookshop carries Caribbean authors and international magazines. ☎ 758-452-2322.

Banana Beach has a great swimsuit selection and carries beaching brands such as Nautica, Speedo, Reef and Teva. ☎ 758-458-0160.

Body, Mind and Soul is a chill-out place to buy gifts and something special for yourself. ☎ 758-458-0224.

Best clothing stores at JQ Charles:

American Classics is the place for Tommy Hilfiger fashions. ☎ 758-452-0856.

Collettas Boutique has a good selection of women's clothes, including plus sizes, as well as shoes and accessories. ☎ 758-458-0530.

Intimate Secret is, of course, lingerie. This is the place to pick up something romantic. ☎ 758-452-9956.

Irie Blue has a bit of this and that, but mostly casual island-style clothes. ☎ 758-458-0689.

Kaycee's is full of dressy outfits, casual wear, shoes, jewelry, cosmetics and purses. If you don't find it in the shop, try online. ☎ 758-452-0061, www.kayceesonline.com.

Kaycee's Men is like Kaycee's, except for those with lots of testosterone. ☎ 758)-458-4303.

SeaIsland Cotton Shop is famous for cool, casual clothing and a wide range of locally made souvenirs. ☎ 758-452-3674.

Basic Blue sells Dockers and Levis. ☎ 758-458-0351.

Natur Pur is a popular shop for women's designer clothing. ☎ 758-458-0228.

Jewelry

Anju Silvers has a nice selection of silver things, but also look over the crystal and leather products. ☎ 758-458-0923.

Anthony's Jewellery does repairs, which is good to know if your necklace breaks or your watch stops running while you're on vacation. The shop also carries all types of luxury jewelry. ☎ 758-458-4394.

This & That

Family Eye Care for designer frames and sunglasses. ☎ 758-458-0334.

Gourmet Kitchen, ☎ 758-458-0179.

House of Wines Spirits, ☎ 758-458-0179.

Mother Earth Natural Health Care, ☎ 758-458-0373.

Joy is a store for children's clothes and accessories, ☎ 758-450-0074.

Toys 4 All has clothes and toys. ☎ 758-458-0112.

Shopping Around the Island

The Art and Craft Cooperative in the little village of Choiseul, just south of the Pitons, is worth a visit. This tiny village has little to recommend it, except a church on the beach, some interesting wooden houses, and the Art and Craft Coop. The workshop, on the outskirts of town, isn't open to the public, but there's a shop where you can purchase baskets, wood carvings, pottery, and other items made by residents from local materials. Prices are good, and the quality is excellent, but service is sometimes indifferent. Go for the unique buys. ☎ 758-453-2338.

Livity Art Studio is on the west coast highway between Choiseul and Soufrière. Stop in to see paintings, sculpture, wood carvings, furniture and unique gifts made by local artists. Sometimes, the craftsmen are working at the studio and encourage you to watch as they create. Ask about the carvings made by Uptight, a wood sculptor whose work is displayed at upscale resorts such as Ladera and Anse Chastanet. There's no phone, but you'll find the studio open weekdays from 9 am until 5 pm.

After Dark

Festivals

Don't miss the weekly Friday night street party in **Gros Islet**. The **jump up** starts at sundown when the streets are blocked off, bands set up on improvised stages, and residents put barbeque grills on street corners to cook skewered conch, chicken, fish, and beef. Tourists and locals crowd into the streets hung with strings of lights to eat, dance, and listen to the drum-heavy beat of the island music.

The weekly event began more than 20 years ago, when Gros Islet was a quiet fishing community. Word spread quickly, helped by coverage in international publications and television shows. Today, the jump up is one of the island's main tourist attractions, which often runs into the early hours of Saturday morning. Plan to take a taxi, because parking is a nightmare, and you don't want to drive home on the narrow roads after partying all night.

A smaller, but similar, event takes place each Friday at **Anse La Raye**. Residents call their event a **fish fry**, but, like the Gros Islet jump up, it's really a street party to kick off the weekend. Anse La Raye began their weekly event in 1999 as an after-work happy hour and barbecue, but it has become almost as popular and almost as publicized as the Gros Islet party. You'll find more than 20 vendors set up along the street near the town jetty grilling right-out-of-the-sea lobster, shrimp, lambi and dorado. Music plays from loudspeakers, and often a live band sets up near the center of the action. This is quite obviously an affair staged for tourists, but you'll meet a lot of locals here, too.

Recently, the small village of **Dennery**, on the Atlantic coast, has started a Saturday night street party, which is called a **Fish Fiesta**. The crowd is made up mostly of locals, but tourists are welcome and encouraged to join in. Tents are set up along the beach and fresh seafood is grilled over open fires. Local musicians sometimes play, but most often recorded soca and reggae tunes stream from a sound system. Don't miss the outstanding hot-off-the-grill accras (fish cakes).

Ashanti at the Jazz Festival

The annual **Jazz Festival** takes place in May, and all nightlife (indeed, all life) during this time centers on international performers who play at outdoor concerts. **Pre Jazz Jam** kicks off the festival at Mindoo Philip Park in Castries with a cross-section of contemporary music. During the week, there are performances throughout the island, with **Tea Time Jazz** at La Place Carenage Shopping Mall, **Jazz on the Square** at Derek Walcott Square, and **Jazz on the Pier** at Pointe Seraphine.

An important part of the festival is **The Fringe**, a mix of music, street theater, arts and craft booths, fashion shows and culinary exhibitions that take place at various venues in conjunction with the international jazz performances. Local and regional bands entertain with Afro-Caribbean sounds that appeal to an audience that may not appreciate jazz. For ticket information and a schedule of events con-

James Carter at the Jazz Festival

tact the **Jazz Shop**, ☎ 758-451-8566, www.stluciajazz.org.

Throughout the year, but especially during major island celebrations such as Carnival, Jounen Kwéyòl (International Creole Day) and Jazz Festival, the large resorts host theme nights with steel bands, reggae singers, and other groups to entertain guests. In addition, piano bars, discos, and night clubs feature special guest performers, and many restaurants host specialty-night buffets with limbo dancers, fire eaters, and dance bands.

For current information about what's happening on the island, pick up a copy of the free monthy publication, Tropical Traveller. You'll find stacks of them at restaurants, hotels and other tourist spots.

A variety of performances are held frequently at the open-air 200-seat **Derek Walcott Center for The Arts**, adjacent to the historic **Great House Restaurant** at Cap Estate, ☎ 758-450-0450. You may be fortunate enough to catch a performance of St. Lucian Nobel Prize-winner Derek Walcott's works or a performance by the renowned Trinidad Theatre Workshop. At other times, the center hosts dance, music and drama programs.

Other cultural performances are scheduled through the **Folk Research Centre** on Morne Pleasant, ☎ 758-452-2279. Traditional island songs and dances are performed throughout the year, but the best take place during Carnival. If movies are more your style, call to see what's showing at **Cinema 2000** near Rodney Bay, ☎ 758-452-8802.

The famous award-winning Chef Harry hosts entertainment at **The Green Parrot Restaurant** on Morne Fortune every Wednesday and Saturday. On Monday nights, ladies who wear a flower in their hair dine free, if they are accompanied by a well-dressed gentleman. Dress up for this restaurant. You'll be in the company of St. Lucia's elite residents. Views of

Castries' lights below are spectacular. Reservations are essential, and call early enough to request a table beside the windows. ☎ 758-452-3399.

Rodney Bay Clubs

You can depend on a lot of action all along the road fronting Reduit Beach and around the harbor at Rodney Bay on most nights, especially on weekends.

Indies is one of the most popular clubs, with three bars and a two-level dance floor. A DJ takes requests and keeps the place hopping with a nice mix of popular music from Europe, South America, the US and throughout the Caribbean. Patrons are upscale and outfitted in the latest tropical fashions. In fact, a dress code is strictly enforced, so no beachwear, hats, tank tops, flip-flops or shorts. At the back of the club, a bar called **The Back Door** plays a variety of music more suited to talking than dancing. You can also get bar food and drinks there until 3 am. The main club opens at 11 pm and closes around 4 am on Wednesday, Friday and Saturday nights. Men pay a cover charge of US$10 and women get in for US$5.50. ☎ 758-452-0727.

Most nights, a solo musician or band entertains in the courtyard at **The Lime**, a casual and moderately priced restaurant. But, if you're looking for a party, you want **Late Lime**, the club next door, where a lively group dances until the wee hours of the morning. Doors open around 11 pm on Wednesday, Friday and Saturday nights, and the nicely-dressed young crowd parties until four the next morning. The cover charge is US$5. ☎ 758-452-0761.

Shamrocks Pub is an Irish-style bar with pub food, beer, pool tables, dart boards, and a jazz group on Wednesday evenings. On Saturday nights, a live dance band plays a mix of Caribbean and internationally-popular music. ☎ 758-452-8725.

Razmataz is a more low-key place to spend the evening. It's a favorite restaurant for those who like authentic Indian food, and there's always some type of entertainment. Perhaps a band playing soft dinner music, or a waiter spontaneously breaking into a round of Bob Marley songs, or, and this is everyone's favorite, a belly dancer making the rounds from table to table. Just a fun place to linger over great food, but not a rocking dance spot. ☎ 758-452-9800.

Around midnight, stop in at **Rumours**, a popular sports bar on the road leading from the Gros Islet Highway to Reduit Beach, where a lot of locals and tourists hang out late at night snacking on inexpensive bar food and enjoying a couple of drinks. ☎ 758-452 9249. Also, try **Charlie's**, a sports bar known also for good music and a friendly crowd. ☎ 758-458-0565.

Around the Island

Rodney Bay has the largest selection of places for late-night entertainment, music and dancing, but most restaurants and bars around the island offer some type of lure to reel patrons in. Happy Hour is a certainty at almost every establishment, and many places offer half-price on certain drinks or two-for-one beer specials all day. Other bars offer reduced-price drinks or free admission on weekly Ladies' Nights.

The restaurant at the **Hummingbird Beach Resort** in **Soufrière** hosts a Creole Night on Wednesdays with special dishes on the menu and dancing to the music of The Family Affairs Band. Make a reservation. This is a popular event and tables fill quickly. ☎ 758-459-7232.

Marigot Bay is surrounded by great restaurants and lively bars. On Tuesday and Sunday nights, **Doolittle's** has live entertainment during a special theme-night dinner (☎ 758-451-4974). **JJ's Paradise Resort** is popular with the boat people, who pull their luxury yachts right up to the dock and head straight to the bar. Every night is party night featuring either limbo dancing, fire-eating shows, a jazz band or calypso music. Call to find out what's planned and make a reservation if you plan to have dinner (☎ 758-451-4076). On Tuesday nights from 5 until 11 pm, **Chateau My'Go** offers two-for-one drinks and live music (☎ 758-451-4772).

In Vieux Fort, try **The Dead End Pub** on Bridge Street. This rum shop is built of bamboo against the back wall of the cemetery and run by an interesting couple, Basil and Priscilla Blasse. Guarantee: You will not be bored here. Priscilla is a graceful beauty and a graduate of the Australian Royal Academy of Dance. Basil is a champion limbo dancer and martial arts master. Ask him about performing in *Return of the Dragon* with Bruce Lee. The two owners speak a dozen or more languages, which brings in an interesting international crowd. Drop in any evening after sundown and plan to stay well into the night. ☎ 758-454 8241.

*For current information about what's happening on the island, pick up a copy of **Tropical Traveller**, a free publication that keeps up with local bands, special events, and activities of interest to both locals and visitors. You'll see stacks of them at restaurants, hotels, and tourist spots.*

Where to Stay

ecently, St. Lucia has undergone a prodigious growth spurt. With eyes set on becoming one of the region's top destinations, the island has lured high-end developers to increase accommodations by about 20%, especially along the once-ignored east (Atlantic) coast. As a result, visitors have a wider choice of lodging throughout the island.

The majority of hotels are clustered around the most picturesque bays on the west (Caribbean) coast. Rodney Bay, with its harbor and fantastic beach, is just north of the capital city (Castries) and extremely popular with visitors, who enjoy an active nightlife as well as water sports. Some of the island's most luxurious resorts line the shore northward to the St. Lucia Golf and Country Club at the island's northern tip, and southward to Castries. South of the capital, a series of large resorts, boutique hotels and small inns are tucked into secluded bays that cut into the shore all the way down to the landmark Piton Mountains.

Ironically, Vieux Fort, on the southern tip of the island, has few hotels, although it is home to the island's international airport and a popular area for surfers. Recently, Coconut Bay Resort took over a nearby coastal stretch that once belonged to Club Med. Just to the north, the Westin-managed Le Paradis Resort now sprawls along the Atlantic shore and features a golf course designed by Greg Norman, a marina, and exquisite private residences.

Tips on All-Inclusives

You may find the all-inclusive concept the perfect answer to budgeting for a vacation. With one payment, you take care of lodging, food, drinks and most activities and entertainment. You can forget about tipping, leave your wallet locked in your room safe when you go to the beach, and eat and drink as much as you want without worrying about the bill. But, be aware that you may not be the all-inclusive type. If you enjoy sampling a variety of restaurants, nightclubs, activities and attractions, the structured all-inclusive life may be too confining for you.

Before you decide, ask the following questions:

- Are all meals buffet-style?
- Does the menu change from day to day?
- How many restaurants are included in the plan?
- Does the price include both alcoholic and non-alcoholic drinks?
- Is wine served with dinner?
- What activities are included?
- Is entertainment scheduled every night?
- What complimentary sports equipment is available?
- Is complimentary transportation provided for trips into town?
- Is there a program for children, and is baby-sitting available? (Ask, even if you don't plan to bring children, and be cautious not to book a family-style resort if you're looking for an adults-only experience.)

Tips for Renting

Rental properties are scattered along St. Lucia's coast and throughout the lush, rolling countryside. Consider booking one of these multi-room houses if you need extra space for friends or family, enjoy cooking your own meals and snacking out of your own refrigerator, or just want to live like a local. Some rentals include extras, such as a car, transportation from the airport, maid service, kitchen provisioning or an on-call chef.

You can choose from lavish properties with all the modern conveniences and a staff of caretakers, or relax in a homey, well-used cottages that owners vacate when they have a renter. Most are something in between. Avoid disappointment by asking the following:

- Has the rental agent actually been to the property? (Pictures don't count.)
- Is the villa immaculately clean?
- Who does the cleaning? (Professional services tend to do a more thorough job than owners.)
- What personal articles are left at the property by the owner? (Must you squeeze your clothes into a closet already packed with the owners' stuff?)
- How many and what size beds are in each bedroom?
- Does the bathroom have a tub and shower?
- Is hot water available at all times?
- Are all linens supplied? How about a change of sheets? Extra towels? Soap?
- Are laundry facilities available? Are guests expected to wash soiled linens, or are they left in place at departure?
- Are all rooms air-conditioned?
- Are ceiling or room fans available?
- Do windows have screens?
- What appliances are in the kitchen? What is their age and condition?
- Is the kitchen stocked with basic supplies?
- Where is the nearest grocery store, and does it carry a wide range of imported as well as local products?
- How far away are beaches, restaurants, neighbors?
- Is there a restriction or charge for use of electricity or water?
- What insurance covers damages or accidents?
- Is a damage deposit required?

Island-Wide Rental Agencies

Lucian Leisure
P. O. Box 1538
Castries, St Lucia
☎ 758-452-8898, www.lucian-leisure.com

This agency based in Rodney Bay offers a selection of apartments, two-bedroom to five-bedroom villas, and rooms or suites in a few all-inclusive resorts.

Gateway Villas

Gatepark, Cap Estate
P.O. Box 2296
Rodney Bay, St.Lucia
☎ 866-428-3725 (US & Canada), 758-450-8611 or 758-452-0052, www.gatewayvillas.org

Gatepark is a seven-acre gated condominium community overlooking Rodney Bay Marina. In addition to managing these condos, which include studios and one-, two-or three-bedroom units, Gateway handles other luxury rentals throughout the island.

Castles in Paradise

P.O. Box 660 GM
Vieux Fort, St. Lucia
☎ 758-454-8572, www.castlesinparadise.com

Castles in Paradise are two-bedroom, three-bath villas near Vieux Fort and the international airport. The agency also represents Top of the World Apartments, each with one bedroom, and the two-bedroom, two-bath Top of the World Villa near Castries, Choc Bay and the regional airport.

Villas of Distinction

Petaluma, California
☎ 800-289-0900, 914-273-3331, www.villasofdistinction.com

With more than three dozen listings on St. Lucia, VOD is sure to have a perfect match for you. Click "Specials" for good bargains.

Caribbean Villa Owners Association

☎ 877-248-2862, www.cvoa.com

This association has pages of villa listings for St. Lucia. You contact the owners or managing agents directly after you find a listed villa that meets your requirements. Once a reservation is set up, check back with the association for wholesale airfare.

Tropical Villas St. Lucia

P.O. Box 189, Castries

☎ 758-450-8240 or 758-450-0349, www.tropicalvillas.net

With offices in Castries, this agency handles villas with one to nine bedrooms in the luxurious neighborhood of Cap Estate, the active Rodney Bay area, or near the Pitons in Soufrière All the properties have private pools and are fully staffed.

Camping

The National Trust runs St. Lucia's only campground at **Anse la Liberté**, south of the village of Anse la Raye. Permanent tents are set off the ground on wooden decks, and facilities include barbecue grills, showers, toilets and a communal pavilion powered by solar energy. Six miles of nature trails wind through the 133-acre campground, which slopes down to a rocky beach on a lovely bay. A bare site without a tent rents for about US$20; permanent tents on platforms and teepee-like huts rent for around US$75. Call ahead for reservations, ☎ 758-452-5005, www.slunatrust.org.

St. Lucia's hotels add an 8% government tax and a 10% service charge to basic room rates. These charges may be included in the quoted price, but be sure to ask. Rates at all-inclusive resorts have taxes and service charges built in, and most small inns include them in their prices.

Hotel Price Guide

Hotel rates fluctuate seasonally in the Caribbean. The prices shown for our recommended accommodations are the high-season range for two people sharing a double room, suite or villa. Meal and activity packages are not included, unless the property is strictly an all-inclusive resort, in which case the rates are the all-inclusive rate per couple, per night. Expect to pay the lower rate for a basic non-view room and the higher rate for the best possible accommodations. Summer and shoulder-season rates are usually offered at a discount.

Sleeping with the Stars

Adventure Travel Guides review a wide scope of accommodations throughout the island. Every listing is recommended within its class, so you can choose with confidence the type of lodging that meets your needs within your budget range. Properties marked with one star (★) are highly recommended and considered outstanding for location, facilities, service or atmosphere. Those earning two stars (★★) are considered to be exceptional and worth a splurge. The very few that rate three stars (★★★) are simply the best of the best – on the island or, perhaps, in the Eastern Caribbean region.

Telephone Tip: The 800 numbers below are toll free when calling within the area in parentheses. Use the 758 numbers when you're in the Caribbean, unless a specific toll-free number is listed. When you're on St. Lucia, dial only the 7-digit local number. Do not dial the 758 area code. You can call St. Lucia direct from the US just as you would any long-distance location: 1 + 758 + xxx-xxxx.

All-Inclusive Resorts
Northwest Coast

★★ East Winds Inn

Labrelotte Bay

☎ 800 347 9154 (US), 020 8874 9534 (UK), 758-452-8212, www.eastwinds.com

30 rooms

$760-$1,080, all-inclusive

If you're looking for a quiet, refined inn with five-star European-style elegance and grace, you'll find it here, tucked away on a secluded beach just five miles from the capital. Recently, East Winds was bought by George and Marilyn Reti, who have been annual guests at the inn for many years. They've made some changes, all for the better, but the exquisite property retains its beachcomber-chic ambiance.

Ideally located at the end of a long road off the main highway between Castries and Rodney Bay, the inn consists of 30 rooms in 15 duplex cottages scattered over eight acres of lush gardens that ring with wild-bird songs. A central open-air lounge is furnished with comfortable seating and a selection of books and games that invite relaxation and impromptu gatherings.

Where to Stay

The gourmet kitchen specializes in imaginative meals that please even the most demanding guests. Returning guests, who sometimes stay for several weeks, never complain of a lack of variety. The European-trained and local chefs have won several awards and the restaurant is a member of the prestigious *Chaine des Rotisseurs*.

A large free-form pool with a wide deck lures guests in the afternoon. The cleverly designed swim-up bar is generously stocked so that swimmers can help themselves to a variety of refreshments, including beer, wine, and top-brand liquors. At 4 pm, tea and fresh-baked treats are served pool-side. Late in

the day, most guests head down to the beach to watch the sun set.

Guest rooms in the single-level moss-green cottages are spacious and cooled by gentle trade winds assisted by ceiling fans. The bedrooms feature lovely furniture and fabrics, and the large bathrooms have unusual stone-lined indoor-outdoor showers that allow guests private-but-open bathing. Each room opens onto a private patio outfitted with a small refrigerator, sink, table, and chairs.

Almond Morgan Bay

Choc Bay

☎ 800-4-ALMOND (US), 0871 871 2828 (UK), 758-450-2511, www.almondresorts.com

238 rooms

$850-$1,200, all-inclusive

Formerly known as the St. James Club, Almond Resorts (popular in Barbados) took over late in 2005 and completely remodeled. The impressive open-air lobby provides a sweeping view of the Caribbean, and the lovely grounds include landscaped lagoons, tennis courts, a large free-form swimming pool and full-service beach facilities.

This is one of the most prestigious resort chains in the Caribbean, and the only thing that prevents Morgan Bay from being outstanding in the all-inclusive category is inconsistent service, perhaps due to under-staffing and the recent management changes. This inconvenience should improve with time and, until it does, may or may not effect

your vacation experience, depending on your temperament and expectations.

We suggest you overlook the small, infrequent annoyances and concentrate, instead, on the small soft-sand beach located on Choc Bay between Castries and Rodney Bay. You'll be well-situated to join all the tourist activity and nightlife, but you may prefer to settle in and never leave the property. This is a family resort, with a full-day program for kids, as well as an adults-only pool with a swim-up bar and activities specifically for grown-ups. Massages, facials, and body treatments are available at the full-service spa. Down on the soft-sand beach, you'll have unlimited use of all types of watersports equipment.

Four restaurants serve a variety of excellent dishes at a buffet breakfast, menu-ordered lunch (plus a cookout on the beach), and a selection of dinner venues in the evening. In addition, there's a proper British tea served each afternoon with sandwiches and desserts. The bars pour premium-brand drinks and offer a good selection of beers and wines. Comfortable rooms provide everything a first-class hotel should, including a welcome retreat from non-stop activities.

★ Windjammer Landing Beach Resort

Labrelotte Bay

☎ 800-345-0356 or 800-743-9609 (North America), 800-316-9797 (UK, Europe), 758-456-9000, www.windjammer-landing.com

292 suites and villas

$225-$350 (rooms), $350-$775 (one- & two-bedroom villas), all-inclusive optional

Driving down the steep road that leads through this vacation village to the lobby, you pass white stucco Mediterranean-styled villas with arched windows and red-tiled roofs connected by brick pathways and partially hidden by flowering vines and tall trees. After check-in, you'll be escorted to a villa with one to four bedrooms, a living/dining area, and a full kitchen. Each  is decorated with bright Caribbean colors, and doors open onto a large private terrace with majestic ocean views. Some of the one-bedroom villas and all larger villas also have splendid private plunge pools.

Even standard suites are special at Windjammer. Each features air-conditioning and ceiling fans, mini-fridge, coffee maker, satellite television, and a private terrace with a garden view. Deluxe units have all the amenities of a standard room plus a private terrace and sundeck with an ocean view and private plunge pool.

On 60 acres of lushly landscaped hillside, the resort offers four restaurants, three bars, a shopping arcade, on-site car rental, a gym and spa, tennis courts, a fully-staffed activities desk that organizes daily programs, and a supervised children's program. The place is so large, a complimentary shuttle runs continuously up and down the steep hills transporting guests from one spot to another.

The new culinary director, Didier Le Berre, is a world-class French-trained chef with a talent for creating unlimited imaginative dishes. If you choose one of the optional meal plans, you will not be bored or underfed. One option is called *Villa Dining*. This is a great way to celebrate a romantic evening on your private patio or to entertain friends. A chef helps

Where to Stay

you plan the menu, then comes to your villa to prepare your private dinner party.

Down on lovely Labrellote Bay, the long sandy beach is lined with palm trees and dotted with lounge chairs. A sports center offers all types of water toys for both kids and adults, including waterskiing, banana-log rides, paddle boats, kayaks, and snorkeling equipment. The dive shop arranges excursions to the best scuba areas around the island, and offers both introduction and certification courses.

The beach at Windjammer Landing (Paul Sullivan)

Four freshwater pools provide plenty of room for swimming, floating, and water games. Almost every afternoon, one of the activity directors encourages guests to join in a game of water volleyball or other sports. For an additional charge, the hotel will arrange horseback riding, Jeep excursions, and boat trips. Each night, there's some type of entertainment in one of the bars or restaurants.

The Body Holiday at LeSport

Cariblue Beach, Cap Estate
☎ 800-544-2883 (North America), 870-220-2344 (UK), 758-450-8551 or 758-457-7800, www.thebodyholiday.com
154 rooms and suites
$700-$830 (rooms), $875-$950 (suites), all-inclusive

Not actually a health spa, but more than a resort, LeSport promotes its product as a "Body Holiday." This means that for one price, guests at this 18-acre facility can have an active resort vacation while enjoying the pampering treatments usually found at upscale spas. You can laze about in your robe, take a yoga class, work up a sweat in the gym, or explore the island by bike. The program is completely up to you.

LeSport (Paul Sullivan)

Consider this resort if you are a solo traveler. LeSport has set aside a block of rooms priced for single occupancy. They are large, nicely furnished rooms with queen-size four-poster beds, and each has a view of the gardens. Standard double rooms are large and handsomely decorated with cool tile floors, marble baths, four-poster king-size beds and a private terrace.

Breakfast and lunch are served buffet-style, and dinner is à la carte, except for special theme nights. Meals are nutritious and filling, and while you may tire of the repetition, the dishes are tasty and well-prepared. Wine and dessert accompany

Oasis Spa at Le Sport

every meal, so you will hardly feel deprived. If you want to diet, simply choose from the selection of light cuisine. Live bands entertain during dinner, and you can stay on for the floor show and dancing afterwards.

The resort is known for its excellent sports programs and sports instruction. Scuba lessons are given for beginners, and certified divers can dive to 70 feet right from the shore. Waterskiing and windsurfing equipment and instruction are available, and you can also join an aerobics class in the pool.

Bike tours are scheduled daily, and there are several jogging routes in and around the resort. Classes include stretching, yoga, t'ai chi, aerobics, and stress management. You may be interested in a cocktail-mixing class or even learning to calypso. Beauty and rejuvenation treatments in the tranquil Oasis spa include massage, hair treatments, sauna, and facials. Save time each day to enjoy the sandy beach.

Rendezvous

Malabar Beach

☎ 800-544-2883 (US), 416-693-6588 (Canada), 870-389-1930 (UK), 758-452-4211, www.theromanticholiday.com

100 rooms and suites

$475-$625, all-inclusive

Rendezvous with your significant other at this couples-only resort tucked away on seven acres of lushly landscaped grounds merging with two miles of Caribbean beach. You can get married, renew your vows or simply bask in the luxury of being alone together on vacation.

The agenda at Rendezvous is geared toward pampering twosomes with plenty of individual and group activities in an intimate environment. Catamaran cruises, scuba diving, windsurfing, and waterskiing are all complimentary, but if you prefer you can wander hand-in-hand through the garden, loll on the beach, or spend all day in the hammock on your private patio.

Guests enjoy two pools, a sauna, hot tub, gym, and two lighted tennis courts. In the evening, there's live music during dinner, and the piano player will stay at the bar as long as someone stays on to listen. Meals are served in the casual open-air **Terrace Restaurant** or the more formal air-conditioned **Trysting Place**. A pair of chefs, plan and prepare a variety of menu choices, and you're unlikely to tire of either the buffets at the Terrace or the multi-course meals served at Trysting Place.

All rooms are air-conditioned and have ceiling fans and king-size four-poster beds. If you choose a standard room (called *superior*), ask to be on the top floor so you can see the water.

These rooms are relatively small, but they all have a balcony or patio. The upper-category rooms are larger, with good views of the sea, and the suites are exquisitely decorated with special amorous touches. There are no TVs on the property, but no one ever notices.

Rex Resorts

St. Lucian Resort by Rex

Reduit Beach
☎ 758-452-8351, www.rexcaribbean.com
120 rooms
$230-$350, all-inclusive Optional

★Royal Resort & Spa by Rex

Reduit Beach
☎ 452-9999, www.rexcaribbean.com
96 rooms and suites
$350-$775, all-inclusive optional

Papillon by Rex

Reduit Beach
☎ 758-452-8351, www.rexcaribbean.com
140 rooms and suites
$425-$650, all-inclusive

As sister resorts on St. Lucia's longest beach, these three Rex properties cover a wide range of vacation preferences. Papillon is all-inclusive only; the Royal and St. Lucian offer an optional all-inclusive package.

The Papillon

The **Papillon** has recently had a good sprucing up and is lovelier than ever. It's now a non-smoking property and the large, tile-floored rooms are decorated in fresh tropical fabrics. Beachfront accommodations have a sitting area and refreshment bar. Meals are served in both the main restaurant, **The Monarch**, or in the casual beach bar café. Entertain-

Papillon beach

ment is presented nightly in the **Tropigala Lounge**, and day-time activity centers around watersports on the beach or in the butterfly-shaped swimming pool.

On a recent visit, **The St. Lucian** was showing signs of wear, but the large rooms are clean and have either a balcony or patio. Perhaps an update is needed because of the resort's popularity and year-round full occupancy. Repeat guests come back year after year because of the relaxed ambience,

The St. Lucian

lush Eden-like gardens, a wide-range of watersports and comparatively low rates. Energetic guests spend time in the pools, on the tennis courts or at the fully-equipped gym. Others prefer to browse through the shopping arcade or enjoy some pampering at the Royal Spa,

Beach at the St. Lucian

Where to Stay

which is next door at the Royal Resort.

When choosing your accommodations, be aware that pool-side rooms are in the midst of all the action, while upgraded accommodations are set back in the quiet tropical gardens. If you want extra room and a spectacular view of the Caribbean, book one of the beachfront rooms.

Guests can dine buffet-style at the casual **Mariners Restaurant**, where Caribbean and international dishes are served, or order à la carte from the Asian menu at the **Oriental Restaurant**. Evening entertainment includes live band music and dancing at the **Admirals Lounge**.

The Royal St. Lucian

The **Royal St. Lucian Resort & Spa** is the most luxurious of the three Rex properties, and offers exquisite accommodations in a variety of suites. Deluxe suites overlook the gardens and waterfall pool. All have separate air-conditioned bedrooms, sitting rooms with ceiling fans, fabulous bathrooms with two sinks, soft robes, cable TV, and a mini-bar. If you want an ocean view, book a Seaview suite; for direct waterfront access, ask for a Beachfront suite, which also has a larger living area. Go all-out with a Grand Deluxe suite, which features oversized rooms and a dining terrace.

Since meal plans are optional at the Royal, you can choose to try the nearby restaurants on Rodney Bay, or dine at the restaurants located within the lushly landscaped Rex complex.

At the Royal, **Chic!** serves French-inspired cuisine, and the award-winning **L'Epicure** offers Creole specialties and international classics.

Sandals Resorts

Sandals Halcyon

Choc Bay
☎ 800-SANDALS (US), 800-545-8283 (Canada), 800-742-0207 (UK), 758-453-0222 www.sandals.com
170 rooms
$680-$960, all-inclusive

Sandals Regency Golf & Spa Resort

La Toc Bay
☎ 800-SANDALS (US), 800-545-8283 (Canada), 800-742-0207 (UK), 758-452-3081, www.sandals.com
327 rooms and suites
$720-$1,240, all-inclusive

★ Sandals Grande Beach Resort & Spa

Pigeon Point
☎ 800-SANDALS (US), 800-545-8283 (Canada), 800-742-0207 (UK), 758-455-2000 www.sandals.com
283 rooms and suites
$625-$1,020, all-inclusive

The view from Sandals Halcyon

The well-known Sandals Resorts cater to couples and specialize in all-inclusive luxury vacations. Three St. Lucia resorts belong to the group; you can stay at one and play at all three. This means you have access to four oversized swimming pools (three with swim-up bars), six whirlpools, two health spas, 14 restaurants and a lush golf course.

Sandals Halcyon is north of Castries on a splendid beach. If a comparison must be

Where to Stay

Pool at Sandals Halcyon (Paul Sullivan)

made, this Sandals is a bit more laid-back than the others, but it lacks none of the trademark sophistication and romance. Tropical gardens surround the classic Caribbean-style buildings, and every room is furnished in fine wood, cool tile and bright island prints. A king-size four-poster bed faces the satellite TV for late-night snuggle-viewing. On-site facilities include three restaurants, tennis courts and a watersports hut.

Sandals Regency Golf and Spa Resort is south of Castries on 210 secluded acres fronted by white sand on crescent-shaped La Toc Bay. The energetic staff keeps things moving at a rapid pace, but guests can escape to their room or suite. All accommodations are tucked into soft-colored hillside villas

The Sandals Regency

that are elegantly decorated with mahogany furniture and elegant fabrics. Each room has a king-size bed and satellite TV, while suites include concierge service, sitting rooms, larger bathrooms, robes and an in-room bar. Hilltop suites on Sunset Bluff have private plunge pools. The complex has two pools, and the largest features a waterfall and swim-up bar. In addition, guests of all three resorts have use of Regency's nine-hole golf course, five tennis courts, health spa, fitness center and six restaurants.

Sandals Grande is a colonial-style resort sitting on 17 acres along the narrow strip of land that connects the main island with Pigeon Point, a national landmark and home to the island's national park. Water is an important feature here; every guest room and all public areas have sweeping views of either the beach and Rodney Bay or the Caribbean. The low-rise complex is

Sandals at Pigeon Beach (Paul Sullivan)

centered around a fantastic one-acre free-form swimming lagoon trimmed with grottoes, waterfalls, and tropical landscaping. Each spacious air-conditioned room is elegantly decorated and includes every convenience. You'll be reminded of gracious plantation living by the antique reproduction furniture, bright island colors, and native art. Five restaurants are within the complex, with specialties ranging from classic Italian to gourmet international favorites.

Club St. Lucia by Splash

Anse du Cap, Cap Estate
☎ 758-450-0551
www.splashresorts.com
372 rooms and suites
$275-$425, all-inclusive

Far on the northern tip of the island, this everything-to-everybody all-inclusive resort is St. Lucia's largest hotel complex. Five vacation villages sprawl across 65 garden-like acres with two beaches, five swimming pools, five restaurants, and a staggering list of activities to please every child, couple, single adult and teenager.

You can get married in one of the wedding chapels overlooking the sea, play unlimited tennis on one of the lighted courts, exercise in the gym, take a sailboat or kayak out for a spin around the bay, drop the little ones at the supervised Kid's Club for the day, or join a volleyball game on the beach. Better yet, enjoy a massage at the spa, then sprawl on a hammock stretched between two palm trees, order a fruity rum drink from the bar, and ask someone to wake you in time for dinner. Even teens enjoy their holiday at a club set up just for them, which has an inline skating track and an e-mail system. Snacks and drinks are available throughout the day at pool-side food stations, and some type of live entertainment is scheduled every evening.

You'll get all this and more at a bargain price, by Caribbean standards, which is why most of the rooms are full year-round. If you want to get away from some of the endless action, book a room in the adults-only Hummingbird Village. Throughout the complex, each village is made up of colorful multi-unit bungalows scattered among the hills. Each spacious air-conditioned room has a king-size bed, ceiling fan, cable TV, and a private patio. Larger suites have separate living areas that can be converted into sleeping space.

Southwest Coast

★★ Jalousie Plantation

Eden Bay, Soufrière
☎ 800-544-2883 (North America), 870-389-1931 (UK and Europe), 758-456-8000, www.thejalousieplantation.com
112 rooms and villas
$520-$725, meal plan optional

Surprisingly, this expansive 325-acre resort is quite intimate and almost hidden on a steep, densely forested slope between the twin Pitons. The haven has won environmental awards and is designated a rainforest nature sanctuary. The bay spread at its feet is a national marine reserve.

As a guest at this luxurious retreat, you'll stay in one of the plush cottages scattered among native fruit trees and flowering shrubs. A shuttle runs continuously up and down the hillside, but if you want to be nearer Eden Beach and all the facilities, book one of the Sugar Mill suites. They are closer to all the action, which is good if you're traveling with kids or don't want to either walk the inclined paths or wait for a shuttle every time you leave your room. Each suite is spacious, with sitting and dressing areas and a private terrace.

Get away from it all in one of the suites or villas farther up the hill. Room numbers increase as you move up the hill, so stick with something in the 300s if you want to be near the main resort buildings, and something in the 700s to 900s to guarantee more privacy. Each has either a mountain or ocean view,

both air-conditioning and ceiling fans, a mini-bar with a coffee maker, and satellite TV with a VCR. Every guest is given a bathrobe to use during their stay, which is especially nice if you have a unit with a private plunge pool. All of the ample-sized bathrooms are outfitted with bidets, hair dryers and make-up mirrors.

The amenities, facilities and services are, of course, five-star quality. You have a choice of four dining areas spread throughout the resort, including pool-side and beach-side service. In addition, the wonderful world-class spa offers all the latest health and beauty treatments, including outdoor massage and services designed specifically for men.

The fitness center is well-equipped, and there are four tennis courts and a complete watersports center with snorkeling, waterskiing, windsurfing and a PADI dive shop. Tons of white sand have been brought in to transform the naturally rocky, black-sand beach, and buoys anchored in the bay designate a safe area for snorkeling and diving near the sheer underwater wall of Petite Piton. Since the bay is a marine reserve, anchoring and fishing are prohibited, so the reef is healthy and sea life is abundant.

★★Coconut Bay Resort & Spa

Vieux Fort
☎ 866-978-6226 (US), 44-58-279-2260 (UK & Europe), 758-459-6000, www.coconutbayresortandspa.com
254 rooms
$380-$440, all-inclusive

Coconut Bay Resort & Spa is St Lucia's newest all-inclusive beachfront resort. It sprawls across 85 acres of handsomely landscaped beachfront property, less than five minutes by car from Hewanorra International Airport on the island's less-

Facing page: Jalousie Resort (Paul Sullivan)

developed southeast coast. The resort strives to be all things to all visitors, and it makes a remarkably good show of it.

On the one hand, it is an excellent choice for couples seeking privacy and romance. The waterfront wedding gazebo is one of the most picturesque spots on the island for exchanging vows, and the palm-shaded adults-only pool and garden area promise tranquility and seclusion. Honeymooners and those suffering from any type of burnout could not ask for a more perfect retreat.

On the other hand, the resort is also ideal for families with kids and all vacationers with energy to burn. The entire north side of the property is designed for fun in the sun and features a huge water park. Let go of all inhibitions and enjoy. You won't be the only fully-grown adult going down the water slides or tubing in the lazy river.

Should you tire of water play, head for the marvelous spa, Kai Mer, which is Creole for "Sea House." There you can partake of an outdoor massage, enjoy a 12-head Swiss hydro-shower, relax in the wet and dry saunas or try one of the signature services offered in the open-air treatment rooms.

Dining options are designed to please both adults and kids. Grownups can choose one of two gourmet restaurants, **Silk** (Asian cuisine) and **Bellagio** (Italian dishes), or join families with kids at the **Coconut Walk** buffet. Snacks and drinks are served throughout the day at **Bites**, the waterfront grill, and all types of beverages are available at three bars and a swim-up pool bar.

If you're traveling with kids, book one of the rooms in the north-side building. Couples and single adults will want to stay in the south zone. Ask for a room on the fourth floor for a spectacular ocean view. Every unit has a balcony and either a king-size or two queen-size beds plus a sitting area. Families can ask for adjoining rooms that allow a connecting door to open and create a two-room suite.

The only drawback for some visitors is the beach. It's beautiful, with soft white sand, but it's on the Atlantic, which means it can be a bit choppy and windy. Some guests also have complained about the build-up of seaweed, but on a recent visit, we didn't find it to be bad. In fact, we got snorkeling gear from the beach bar and saw some interesting fish. Wind-and-wave watersports are available nearby, and a calmer beach is within walking distance. Most guests prefer to spend their time in one of the three pools or at the water park.

Tipping is not allowed, so the all-inclusive rates really do include everything.

Resorts, Hotels & Inns

★★★ Anse Chastanet Resort

Anse Chastanet, Soufrière
☎ 800-223-1108 (US), 758-459-7000, www.ansechastanet.com
49 rooms and suites
$465-$795, including breakfast and dinner (optional in summer)

If you like posh and polish, skip this fabulous-but-earthy resort that caters to divers, nature lovers and reckless romantics. Your first clue to the drama here is the brain-bouncing, rut-ravaged dirt road that leads to the magnificent marine reserve off the beach at Anse Chastanet. If you survive the ride, you're rewarded with paradise.

The resort climbs the hill that rises steeply from the black-and-white-sand beach. Rooms were cleverly designed by Canadian owner Nick Troubetzkoy to be open to nature but screened from the view of other guests. All are large and rusti-

Anse Chastanet Resort

cally elegant, with high ceilings, open walls, and balconies that wrap around trees. You'll have the pleasant sensation of being outdoors while enjoying the comfort of inside conveniences. The furniture is hand-crafted from local wood that blends perfectly with the island art, West Indies red-and-yellow plaid fabrics, tree-house views and the close-by sounds of nature that pour in from every direction.

Ask for one of the premium or deluxe rooms at the top of the hill. It's a precipitous climb, but you'll be rewarded with breathtaking vistas of the Pitons and sea. Standard rooms are similar, but with less dramatic views and a bit less space. Each opens onto a balcony and has a ceiling fan, small refrigerator, hair dryer, and coffee maker – but no phones, TVs or air-conditioning.

The **Piti Piton** and **Trou-au-Diable** restaurants are in the talented hands of Executive Chef Jon Bentham, a mild-mannered Englishman who enjoys the challenge of fusion cuisine. His menus mix and mingle West Indies, Mediterranean, French and Asian recipes into what he calls "Tropical World Cuisine." Patrons call it delicious, and it's possible to eat at the resort all week and still be surprised by the choice of creative dishes. On Tuesdays, the resort throws a beach party featuring a Caribbean buffet. East Indian-Caribbean fusion dishes are served in the Trou au Diable restaurant Wednes-

Hillside Deluxe suite

day through Monday evenings. For the afternoon munchies, snacks are served every afternoon at both the Piton Bar and Beach Bar. During the winter season, the Modified American Plan (MAP, breakfast and dinner) is mandatory and adds about $70 per person to the rate. Off-season, you have the option of accepting or declining the meal plan.

Couples often choose Anse Chastanet for their wedding and honeymoon. The resort has been voted "One of the World's Top Ten Most Romantic" by A&E television, and their wedding package is among the most complete and

Beachside Deluxe suite

worry-free on the island. A wedding coordinator works with the couple to design the perfect ceremony, reception and honeymoon, then arranges every detail, start to finish, so the bride and groom can relax and enjoy.

Anse Chastanet also has a soft adventure program that appeals to guests who want a bit of excitement. The resort is known for its direct-from-the-beach access to the marine reserve, which has superb visibility and extraordinary coral, sponges and sea creatures. Guests have complimentary use of snorkel gear and a variety of water toys, so seeing all the underwater sights and enjoying watersports is one of the daily bonuses of staying at the resort.

Where to Stay

Scuba St. Lucia, a five-star PADI operator with a legendary reputation for excellence, is located directly on the Anse Chastanet beach. Recently, the resort has added **Kayak St. Lucia** and **Bike St. Lucia** to its offerings. The 600-acre resort property has miles of biking and hiking trails, including **Tinker's Trail**, named after the Olympic mountain-bike champion and frequent resort visitor, Tinker Juarez.

The new **Kai Belté Spa** is the perfect place to relax and refresh between active pursuits. Ayurveda treatments are the highlight, but you can also enjoy an outdoor massage, take a bit of aromatherapy or submit your face to a cellular-repair treatment.

This resort repeatedly makes every credible international list of the

Kai Belté Spa

world's best, and you will immediately understand why – if you make it down that darn entrance road in one piece.

★★★ Jade Mountain

Morne Chastanet, Soufrière

☎ 800-223-1108 (US), 758-459-7000, www.jademountain-stlucia.com

24 suites

$1,150-$1,600, meal plan optional

Jade Mountain is almost too breathtakingly extraordinary to describe. It deserves more than the three-star maximum rating awarded to the most outstanding resorts reviewed in this guide. It's that magnificent.

However, if you can and will pay more than a thousand dollars per night for accommodations, this is certainly a fabulous place to do it. If you're honeymooning, celebrating a big occasion or just rich, by all means book a night or a week or eternity at Jade Mountain.

This newly-opened resort was designed and built by architect-owner Nick Troubetzkoy and his wife, Karolin. They also designed, built and own Anse Chastanet Resort, which is on the

Jade Mountain Infinity Pool suite

beach just a short distance down the steep hillside. Designed to look like a ship, Jade Mountain seems to float both on the mountaintop and on the sea behind it. A separate gangplank leads to every suite (each costing a smidgen over US$1 million to build) giving you the sensation of entering your own luxury yacht. Within, the room is open to nature on one side with a private glass-tiled infinity pool seemingly merging with the sea below and the twin Pitons beyond.

Another suite

Once you catch your breath and turn your gaze away from the view, you notice several ceiling fans hanging from the 15-foot ceiling to cool the room and shoo away flying insects. Curved

Where to Stay

half-walls shield the raised bathroom from view and magnificent furniture fills the living/sleeping area. If you are an environmentalist, you'll be glad to learn that the resort has won awards for its preservation of the land, conservation of water and utilization of recycled material. It's no surprise that your suite is lacking a computer, television, radio and telephone. If you need something from room service or housekeeping, you simply pull the bell cord that summons a pleasant staff member.

After you settle in, the Jade Mountain concierge will help you choose activities and excursions to suit your individual interests. You might want to work out in the fitness room, enjoy an exotic treatment in the private spa rooms or spend time at the Jade Mountain Club – a casual bar and grill. The limousine shuttle will take you down the hill to the beach, and you'll have access to all the facilities and activities of the 600-acre Anse Chastanet Resort

Northwest Coast

★Villa Beach Cottages

Choc Bay Beach
☎ 758-450-2884
www.villabeachcottages.com
14 suites & cottages
$110-$155 (suites), $220-$240 (cottages)

Located four miles north of Castries, and right on the sand at Choc Bay, these gingerbread-trimmed one- and two-bedroom air-conditioned cottages have four-poster beds, ceiling fans, living areas, a fully-equipped kitchen, and large balconies with hammocks. If you're celebrating a special occasion, ask for the two-level Honeymoon Villa, which has a spiral staircase leading up from the ground-floor living/dining area to a large bedroom.

The resort is thoroughly modern, but decorated to appear "old Caribbean." Original local art hangs on the walls (some by the St. Lucian Nobel Prize-winner Derek Walcott), and the little swimming pool that overlooks the sea has a unique rock waterfall.

Villa Beach Cottages (Paul Sullivan)

As a guest, you get a lot of amenities you might not expect from such a tiny resort. **Coconuts Restaurant** prepares and serves meals on request, all types of watersports equipment is available on the beach, and you can shop at the gift store, pick up necessities at the mini-mart, and rent a car from the on-site rental desk.

La Dauphine Estate in Soufrière is a sister resort, so you may want to split your time between the two locations. (See review under *Southwest Coast*, below.)

Bay Gardens Hotel

Rodney Bay
☎ 877-620-3200 (North America), 758-452-8060
www.baygardenshotel.com
79 rooms and suites
$120-$160

Reduit Beach and all the facilities of Rodney Bay are within walking distance, which makes this medium-sized hotel popular with vacationers who don't have a car. If you don't want to leave the property, you can lounge around the two swim-

Bay Gardens

ming pools, order drinks from **Cinnamon Bar**, and have all your meals at the award-winning **Spices Restaurant**.

Air-conditioned rooms are either standard or superior, but both are spacious and feature patios or balconies, small refrigerators, Wi-Fi access and cable TV. The superior rooms have a few more amenities, such as Jacuzzi bathtubs and ceiling fans. Executive suites have a small kitchenette and a sitting area with a sleeper sofa. If you need more room, book one of the new two-bedroom **Croton Suites**. Each is actually a full apartment with a kitchen, living-dining area, and a furnished balcony overlooking Rodney Bay Marina.

This isn't a luxurious resort, but the rooms are bright and clean, and the staff wins awards for everything from management to cooking. You get a lot for your money here. If the location were directly on the beach, rates would be much higher. As it is, you'll save a few dollars and still be within walking distance of Reduit Beach and all the restaurants, shops, and nightspots of Rodney Bay.

Bay Gardens Inn

Rodney Bay

☎ 877-434-1212 (North America), 758-452-8200, www.baygardensinn.com

33 rooms and suites

$110-$160

Bay Gardens Inn

Right next door to Bay Gardens Hotel, the Inn is a popular retreat and often booked up early for the winter season. Standard rooms are small and seem a bit crowded, but the deluxe rooms are fairly spacious and have plenty of space for the king-size bed and all the modern conveniences. All rooms are air-conditioned and come with a private terrace, cable TV and a refrigerator. The inn has its own pool, but guests can use the pools and other facilities at the hotel next door.

Tuxedo Villas

Rodney Bay

☎ 758-452-8553 or 800-600-2688, fax: 452-8577.

10 apartments

$100-$120

Tuxedo Villas

These new apartments across the street from fabulous Reduit Beach provide guests extra space in one- or two-bedroom units. Housed in a two-story building with a central pool and courtyard, each air-conditioned apartment has a living room, dining area, fully-equipped kitchen, and either one or two bathrooms. Perfect for families or friends sharing expenses,

Tuxedo has its own restaurant, bar, mini-market, and coin-op laundry. There's no need for a car, since all the facilities of Rodney Bay and Reduit Beach are within walking distance

★Coco Palm

Rodney Bay
☎ 866-588-5980 (North America), 758-452-0712, www.coco-resorts.com
83 rooms and suites
$145-$290

Coco Palm

This new resort in the center of Rodney Bay Village is a real attention-getter. The four-level Caribbean colonial-style building is painted yellow, with a red roof. Impossible to ignore, and you shouldn't. It's a great little hotel with good rates in an ideal location.

Each room is decorated in splashy tropical colors and outfitted with cable TVs (some are flat-screen), Wi-Fi, both air-conditioning and ceiling fans, CD players and a small refrigerator. Some of the suites also have iPods and DVD players, plus separate living areas and an extra bathroom.

The rooftop is a multi-use area with fantastic views. During the day, you can book an open-air massage up there, and in the evening arrange for a butler to serve you and your guests a private dinner. **Kafe Kaiso** is open around the clock to serve drinks and snacks and provide entertainment. **Ti Banane**, the poolside bistro, serves meals throughout the day, and all the Rodney Bay restaurants are within walking distance. The swimming pool is large and surrounded by lounge chairs and tables with umbrellas. You have a choice of several nearby beaches, including Reduit.

Coco Kreole

Rodney Bay

☎ 866-588-5980 (North America), 758-452-0712, www.coco-resorts.com

20 rooms

$95-$105

Coco Kreole

This wonderful little bed-and-breakfast inn is a sister to Coco Palm, so you can use all the facilities at both properties. Kreole opened in 2003 and Palm opened in 2005, so both are modern and maintain high standards set by owner Allan Chastanet and managing director Feolla Chastanet, including especially friendly staff. Rates are a few dollars lower at the Kreole, so choose this inn if you're on a budget. It's probably the best value on the island.

Ask for a pool-side room, since the yellow inn is directly on a main road, and traffic noise on the street side can be annoying. Rooms are small, but each is bright, fresh and outfitted with air-conditioning, TVs with VCRs, CD players and ceiling fans. If you're traveling with family or friends, ask for interconnecting rooms. In addition to the small swimming pool, Kreole has its own bar.

Green Parrot Inn

Morne Fortune, Castries

☎ 758-452-3399, www.greenparrotinn.com

55 rooms

$75-$100

The motel-style rooms are showing their age, but the views from this hillside inn set above the capital's harbor are terrific. If you aren't drawn by the setting and low room rates, try

Green Parrot Inn seen from its dock

the food. You'll be hooked for sure. Chef-owner-manager Harry Edward Joseph is a worldly epicurean who enjoys showing off his culinary talents. The restaurant is his true love. The inn is an afterthought.

If you're on the island for business or a short layover, the location is good for easy access to Castries and the regional airport. Be sure to ask for a room with a view. There's no difference in price, and you don't want to miss the best feature of the inn. All rooms are air-conditioned and have cable TV, but the furnishings and décor are merely basic. Guests have a panoramic view from the swimming pool, bar and restaurant.

See *Where to Eat* for details about the **Green Parrot Restaurant**.

Cara Suites

La Pansee, Castries
☎ 758-452-4767, www.carahotels.com
54 rooms
$115-$125

Business travelers recognize Cara Hotels as a reliable chain in the southern Caribbean. On St. Lucia, Cara Suites are on a hillside overlooking the east side of the capital with a well-equipped business center and quick

Cara Suites

access by shuttle into town. Each of the modern economy-priced air-conditioned suites opens onto a balcony and has one king-size or two queen-size beds, a refrigerator and coffee-making supplies. There's a small swimming pool, the business center offers computers with high-speed Internet and Wi-Fi access, and the **Mandolin Restaurant** is open for all meals throughout the day. This is a good choice if you're only on the island for a short layover or a few days of business meetings. Otherwise, you'll soon tire of hassling with city traffic every time you leave the hotel grounds.

Mid-West Coast

★★Discovery at Marigot Bay
Marigot
☎ 800-766-3782, 758-458-5300, www.discoverystlucia.com
124 rooms and suites
$350-$775

Recently opened as part of the new upscale Marina Village, Discovery Resort gives island visitors yet another choice in luxury accommodations. While Marigot Bay has a long-standing reputation for old Caribbean charm and natural beauty, Discovery and its adjacent marina, restaurants, shops and spa are meant to lure travelers who favor New World conveniences and futuristic style.

Each suite is a dramatically comfortable air-conditioned setting with white walls and hardwood floors. As you look around, you'll take in the up-to-date technology and top-of-the-line features: flat-screen TVs with DVD players; high-speed WiFi Internet access; pillow-top beds made up with Egyptian cotton sheets; large, luxurious bathrooms with slate tile, drench showers and bidets; kitchens outfitted with stylish Italian appliances. Every room opens out onto a large balcony with a view of the bay, and half of the units have a private plunge pool.

Guests take a water taxi across the bay to Marigot Beach, which is a hindrance to some. Since the resort has two pools (one with a swim-up bar), and many of the units have a pri-

Discovery at Marigot Bay

vate plunge pool, most guests don't miss easy access to the beach.

Kitchens in each unit are so sleek and modern, you may prefer to prepare some of your own meals. If you decide to dine out, the choices are vast. On the property, **Hurricane Hole** has great views of the bay and features an excellent lunch menu, including the soon-to-be-famous Big Mouth Burger. **Boudreau** serves breakfast, lunch and dinner in a stylishly relaxed French-colonial setting. You can hang out with all the beautiful people, both local and visiting, at **Pink Snail Bar**. Try the Rosy Cheeks, a cranberry juice and champagne drink spiked with a dash of triple sec.

As for spas, **Lapli** is among the best on the island. It has private treatment rooms with their own sun deck and outdoor shower. The adjoining Zen garden features massage cabanas and wooden soaking tubs.

The resort and village complex is lavish and chic in every respect. And the staff is extremely friendly. They go the extra step to make you feel comfortable and are quick to offer advice, assistance and a slice of island lore.

Marigot Beach Club Hotel & Dive Resort

Marigot Bay

☎ 888-790-5264, 758-451-4974, www.marigotdiveresort.com

25 villas

$185-$208. Breakfast, lunch and dinner are included for an additional $55 per person per day.

This popular resort depends on its outstanding location and relaxed atmosphere to draw repeat guests year after year. It's set on the north side of gorgeous Marigot Bay, and all of the breezy units are either beach-front or beach-view.

Marigot Beach Club Hotel & Dive Resort

Some of the well-equipped villas accommodate up to 10 guests, and the snug studios are a perfect hideaway for two. All are cooled by ceiling fans, but you can flip on the A/C if you get too warm. Studios have a small kitchenette, larger villas feature full kitchens, and every unit has a king-size bed and its own furnished patio.

Breakfast is included in the rate and full-meal and dive packages are available. Doolittle's Restaurant and Big Bamboo

Balcony view

Tiki Lounge are just steps away, with special drinks, theme-night dinners and evening entertainment. Diving is the main passion for most guests, and a PADI dive shop offers training and scuba/snorkeling trips. In addition, there's a swimming pool, white-sand beach, watersports center, gym and spa.

★ Oasis Marigot

Marigot Bay
☎ 800-263-4202 (North America), 800-2785-8241 (UK and worldwide), 758-451-4185, www.oasismarigot.com
21 suites, cottages and apartments
$155-$455

Oasis Marigot (Paul Sullivan)

Several types of accommodations are available at Oasis Marigot. Our review and rates are based on two people staying in one of the basic suites or cottages. Luxuries and prices escalate when you opt for a larger unit or extras, such as a private pool. Look carefully at the descriptions on the website or call the office manager to find out exactly which unit is right for you. Some of the houses and villas are owned by individuals, and some of the cottages are part of a timeshare operation, so decorations, furnishings and amenities differ throughout.

The Ocean Cottage has four self-contained apartments. Each features a luxuriously furnished living area, bedroom with a king or queen bed, tiled bathroom with shower, fully outfitted kitchen, and a private terrace shaded by tropical landscaping. You have a choice of walking to the nearby beach and restaurants, or staying "home" to enjoy the pool, sauna, and barbecue on the open wood-fire pit.

Facing page: View from Oasis Marigot (Paul Sullivan)

The Vacation Club is a cluster of 12 private sea houses scattered on a steep hill that overlooks the bay and beach. Each modern two-story house is individually decorated and features a master bedroom, living room with a sofa bed, and fully-equipped kitchen. Both the upstairs living area and downstairs bedroom have double French doors that open onto verandas with views of the bay. Some are air-conditioned and all have ceiling fans.

Villa St. Lucia has two levels; each can be rented separately or the entire house can be reserved for up to six people. The main upper level has two air-conditioned bedrooms with king-size beds, private bathrooms, a fully-equipped kitchen and a covered, furnished veranda. Rented separately, it is perfect for four guests. The lower level is actually a large suite for two with its own kitchen, separate air-conditioned bedroom, private bathroom and a a screened terrace.

The Great House is pure self-indulgence, with breathtaking views of the bay, mountains, and sea. It accommodates up to six people in three private bedrooms (two with private baths, a third bath is off the common area). Built in the tradition of the original great houses that once overlooked thriving Caribbean plantations, it has a grassy lawn edged with tropical plants and royal palms, a huge cliff-side verandah, and freshwater swimming pool. Inside, classic-style columns form a grand entry into the vast living area with its 20-foot vaulted ceiling and entertainment system. A formal dining room sits adjacent to a kitchen that offers every modern convenience. A housekeeper and gardener maintain the house and grounds, and guests can request a cook, chauffeur or nanny.

Other accommodations above the bay include the exquisite two-bedroom **Emerald Hill Villa** and the nearby, but secluded, **Caribbean Blue Suite**, which is ideal for honeymooners.

★★ Ti Kaye Village

Anse Cochon
☎ 758-456-8101, www.tikaye.com
33 cottages
$200-$380

We think this lit-
tle hideaway is a
real bargain.
Developer Nick
P i n n o c k
designed the
resort along with
Wayne Brown (a
co-founder of
Anse Chastanet
Resort) to insure
maximum pri-
vacy and great
views by tucking

Cottage at Ti Kaye Village

each cottage into the lush foliage that grows on the hillside above secluded Anse Cochon, one of the best diving and snorkeling bays on the island.

For a very reasonable price, you get more than 750 square feet of air-conditioned space, a large veranda furnished with rocking chairs and a two-person hammock, an oversized open-air garden shower, a four-poster king-size bed, and breakfast each morning in the dining pavilion. Some of the cottages have a plunge pool, and a few are configured as duplexes with adjoining doors on the balcony, which are ideal for families with teenagers or friends traveling together.

The mile-long road leading from the highway to the resort entrance is every bit as horrific as the famous rutted entrance to Anse Chastanet Resort. If you make it unscathed, you'll be faced with 166 wooden steps down (and back up) the steep hillside from the resort to the beach. But, no matter, you'll soon get used to the trip, and it's fine exercise for burning off the calories consumed at the beach-side **Ti Manje** bar and grill.

No one under age 12 is allowed, so the resort is quiet and peaceful. You can spend all day lazing in your hammock, or walk down the steep stairs leading to the bay to snorkel in the clear water or to nap on the sandy beach. Since the resort is remote, you'll be wise to sign up for the optional meal plan. The cuisine at **Kai Manje**, the main restaurant, is superb, and the open-air dining pavilion is a romantic spot with splendid views.

Ti Manje at Ti Kaye Village (Paul Sullivan)

Southwest Coast

La Dauphine Estate
Soufrière
☎ 758-450-2884, www.villabeachcottages.com (click La Dauphine Estate at the top right)
Six rooms
$110-$260
This 200-acre former plantation is a sister property to the Villa Beach Cottages, near Castries. If you want to stay in a small inn on the south end of the island, La Dauphine is a

good choice. It's in the hills about five miles from Soufrière, a short drive from lovely beaches and many of the island's top attractions.

Four of the six estate rooms are in the Great House, which share one full bathroom, a half-bath and an outdoor shower. In addition, the house has a living room, a dining room with a table that seats 10, and a wrap-around veranda. A master bedroom and a smaller bedroom share a bathroom in Chateau Laffitte, which is about 200 yards downhill.

This is a lovely property. Very old Caribbean. If you have a group traveling together, consider taking over both houses, which were built in the late 1800s and recently restored in their original style with modern upgrades. You'll live like a local and can arrange for the housekeeper to prepare meals. However, if you want a private bathroom, Villa Beach Cottages are a better choice.

La Dauphine Estate

The Still Plantation & Beach Resort

Soufrière
☎ 758-459-5049, www.thestillresort.com
20 apartments and studios
$110-$145

With two properties and one name, this resort plantation offers guests several options. The **Plantation** has 14 apartments, each with one or two bedrooms and either a kitchenette or full kitchen. It is a 400-acre working estate located short distance inland from the coast on the Fond St. Jacques Road, about a five-minute walk from Soufrière. All the spacious units have a sitting area and ceiling fans; most also have air-conditioning, and there's a large swimming pool. **The**

Still Plantation & Beach Resort

Beach Resort is on the north end of Soufrière Bay. Two studio apartments and three one-bedroom apartments are on the upper level of the beachfront building and have wonderful views of the Pitons. All units are cheerfully decorated and cooled by ceiling fans; some have a kitchen. A shuttle bus runs between the two properties, but they are within walking distance and guests have privileges at both. When combined, there are two restaurants, two bars, a swimming pool, a gift boutique, and a nearby scuba shop and horse stables.

Hummingbird Beach Resort

Soufrière
☎ 800-223-9815, 758-459-7232, www.nvo.com/pitonresort
11 rooms, suites and cottages
$70-$170

On the beach at the northern edge of Soufrière, the Hummingbird is the ideal low-cost retreat. Its enchanting cabins overlook the Pitons and Caribbean Sea, and you can walk into town in about five minutes. Most rooms have a private bath,

Hummingbird Beach Resort

but one suite and two standard rooms share a bath. One cottage has two bedrooms, a sitting area, and kitchen. The resort is rustic and cooled by ceiling fans, but there are occasional elegant touches, such as stone walls, cathedral ceilings, and mahogany four-poster beds in three of the deluxe rooms.

Guests enjoy swimming in the attractive freshwater pool and watching the sun set from the beach-side bar. The **Lifeline Bar and Restaurant** has a reputation for serving some of the best food on the island; it's a popular hangout for locals and visitors arriving by private yacht. Owner Joan Alexander Stowe, whom everyone calls Joyce, is a native St. Lucian and gifted artist. When she's not busy overseeing the resort, she operates an on-site studio and gift shop that features her colorful batiks.

Stonefield Estate Villas

★ Stonefield Estate Villas

Soufrière

☎ 758/459-7037, www.stonefieldvillas.com

20 one- to three-bedroom villas

$190-$350

If you want to totally escape, make reservations for one of these villas designed for solitude and, if you wish, romance. The 20 plantation-style villas scattered across 26 acres at the base of Petit Piton have one to three bedrooms, gorgeous views and fully-equipped kitchens. Each is different, but all have four-poster queen-size beds, ceiling fans and CD players. Most also include a private plunge pool and secluded outdoor showers.

Join other guests around sundown to enjoy a cocktail and gaze out at the awesome view of the Pitons from the resort pool, which is one of Stonefield's best features.

The estate has been in the Brown family for more than three decades but Aly Brown only recently began to convert the plantation where he grew up into a vacation paradise. He's done a spectacular job and is a welcoming host. The entire staff, in fact, will treat you like a val-ued friend, especially at

The most luxurious Stonefield villa

the on-site **Mango Tree Restaurant**, where excellent dishes are served at a leisurely pace.

You'll be near the town of Soufrière and the white-sand Jalousie Resort beach; a complimentary shuttle will take you to either at any time. Or you may choose to just stay on the lovely resort grounds. Each cottage is surrounded by tropical plants and tall trees, and you'll have a shady hammock for napping or reading. If you need a bit of exercise, take the nature trail down to the little rocky beach and stop along the way to inspect ancient petrographs

★★ Ladera Resort

Soufrière
☎ 800-738-4752 (North America), 758-459-7323, www.ladera. com
27 suites and villa suites
$420-$560, meal plan available

Ladera rivals Anse Chastanet Resort for the title of most unusual hotel on the island. Each room is different, and each is missing a west wall, allowing guests unrestricted views of nature and the setting sun. Positioned 1,000 feet above the Caribbean Sea on a hillside between the Piton peaks, the resort is designed so that all rooms, though open on one side, are completely screened from anyone passing by. Trade winds

Ladera Resort (Paul Sullivan)

prevent a problem with flying insects, and the lofty location guarantees cool temperatures for sleeping.

Some accommodations feature private waterfall pools and kitchens, others have small plunge pools. All are exquisitely furnished with four-poster beds, antiques and local art. One of the villas accommodates up to six guests and has a heated indoor plunge pool, an open-air master bedroom and bath, a separate second bedroom and bath, and a third sleeping area. Another villa also sleeps six and has a private garden swimming pool and a dining area. The grounds are lavishly landscaped and include a lovely swimming pool and sun deck with dramatic views of the Pitons and Caribbean.

This resort doesn't meet the expectations of everyone. There is no beach, though Jalousie Plantation's tons of white sand are clearly visible directly below. A shuttle takes guests down to the Jalousie beach, but it's a 15-minute ride, and many guests decide to skip it. Those who don't have a private pool in their suite, use the resort pool, where staff is always on hand to bring fresh towels or fetch a cold drink.

Dasheene Restaurant (Paul Sullivan)

Dasheene Restaurant is famous for its views and its excellent cuisine. Lunch is a casual affair on comfortable sofas and chairs scattered around the bar/lobby. Dinner and Sunday buffet brunch are dressy occasions in the upper-level open-air dining room. The restaurant has an international reputation for award-winning dishes created by Head Chef Nigel Mitchel and celebrated Executive Chef Orlando Satchell.

Ti Kai Posé Spa has four deluxe treatment rooms and services also are available in the guest suites. Newly-constructed pools filled with water from the Diamond Mineral Baths are located in the spa gardens, and guests are encouraged to soak in the pools for relaxation and therapeutic results.

Fond Doux Estate

Soufrière
☎ 759-7545, www.fonddouxestate.com
12 suites and cottages
$120-$350, meal plan available
Three miles from Soufrière and a popular tourist attraction, this working cocoa plantation now offers first-class accommo-

Facing page: Pool at Ladera (Paul Sullivan)

dations. The least expensive rooms are in the main plantation house. Rates in the newly constructed cottages are considerably more. All rooms are lovely and have private baths, king- or queen-size beds, fresh flowers from the gardens and a mini-bar with a complimentary bottle of champagne. Rates include breakfast each morning.

Fond Doux was built in the mid-1700s on land granted to some of the island's original French settlers. Today, the estate's primary purpose is growing cacao beans and turning them into chocolate for the Hershey Company.

Fond Doux cottage

Processing cocoa at Fond Doux Estate

As a guest, you'll be able to stroll through the lavishly landscaped grounds that include thriving cocoa, banana and coconut trees, military ruins and other historical structures. The aroma of chocolate mingles with the scent of flowering plants and fresh sea air. If you need a bit of exercise, take a strenuous hike up Chateaubelair hill to the high point of the estate, where you'll have a breathtaking view of the Pitons and the Caribbean Sea.

South Coast

Juliette's Lodge

Vieux Fort

☎ 888-970-5264, 758-454-5300, www.julietteslodge.com

27 rooms and three apartments

$100-$135

This pink four-level building is owned and managed by a friendly St. Lucian couple, Juliette and Andrew. She runs the kitchen. He oversees the hotel. The air-conditioned rooms are comfortable and spacious with patios, TVs, and one or two beds. Apartments have one or two bedrooms and a living area. There's a small round swimming pool, and mountain bikes are available at an extra charge, but most guests spend their days wind- or kitesurfing. **Reef Kite & Surf** is a short walk or bike ride from the lodge, and you can arrange for special package rates that include lodging and equipment. Most of the guests are adventure lovers who enjoy hanging out at the pool or bar after a day at the beach or hiking through the rainforest. The restaurant serves all day (meal plans are available) and the menu offers West Indies dishes as well as popular international choices.

East Coast

★ Fox Grove Inn

Mon Repose

☎ 758-455-3271, www.foxgroveinn.com

14 rooms and apartments

$55-$65 (rooms, including breakfast), $595-$700 (apartments per week), meal plan available

This is the spot for hikers, surfers, bird watchers, and anyone who wants to be off the beaten path but supremely comfortable. Just south of Dennery, the hillside estate offers easy access to south-coast beaches, the central rainforest and the east-coast nature reserves. Mamiku Gardens are within walking distance and owned by Franz Louis-Fernand, who worked as a chef in Europe for many years, and his Swiss wife, Esther.

Fox Grove Inn

The rooms are basic motel-style doubles, with ceiling fans and private bathrooms as their only luxuries. Half of the units have a balcony with a view of the Atlantic, and there are new one- and two-bedroom two-bath apartments with kitchens and a private terrace. Everything, inside and out, is white-glove clean.

The large swimming pool, surrounded by a spacious sun deck, is a lovely place to relax and enjoy the views, and the grounds are attractively landscaped. The real treasure here is the inn's **Whispering Palms Restaurant**. Franz is master of the kitchen and a talented chef. He uses fresh-from-the-bay fish and locally-grown produce to create luscious meals that are among the best on the island. You'll recognize the gourmet touches he learned over the years in some of the best hotel kitchens in England, Belgium, France, and Switzerland. Eat inside or out, and allow time to admire the magnificent ocean views from the restaurant's large patio.

You'll be just a short drive from the international airport, **Mamiku Gardens** are within walking distance, and **ATV Paradise Tours** will take you off-road through spectacular undeveloped parts of the island. Nearby, the new Westin Le Paradis St Lucia Beach & Golf Resort has taken over much of Praslin Bay, but you still can book a nature tour along the northern section of the trail or go inland for a guided hike through the Forest Reserve. Staff at the inn will help you arrange tours or rent a car.

Where to Dine

t. Lucia has an abundance of splendid places to eat, from sophisticated to casual. Many serve customers outdoors on scenic patios, others are open-air pavilions with lovely views and some offer a choice of dining in an air-conditioned dining room or on a breezy terrace. Menus feature international as well as West Indies (African influence) and Creole (French-inspired) cuisine. Chefs are often trained in Europe or the US, and their cooking style reflects this diversity. The best kitchens are just as likely to be under the direction of an award-winning world-class chef or a self-taught resident with innate talent.

Expect prices to be high, since many items must be imported. Dishes prepared with local ingredients are usually bargains, and you'll find particularly good and original meals at little beach-side cafés. The best buys are fresh fish cooked over an open fire, rotis made of curried produce baked in a fresh-dough wrapper, ice-cold locally-brewed **Piton** beer and creative drinks mixed with island-made **Bounty** or **Old Fort Reserve** rum.

Many visitors come to St. Lucia on an all-inclusive resort plan. If this is your choice, read a few reviews to be sure you'll have a wide variety of menu choices during your vacation. Most resorts strive, in fact compete, to please guests with award-winning international cuisine. Still, you'll find it worthwhile to try the great food served by unpretentious bistros, beach vendors and small family-owned cafés.

Don't miss the weekly **Fish Fry** hosted by villagers in Gros Islet, Anse La Ray and Dennery. These outdoor feasts give you a chance to eat as the locals do. Try the little fish that the Lucians call *tatiri,* which is grilled or deep fried and popped into the mouth whole. If that doesn't sound delicious, order a thick tuna steak, cut from a freshly-caught fish and grilled over the open flames of a wood fire. The bill for a complete meal at one of these village fish fries will be around US$8-$10, and may include rum punch or a Piton beer.

If you're looking for more elegant dining, you'll have many choices. Caribbean chefs frequently hold regional competitions to show off their best creations, and several St. Lucian festivals include cooking demonstrations and contests. Internationally trained chefs seek jobs on the islands, not only because of the year-round good weather, but because of the concentration of deluxe resorts and restaurants with renowned reputations.

Islanders treat dinner as relaxing evening entertainment, so plan to spend time lingering over a cocktail or appetizer while you wait for your main meal to be served. Desserts and after-dinner drinks can take you right up to bedtime.

Only the most luxurious restaurants have a dress code. Shorts, slacks or jeans topped with a casual shirt is appropriate attire most places, but women may prefer to wear a colorful sundress in the evening. If an establishment does have a dress code, it's strictly enforced, so ask when you make reservations. Beachwear isn't appropriate anywhere, except at a beach bar or waterfront café during the day. Even then, you'll be expected to wear a modest coverup and shoes or sandals if you go inside or sit at a patio table.

During the off-season, some restaurants close entirely for several weeks, and others may operate on a limited schedule. Call ahead to avoid disappointment. Throughout the year, tables at the most popular restaurants book up quickly, so phone early for a reservation.

Most restaurants accept major credit cards, but remote cafés and small operations (beach vendors, market stalls and some family-run places) may require cash. Almost every one will accept US dollars, but expect change in Eastern Caribbean currency.

An 8% government tax will be added to your bill, but also look for an additional service charge. It's customary for a 10% fee to be added automatically, which is meant to be a tip, but the wait staff may never receive it. Consider giving an additional 5% to 10% cash tip directly to your server if you think the service was worthy. Upscale restaurants probably give at least part of the service charge to the service staff, but it's customary at these places to leave an additional tip for excellent service.

RESTAURANT PRICE GUIDE

Use the menu price ranges listed for each restaurant as a guide for the cost of a typical dinner, excluding drinks, tax and service charge. St. Lucian menus often list prices in Eastern Caribbean dollars, but the following scale is based on US dollars. Restaurants in tourist areas commonly print prices in US dollars, either instead of or in addition to EC dollars, but if the menu prices seem unreasonably high, verify the currency. Also, check the bill and any currency conversion that's been done by the restaurant. Expect lunch portions to be smaller and prices to be lower than those quoted below. (US$1 = EC$2.67)

Dining With the Stars

Every *Adventure Guide* listing is recommended and considered above average in its category. Restaurants with one star (★) are highly recommended, and those earning two stars (★★) are considered to be exceptional. A few restaurants rate three stars (★★★), which means they are worthy of a special occasion splurge, and you should make an extra effort to dine there.

Where to Dine

Castries

Castries Central Market

An alleyway lined with food stalls and out-door tables is located at the south end of the **Central Market** in Castries. This is a place for locals, so prices are low and the quality is good. Try curried meats, coal pot stews, and fresh coconut drinks. The stalls are open Monday through Saturday 6 am until 5 pm.

If you have a craving for a familiar back-home meal, look for one of these American-style fast-food joints: **Dominos Pizza** in Rodney Bay, ☎ 758-458-0002; **Kentucky Fried Chicken** on Bridge Street in Castries, ☎ 758-452-6444, on New Dock Road in Vieux Fort, ☎ 758-454-8576, and at the JQ Charles Mall in Rodney Bay, ☎ 758-452-8300; **Burger King-Popeyes Chicken** on Jeremie Street in Castries, ☎ 758-458-2518, and at the JQ Charles Mall in Rodney Bay, ☎ 758-458-0742.

On the upper level of La Place Carenage, on the downtown waterfront, **Caribbean Pirate Restaurant** serves reasonably-priced breakfast and lunch specials from 8 am until 6 pm Monday through Saturday. ☎ 758-452-2543.

Across the bay, near Pointe Seraphine Mall, **Auberge Seraphine** has a garden-like covered patio restaurant overlooking the harbor. It serves a wide variety of light meals and has a good selection of wines and a well-stocked bar. ☎ 758-453-2073.

Kimlans, upstairs on Micoud Street at the north end of Walcott Square, serves bargain-priced local dishes, including curries and rotis. Cool off with a fresh fruit juice drink on the balcony overlooking the square from 7 am until 11 pm Monday through Saturday. ☎ 758-452-1136.

Green Parrot Restaurant

Morne Fortune
☎ 758-452-3399
French/International
$15-$25 (entrée), $35-$40 (fixed-price dinner)
Daily 7 am-midnight
Reservations required

Green Parrot Restaurant

Weekdays, this exquisite hotel restaurant serves an inexpensive business lunch from noon to 3 pm. In the evening, a more elaborate four-course dinner is laid out on crisp table linens. Men are required to wear jackets and women dress to match. London-trained chef Harry Joseph Edwards specializes in French-inspired cuisine using local ingredients, but the menu includes such things as taco shell appetizers, Indian curries, and Créole fish. You can also order shrimp, lobster, and steaks.

Request a table near the window so you'll have a view of the lights in Castries and the harbor during

The cabanas at Green Parrot

Where to Dine

your meal. On Wednesday and Saturday, Chef Edwards comes out of the kitchen to get everyone involved in dancing to the live band. On Monday nights, all women who wear a flower in their hair and are accompanied by a well-dressed man receive a free dinner. Be sure to make reservations well in advance if you want to dine at the Green Parrot on any of these special evenings.

Bon Appetit

Morne Fortune
☎ 758-452-2757
Seafood and steaks
$20-$45
Monday through Friday, 11 am to 2 pm and 6:30 to 9:30 pm
Saturday and Sunday, 6:30 to 9:30 pm
Reservations required.

The views of Castries and the harbor are spectacular at this cozy five-table restaurant. The food is outstanding, but portions are on the small side; you pay for the ambience and views. Soups and appetizers are especially delicious, and the restaurant specializes in cooked-to-order steaks. The wine list is impressive and pricey, with selections that perfectly match your dinner choices.

★★★ Coal Pot

Vigie Cove Marina
☎ 758-452-5566, www.coalpotrestaurant.com
Nouvelle Caribbean
$12-$20 (lunch), $20-$30 (dinner)
Monday-Saturday, noon to 3 pm and 7 to 10 pm
Reservations essential

This popular spot with only 10 tables gets crowded quickly, so arrive early for lunch and make reservations for dinner. Artist Michelle Elliot and her French-chef husband, Xavier Ribot, have a long-running reputation for friendly service and excellent cuisine, distinguished by the mingling of island products and classic preparation. Lunch specials feature fresh fish and seafood salads, while dinner highlights include smoked salmon, Coquilles Saint-Jacques, lobster, and curried meats. You have a large choice of wines, including some fine

vintages from
France and
Chili, to accom-
pany your meal.
The open-air
restaurant is
decorated with
Michelle's color-
ful paintings,
which give the
old wood-and-
stone landmark
a fresh spirit.
This is a don't-
miss dining experience.

Coal Pot

★ Jacques Waterfront Dining

Vigie Marina
☎ 758-458-1900
French
Monday through Saturday, noon until midnight
$12-$15 (lunch) $20-$30 (dinner)
Past visitors may remember this little bistro as Froggie
Jack's. It's the same place and the same owners, Jacky and
Cathy Rioux, but there have been some changes, including
the brightly painted Caribbean Perfume shop that now sits in
the garden.

Jacques calls himself Jacky, a simpler, more familiar name.
His cooking style reflects this same easy casualness. He has a
Frenchman's talent with sauces and creative flourishes, but
he's an islander at heart. He lived among the fishermen in
Soufrière for several years and has inside connections for
snagging the best of the catch right off the boats each morning. Seafood is a restaurant specialty, but Jacky also tours the
local market every day, and his menu includes amazing mat-
ings of local spices with fresh produce.

The daily lunch menu is written on a blackboard and features
soups, grilled meat and vegetables, plus other light offerings.
In the evening, low lights come on to illuminate the waterfront and add a touch of romance to the garden. The menu
changes to à la carte specialties with an emphasis on seafood

Where to Dine

and smoked meats. Almost everything comes with a sauce or imaginative seasoning.

You won't be surprised to know that Jacky and Cathy have a great knowledge and love of good wines. The list is long, international and impressive. If you want advice or a tad of education, it will be provided without a hint of condescension. The cocktail menu is equally extensive and has all the old favorites, as well as some unique concoctions dreamed up by the staff.

Rodney Bay

Rodney Bay is a lively area with an abundance of good to great restaurants. You can't go wrong with any of them. Park your car and stroll around to let your appetite build and check out the offerings. A few eateries are actually on the water side of the avenue that parallels Reduit Beach; more line up along the other side of the street.

The greatest number of restaurants cluster on both sides of the main road that breaks away from the Castries-Gros Islet Highway near the JQ Mall, leading to the village and beach. This is known as Restaurant Row, and with good reason. The area is saturated with alluring aromas and enticing settings. The marina, across the bay from Reduit and a bit farther along the main highway, has a few more dining choices.

Kentucky Fried Chicken, **Subway** and **Burger King** are at the mall turn-off. **Elena Ice Cream** and **Pizza Pizza** are down the road, toward the beach. For bakery treats, stop by the **Bread Basket** at the marina complex. The following are our recommendations for an excellent meal in nice surroundings:

★ Scuttlebutts

Rodney Bay Marina
☎ 758-452-0351
Bar and grill
$8-$10 (breakfast), $10-$18 (lunch), $20-$28 (dinner)
Daily 7 am until late

Dinghies tie up right on the pier at this waterfront tavern, and you'll be in the jovial company of yachtsmen from all over the world when you drop in for breakfast, lunch, dinner or

Scuttlebutts (Paul Sullivan)

anything in-between. If you're just in need of refreshment, pick up an icy drink and take a dip in the private swimming pool.

Meals are served in the mariner-inspired main restaurant or on the waterfront deck, and the large menu includes kid pleasers as well as hearty portions of grilled seafood, steaks, burgers and daily specials. The specialty drinks made with Caribbean rum are some of the best on the island, and the wine list is surprisingly good. As long as you're drinking or eating, you can use the communications center, which has high-speed Internet, weather updates and boat-crew news.

Key Largo

Rodney Bay
☎ 758-452-0282
Pizza/pasta
$8-$20
Daily, 7:30 am until midnight

Owners Marie, Carlo, and Val run this landmark pizzeria. You can't miss the large white Spanish-design building circled by a red brick wall. Inside the spacious restaurant the three

Key Largo

owners hustle around making sure their friendly staff keeps up with the constant demand for the island's best wood-fire pizza. You can get all your favorite toppings and even add gourmet touches such as shrimp. Longtime customers have begun to appreciate the expanded menu, which features lasagna, cannelloni and spaghetti *pomodoro e basilico*. Top off your meal with a cup of freshly-ground espresso.

The Lime

Rodney Bay
☎ 758-452-0761
Caribbean
$8-$22
Wednesday-Monday 8 am to 1 am
Reservations suggested

This great place has many faces, all of them happy. It's a full-service bar, a late-night club and a three-meals-a-day restaurant. All the food is delicious and many dishes are accented with traditional island sauces. Try *rotis* or crêpes for a snack or light lunch, and seafood or lamb at dinner. Steaks are cooked to your exact preference over a charcoal fire, but you may want to "go island" with jerk chicken. Prices are reasonable and portions are large, which is probably why you need a reservation to get a table on most evenings. Many customers stay on for the late-night dancing and entertainment at the adjoining club, **Late Lime**.

☆ Spinnakers Beach Bar & Grill

Reduit Beach
☎ 758-452-8491, www.spinnakersbeachbar.com
International
$8-$10 (breakfast), $12-$18 (lunch), $22-$35 (dinner)
Daily, 9 am to 11 pm
Reservations accepted

Spinnakers is on one of the island's most popular beaches, so the place is busy all day. Early risers enjoy a full English breakfast (owners Alison and Michael Richings are British) and, sometime after noon, a hungry crowd spills in from the beach to fill up on lobster salads, sandwiches, cheeseburgers and frosty drinks. Happy hour runs from 6 pm to 7 pm every evening and, after enjoying two-for-one drinks, many patrons stay on for dinner.

You'll find the atmosphere quieter and more romantic after the sun goes down, when diners relax to the sound of waves lapping onto the nearby beach. Menu choices range from fancy French-Caribbean dishes to basic spaghetti with tomato sauce, and you can never go wrong ordering any of the seafood meals. Carnivores will appreciate perfectly grilled steaks, which are brought in from the US, and vegetarians have a choice of several house specialties, including vegetarian lasagna.

Tilly's Restaurant & Bar

Rodney Bay
☎ 758-458-4440
Creole and West Indies
$7-$12 (lunch), $15-$22 (dinner)
Daily, noon until midnight
Reservations accepted

Regular visitors, especially those who arrive by boat, say this is the best Creole restaurant on the island. It's set in a little garden on the main highway a short distance from the marina and serves favorites such as flying fish (fried whole), spicy curries and lambi (conch). If you prefer, there are also grilled steaks and chicken. At lunch, try a roti or hamburger. Dine inside or out, and be sure to arrive during happy hour, which is daily from 5 to 7 pm.

Memories of Hong Kong

Rodney Bay
☎ 758-452-8218
Chinese
$10-$28
Monday to Saturday, 6 to 11 pm
Reservations accepted

Bring friends along to share the multi-person meals at this open-air restaurant across the road from Reduit Beach. Several regional Chinese specialties are offered, and you'll be able to sample more variety if you have some buddies to help you choose and eat the tempting selections. If you must restrict your order to one or two dishes, skip the soup and have rice-paper-wrapped prawns to start. Then move on to one of the roast pork dishes (the Szechuan sauce is especially delicious) or the Hong Kong-style sweet-and-sour chicken. Add Singapore fried rice and enjoy.

The Buzz

Rodney Bay
☎ 758-458-0450
Seafood & grill (vegetarian choices available)
$17-$35 (dinner), $9-$20 (brunch)
Monday-Sunday, 5 pm-midnight; Sunday Brunch 11 am, December-May.
Reservations recommended

We struggled to decide what to order at this lantern-lit hot spot across from the Royal St. Lucian Hotel. Our eyes flew immediately to the desserts, crème brulée, chocolate brandy

The Buzz

cheesecake, warm apple crêpes ($7). "Maybe I'll just have a salad and dessert. But, no, this is a work-related assignment, and we must sample a range of dishes." So, we bravely forged ahead and settled on lobster & crab cakes to start ($9), skipped the salads (but noticed our dining neighbors were enjoying the seafood caesar ($18), and selected both the potato crusted red snapper ($19) and rosemary roasted rack of lamb ($25) for the main course. As expected, everything was perfectly prepared and delicious. We suggest you just close your eyes and point to something at the top, middle and bottom of the menu. You can't make a bad choice. For dessert, we were able to limit our order to the banana pecan bread pudding and the white chocolate mousse. Both were excellent, and we returned the next day to share a slice of cheesecake.

Gros Islet, Cap Estate & Pigeon Point

On Friday nights, the little village of **Gros Islet** throws a **Jump Up** street party and **Fish Fry**. Vendors set up barbecue pits along the roads, which are blocked from traffic, and local musicians hook up their sound equipment. Then the eating and dancing begin and last well into the night. An entire meal will cost you about US$8, and the fun is free.

Should you be hungry on evenings other than Friday, or prefer a proper sit-down meal, give the following restaurants a try.

★★ The Great House

Cap Estate
☎ 758-450-0450 or 758-450-0211
French/International
$18-$35
Tuesday-Sunday 4:30-10 pm
Reservations required

Elegant attire is requested at this grand plantation manor, which brings back memories of a festive, graceful time in St. Lucia's history. It's built on the original foundations of the de Longueville Estate, which was constructed during the 1700s.

You enter the Colonial-style mansion via a grand staircase, and dine by candle light, with polished service, excellent cuisine, and fine wines. Ask about the *prix fixe* meal, which features a choice of fish, steak, or chicken accompanied by an appetizer, soup and dessert. The à la carte menu changes nightly, but on recent visits we enjoyed lobster bisque, scallops gratiné, rack of lamb, beef tenderloin and roast duck glazed with honey.

Plan to arrive for afternoon tea (4:30 to 5:30 pm) or happy hour (5:30 to 6:30 pm). Dinner seating begins at 6:30 and runs until 9:45 pm. Most evenings, a guitarist strolls among the tables playing requests and favorites. **The Derek Walcott Theatre** is next door, and the receptionist at The Great House can tell you if a performance is scheduled anytime during your stay on the island. If so, combine dinner with one of the excellent presentations at this open-air theater.

Jambe de Bois

Pigeon Point
☎ 758-450-8166 or 758-452-0321
Pub food
Daily, 9 am to 5 pm
$8-$17

The food at this amiable café and bar is good and inexpensive, but the drinks and desserts are outstanding. When you visit Pigeon Point National Park, stop here for refreshments or a meal on the waterfront patio. It's a great place for hanging out. There's often live entertainment, with classical music featured on Thursdays and jazz on Sundays. Call for the exact schedule. In addition to well-prepared pub-style food and frozen drinks, the café has Wi-Fi access and a book-swap library.

Marigot Bay

This area has developed rapidly over the past few years, and you will find a half-dozen long-time favorite haunts along with a few new places that are still earning their ratings. In general, you can enjoy excellent meals, abundant drinks and jovial company throughout the day on both sides of the bay. The following are current hot-spots.

Doolittles Restaurant

Marigot Bay
☎ 758-451-4974
International
$8-$12 (breakfast), $10-$18 (lunch), $17-$30 (dinner)
Daily, 6:30 am to 10 pm
Reservations recommended

Unless you're staying on the north side of Marigot Bay, you'll have to take a short ferry ride across the cove to this waterfront open-air restaurant. They have an award-winning chef, and the food is dependably good, but you'll

Doolittles

want to dine here because it's a tradition for all visitors. This is the scenic setting of the well-known movie *Dr. Doolittle*, and several other films that you may be too young to remember. When you return from your vacation, someone will undoubtedly ask if you dined at Doolittles, and you don't want to disappoint them by saying no.

Actually, this is a nice place to hang out all day. A white sand beach with a watersports center is just steps away, and the restaurant serves meals, snacks and drinks all day. Look for a small blackboard announcing the evening's theme dinner. The Saturday night barbecue is probably the best bet and surely the most popular, but you'll have to make a reservation to guarantee a table on any evening, especially during high season. À la carte choices range from American and British favorites to creatively exotic fusions and island specialties that will impress even a seasoned world traveler.

Where to Dine

The only downside is slow service, and you may feel neglected as the wait staff chat among themselves in Creole instead of attending to your needs. But, the view of the bay and the casually lovely atmosphere makes up for any negligence.

JJ's Paradise

Marigot Bay Road
☎ 758-451-4076
www.jj-paradise.com
Seafood
$10-$17 (lunch), $15-$30 (dinner)
Daily, 10 am until late
Reservations recommended

JJ's Paradise

Owner-chef Gerald Felix (JJ) has remodeled his popular waterfront resort and restaurant, and the yachties couldn't be happier. Dozens of powerboats, catamarans and sailboats tie up to the resort's dock at the far end of the bay each day, and vacationers make their way up the hill to join resort guests in the restaurant for food, drinks and entertainment.

We arrived at JJ's for a late lunch. The menu featured the usual sandwiches and salads, and we enjoyed the rotis, which are curried meat and vegetables rolled into a burrito-like wrap. Around five o'clock, the bar was packed with happy-hour revelers speaking a mix of languages. When we returned one evening for dinner, we found the restaurant surprisingly sedate. Romantic, actually. Dinner was good, with large portions of fish accompanied by locally grown vegetables. The real treat was later, when the limbo dancers arrived. They were amazing performers and encouraged everyone to join in. Naturally, the activity and noise levels rose as the night progressed. On Friday and Saturday nights, there's live music, so be sure to make reservations well in advance.

Café Paradis

Marigot Beach Club
☎ 758-451-4974, fax 758-451-4973
Caribbean
$10-$13 (breakfast), $15-$18 (lunch), $18-$35 (dinner)
Daily 8 am-late
Reservations accepted

Set on the waterfront, this attractive open-air restaurant serves gourmet meals from morning until night. Breakfast and lunch are well-priced and casual with typical local offerings, but dinner is a more romantic affair, with the lights of the harbor in the background. Arrive in time for happy hour at sunset, then move to a harbor-side table for a slow, relaxing meal featuring escargot, fish or lamb with a flavorful French-inspired sauce, followed by tropical fruit or a homemade dessert.

★★Rainforest Hideaway

Marigot Bay
☎ 758-286-0511
International, sushi, fusion
$22-$40
Wednesday through Monday, 6 to 10 pm
Reservations essential

The Hideaway has recently undergone a complete update, though it didn't actually need it. But, the new and luxurious Discovery complex was opening across the bay, and award-winning owner-chef Jim Verity and his wife, Carla, thought a little freshening was in order. The results are stunning.

Rainforest Hideaway

You'll be dining in a wonderful little restaurant that deserves every one of the five stars and all the praise it has been awarded. Start in the champagne bar, where you can sip a well-mixed cocktail while you look over the nightly menu, which is written English-pub-style on a blackboard. Permanent printed menus are not possible because Jim doesn't know until he tours the markets each day what will be fresh and available for the evening meal.

Whatever appears on the blackboard will be excellent. Expect such things as seared tuna appetizers, coconut and pumpkin soup, gingered scallops with mint purée, sun-dried tomato risotto, and pan-fried calamari with a fresh tomato salsa. If you don't care for "fussy" food, try one of the grilled meats or delicately sauced fish fillets. Our meal was punctuated with sorbet to cleanse our palates (and cool our tongues after the wasabi-spiked shrimp) and grilled vegetables to accompany the main course. Little hints of Asia were added to almost everything, and the fusions worked perfectly. Don't hesitate to ask for advice on a wine to mate with your meal. The staff is knowledgeable and always happy to make recommendations.

The Shack

Marigot Bay
☎ 758-451-4145
International
$7-$12 (lunch), $15-$25 (dinner)
Daily, noon until 11 pm
Reservations accepted

This popular hangout actually hangs out over Marigot Bay supported by stilts. Guests arriving by water tie up right at the restaurant's deck, and those coming by land park under the tall trees that surround the Shack's garden entrance.

You might expect great burgers and fries here, since the owner is American-born Melanie Ratteray, and you're expectations would be exceeded. But, there's more. Much more. We highly recommend the conch fritters and any of the grilled fish. In the evening, you'll have a list of international favorites, but we suggest you go Caribbean with the Creole-style shrimp or lobster. If you're really hungry, order the huge T-bone steak. In fact, steak lovers shouldn't miss the Tuesday night Steak Blow-Out. You get a steak with salad and French fries for about US$11. Add a Piton beer or one of the specialty cocktails, and you have a great meal for around US$15.

Before you leave, look down into the water to watch fish, attracted by the lights, playing around the poles that hold up the deck. Toss in a bit of bread for a real show. Island entertainment just doesn't get any better than this.

Chateau My'go

Marigot Bay
☎ 758-451-4772
Indian, Mexican and Creole
$7-$10 (breakfast), $8-$12 (lunch), $15-$20 (dinner)
Daily, 8 am to 11 pm
Reservations accepted

Chateau My'Go is a family-owned restaurant run by Doreen Rambally and built right out over the waters of Marigot Bay. Dinghies tie up to the dock, and land-side arrivers park in the lot surrounded by lush vegetation and trees. This is a great place for breakfast, and you can grab a light meal of cappuccino and toast, or linger over a veggie-stuffed omelette or Mexican-style huevos rancheros served with warm tortillas.

Chateau My'go

Locals come here for the thin-crust pizza at lunch time, but you can also get sandwiches, salads and East Indian-style rotis. After sundown, try one of the seafood dishes. These are the restaurant's specialty, following favorite family recipes. You'll have a choice of cooking style and sauce, so ask your waitress for suggestions, and be aware that some of the dishes are made with chopped pieces of fish rather than filets. Every meal comes with side-dishes straight out of local gardens, and vegetarians can make a meal of these exotically spiced and delicately sauced vegetables. On Thursday nights, MyGo features an authentic East Indian menu with complete meals from US$15 to $25.

Happy hour runs all day and all night. You get two-for-the-price-of-one cocktails (the piña coladas are excellent) for US$4.50 and two beers for US$3. On Tuesday nights, the restaurant features live music in the waterfront bar from 5 until 11 pm.

Soufrière

★★Anse Chastanet Resort Restaurants

Anse Chastanet
☎ 758-459-7354
International and island specialties
$12-$18 (breakfast), $15-$25 (lunch), $20-$40 (dinner)
Daily, 6:30 am until 9 pm
Reservations essential

Englishman Jon Bentham is the executive chef who oversees the preparation of "Tropical World Cuisine" at the resort's restaurants. You don't have to be a guest of the resort to dine at the restaurants, but you should call ahead to make reservations and ask about special events. The resort has its own gardens and works with farmers on the island to encourage them to grow crops that are in demand by local chefs. You'll have fresh vegetables, fruits, herbs and spices at every meal served in either **Trou au Diable** or the **Piton Restaurant**.

On Tuesday evenings, Trou au Diable lays out a fabulous Caribbean Buffet with the entire beach lighted by torches. On other nights, the menu features specialties that creatively mix modern East Indian recipes with Caribbean cooking.

Part of the Piton Restaurant is the **Treehouse**, where diners sit surrounded by treetops in an open-air hillside pavilion. At lunch, you can choose to go through the hot-and-cold buffet line or order from the à la carte menu that features salads, sandwiches, burgers and creole specialties.

La Haut Plantation Restaurant

West Coast Road
☎ 758-459-7008, www.lahaut.com
Créole and International
$10-$15 (breakfast), $15-$20 (lunch), $20-$40 (dinner)
Tuesday through Sunday, 9 am to 9 pm
Reservations recommended

You'll have great views from the open-air restaurant at this lovely resort about two miles north of Soufrière. We took our waitress's advice and ordered a bowl of the special clam chowder. You'd be wise to do the same. It's excellent. Other

View from La Haut Plantation

choices were more difficult, because everything looked so delicious. Finally, we settled on coconut chicken and an order of fish cakes. As expected, everything was excellent.

The kitchen specializes in dishes made with local fish, such as dorado, snapper and flying fish, and all meals are served with Creole bread, salad, rice and local vegetables. We highly recommend the lobster seasoned with fresh herbs and butter if it's available.

Before you leave the plantation, take time to look at the views from the three balconies. Outstanding. You'll be able to see the nearby town of Soufrière, the Pitons and the sea. Also, look around the great house, stroll through the tropical garden and stop by the little boutique to browse for a souvenir to take home.

Where to Dine

Lifeline Restaurant

Hummingbird Beach Resort, Soufrière
☎ 758-459-7232
Créole
$8-$10 (breakfast), $12-$18 (lunch), $20-$35 (dinner)
Daily, 6:30 am to 11 pm
Reservations suggested

Set in the garden of the Hummingbird Beach Resort on the waterfront at the north end of Soufrière, this charming restaurant offers excellent gourmet meals, friendly service, and outstanding views of the Pitons. The menu includes French-inspired Creole dishes that are heavy on fish straight from the sea and local vegetables laced with island spices. The wine list is first-class. At lunch, you can order lighter meals, such as salads, sandwiches and burgers. Don't leave without checking out the batik art designed by Joyce Alexander, the talented and gregarious owner.

The Still

Soufrière
☎ 758-459-7224
Creole
$8-$10 (breakfast), $12-18 (lunch), $18-25 (dinner).
Daily, 8 am until 5 pm

The only thing wrong with this restaurant is that there are two dining rooms that seat about 400 people, so tour buses frequently stop here for lunch. If a cruise ship is in port, we suggest you choose another place. Otherwise, this is a wonderful place to eat. All the produce served at The Still is organically grown on the working plantation, so you'll be presented with adventurous items such as breadfruit, callaloo and christophenes. These side-dishes are paired with grilled fish and meats, resulting in delicious meals. Service is good, even when large groups fill the dining room, but it's better and very friendly when the crowd is smaller. Notice the old rum distillery as you drive up the hill onto the estate. Workers still grow citrus fruit and cocoa on the plantation, which has belonged to the same family for four generations.

Camilla's

Bridge Street, Soufrière
☎ 758-459-5379
Vegetarian and Créole
$5-$8 (breakfast), $8-$15 (lunch), $12-$20 (dinner)
Tuesday through Sunday, 8 am until midnight

Right in the middle of town, about a block from the waterfront, this tiny second-floor café with a little balcony is a casual spot serving generous portions of well-prepared food. The staff is friendly and efficient, and the owner, Camilla Alcindor, may greet you herself. Don't expect anything gourmet or pretentious. This is a place for fresh fish, curry, omelets and salads. Skip the steaks and burgers, and try to snag a table on the balcony. There's no air-conditioning, and the sea breeze doesn't compensate on warm days.

★★Dasheene Restaurant

Ladera Resort
☎ 758-459-7323
Nouvelle Caribbean
$10-$18 (breakfast), $12-$20 (lunch), $25-$40 (dinner)
Daily, 8 to 10 am, noon to 2:30 pm and 6:30 to 9:30 pm
Reservations essential at dinner

The view from this restaurant perched 1,000 feet above the coast at Ladera Resort is dramatic and magnificent. You look between the Pitons out toward the sea, so plan to arrive during daylight hours for the best view. Sunsets are spectacular. You would want to eat in this upscale dining room, even if the food was poor, which it is not. In fact, the chef has won several awards for the best cuisine on the island.

We stopped here for lunch, which is casual and inexpen-

Dasheene Restaurant

sive, and ate sitting on a comfortable couch overlooking the pool and sea. It was so breathtakingly beautiful that we didn't want to leave. Finally, we made reservations to return for dinner, and were nicely, but decisively, informed of the strict dress code. Since the restrictions included no bare shoulders (for men or women), we spent some time shopping for a shawl to throw over a quite tasteful, but sleeveless, dress.

We did enjoy every bite of our dinner. Properly attired, we started with a spunky pumpkin soup and a crab salad, then opted for the Dasheene shrimp as the main course. Fabulous. The menu changes regularly, so it's impossible to say what will be featured on your visit. Ask your server for suggestions, and resist the impulse to over-order, so you'll have room for one of the creative desserts. Order something that is flambéed at your table side.

Day-Trips & Inter-Island Travel

S t. Lucia offers sufficient diversity and enough attractions to keep most visitors busy and contented for a week or more. But, if you're the type of independent traveler who enjoys packing as much activity as possible into every trip, consider visiting the nearby islands. Suggestions for convenient day-trips and dual-destination vacations include: the French islands, **Martinique** and **Guadeloupe**, and the untamed nature island, **Dominica**.

It's easy to travel from St. Lucia to all of these islands by modern high-speed catamaran or regional airlines. **L'Express des Isles** zips passengers between St. Lucia, Martinique, Guadeloupe and Dominica in an ultra-modern high-speed catamaran. If you prefer to travel by air, **LIAT**, **Air Caraibes**, **SVG Air** and **Caribbean Airlines** offer inter-island service, and often have island-hopper specials. In addition, **Channel Shuttles** has 12-seat motorboat service to Martinique, **Dominica Air Taxi** provides charter flights to Dominica, and **Sun Link Tours** conducts group trips, including transportation, to Martinique.

Contact Information

L'Express des Isles, ☎ 0596-42-04-05 (Martinique), www.express-des-iles.com.

Dominica Air Taxi, ☎ 268-481-2403(Antigua), www.dominicaairtaxi.com.

LIAT, ☎ 888-844-5428 (Caribbean), 268-462-0700 (US), 758-456-9100 (local), www.flyliat.com.

Air Caraibes, ☎ 877-772-1005(US), 758-452-2463 or 758-453-6660, www.air-caraibes-charter.com.

SVG Air, ☎ 784-457-5124 (St. Vincent), 800-744-5777 (Caribbean), 800-624-1843 (North America), www.svgair.com.

Caribbean Airlines, ☎ 800-920-4225 (North America), 845-362-4225 (UK), 800-744-2225 (St Lucia), 758-452-3778 (local), www.caribbean-airlines.com.

Channel Shuttles, ☎ 758-452-8757, located at the ferry dock in Castries.

Sun Link Tours, ☎ 758-456-9100, www.sunlinktours.com.

Dominica

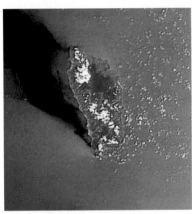

Dominica from space

If you like St. Lucia's extravagant untouched forests and dramatic coastline, consider a side-trip to **Dominica** (dom-in-ĒĒ-ka, not the Dominican Republic). This largely undeveloped island mirrors St. Lucia's towering twin Pitons with forested peaks that jut dramatically from the sea. Hot springs billow from the earth, creating boiling lakes and other geothermal wonders, and hundreds of freshwater rivers and streams wind through the lush landscape. Eco-tourism is the only form of tourism the locals will tolerate, yet the small resorts and inns offer sufficient creature comforts, and restaurants serve excellent meals.

In one day, you can take a taxi tour around the 290-square-mile island, check out the filming sites for *Pirates of the Caribbean 2 and 3*, hike a few of the 300 miles of marked trails, explore the **Morne Trois Pitons National Park** (the first UNESCO World Heritage Site in the eastern Caribbean),

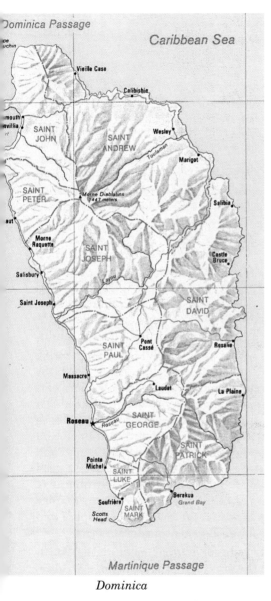

Dominica

or view the tropical rainforest from a gondola-type car on an aerial tram that allows you an up-close canopy view of the raging vegetation (☎ 866-759-8726, www.rfat.com).

If you decide to stay a day or two in this Jurassic-Park like nature isle, reserve a room at **Beau Rive** (☎ 767-445-8992, www.beaurive.com), an exceptional little retreat on the hilly, remote eastern coast. If you prefer a larger hotel near the main town of Roseau, try **Fort Young** (☎ 767-448-5000, www.fortyounghotel.com). Both run about $150 per night for a double room. Not bad for any season in the Caribbean.

Expect to get hooked on this escape-from-reality island. When you do, check yourself into the best all-inclusive eco-retreat, **Jungle Bay**, a 55-acre property overlooking Pointe Mulâtre Bay on the southwest coast. Rates include organic meals, yoga classes, a spa treatment and

The Dominica coast

some type of excursion (snorkeling, hiking, etc.). Rustic-luxury double rooms are in the area of $250 per day per person. Reservations and information is on the web at www.junglebaydominica.com or call the resort directly at ☎ 767-446-1789.

You can eat quite well on Dominica. Grab lunch at **The Mouse Hole**, 3 Victoria Street, ☎ 767-448-4436, Monday-Saturday, 8 am-4 pm, (try the sandwich roll-ups called rotis), then come back for dinner at the upstairs restaurant, **La Robe Creole**. Both eateries are located in a single colonial-style house overlooking a seaside plaza, and the staff at La Robe adds to the ambience by dressing in authentic Creole madras outfits. Lunch and dinner are served Monday-Saturday 11 am-9:30 pm, and main courses run about US$12-$20, ☎ 767-448-2896. A good alternative, especially for lunch, is **Guiyave Restaurant & Patisserie**, ☎ 767-448-1723. Just follow the locals to 15 Cork Street in Roseau. This is where the everyday shoppers and business people gather for good food at moderate prices.

Head out to the countryside for a great meal at the **Rainforest Restaurant** on the grounds of the **Papillote Wilderness Retreat**, ☎ 767-448-2287. This open-air dining room has panoramic views of the Roseau River Valley, and the menu offers fresh fish and Creole-style dishes. Guests of the resort may enjoy all meals at the restaurant, and the public is welcome for lunch every day and, by reservation only, for dinner each night.

For more information about Dominica, contact the tourist bureau, ☎ 888-645-5637 (North America), www.dominica.dm.

Martinique

Martinique is so close (23 miles north) and so accessible by sea and air that you will want to seriously consider adding this very French island to your St. Lucia itinerary. You'll need a passport, but you are welcome to stay for up to 90 days without a visa.

Go for the excellent French and West Indies cuisine if nothing else. You'll be captivated by the lilting French and patois words

Martinique from space

rolling off the tongues of island natives, the gorgeous gardens and the colorful traditions, dances and music. In one day, you can rent a car or tour the island by taxi. Pick up free maps and brochures at the English-speaking tourist office at the airport or dock, then sign on for a scheduled tour or set out on your own to explore the island.

Bananaquit, Martinique

Metered taxis are found at the airport, docks, hotels and on the streets in Fort-de-France (or arrange for transportation or a tour by phoning ☎ 596-63-63-62).

Day-Trips

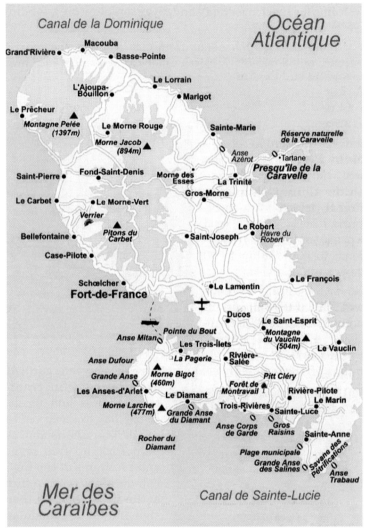

Martinique

You might also try one of the collective taxis, which are much less expensive. Look for the eight-passenger limousines bearing the sign TC, which travel the main roads from early morning until 6 pm.

All you need to rent a car, if you're over 21 years of age, is a valid driver's license, a major credit card and about $50 per day. Rental booths are located at the airport or call one of the international companies, such as Avis (☎ 596-42-11-00), Budget (☎ 596-42-04-04) or Hertz (☎ 596-42-16-90).

The capital, **Fort-de-France**, is a walkable town with a few historical buildings and a shady central park, La Savane, featuring a statue of Napoléon's Empress Joséphine. She was born on a sugar plantation near the town of Trois Islets, which is across the bay from the capital.

A more interesting site is just north at **St-Pierre**, where **Mont Pelée** erupted in 1902 and turned the "Paris of the West Indies" into a Pompeii-like ruin. You can get to the ruins on the **Cyparis Express** (☎ 0596-78-31-41), a small train that travels there for €6/$8, including a guided tour of the ruins.

Art lovers will want to visit the Gauguin Museum in the little fishing village of **Carbet**, where Columbus landed in 1502 and Gauguin lived and painted in 1887. If you prefer nature, head to the **Gorges de la Falaise**, where you will find a waterfall at the end of a trail through the mini-canyons lining a lovely river. Other natural sites on the north end of the island include a rain forest, black-sand beaches and hot springs at **Le Precheur**

Take a ferry from Fort-de-France to **Trois-Islets**, a pretty town and home to **The Pagerie Museum**, which stands on the spot where Empress Josephine was born. Check to see if a musical or cultural event will be taking place at the lovely **Park of the Trois-Ilets,** or schedule a tee time at the Robert Trent Jones-

Martinique beach

designed golf course, **Golf de l'Impératrice Joséphine** (☎ 0596-68-32-81, www.golfmartinique.com).

Connoisseurs consider Martinique rums among the best in the world, and France has awarded them the prestigious *appellation d'origine contrôlée*, which has previously been reserved for French cheeses and wines. Ask at the tourist office for a list of distilleries that welcome visitors and allow sampling. You'll want to buy your customs-limited number of bottles to take home.

Before you leave the island, spend some time at one or more of the fantastic beaches. White-sand covers the beaches south of Fort-de-France, and the best spots are **Plage des Salines**, which is near the town of Ste-Anne and has tall coconut palms and miles of soft sand, and **Anses d'Arlet** at Le Diamant, which features the often-photographed offshore landmark, **Diamond Rock**. If you want a bit of privacy, try **Cap Chevalier** or **Cap Macré**. While none of the beaches legally allow total nudity, the European custom of topless bathing is not uncommon. The public beaches don't have changing cabins or showers, but day guests are welcome to visit most of the hotels and pay a fee for use of the locker rooms and other beach facilities.

Expect the island to capture your heart, mind and body. If you can't leave, reserve a room at one of the 100 small and medium-sized hotels called *Relais Créoles*. They are scattered all over the island and offer true hospitality and charm. A central reservation service is provided by **Centrale de Reservation**, ☎ 596-61-61-77, www.martiniquetourisme.com.

For more information on Martinique, contact the Martinique Promotion Bureau, ☎ 212-838-7800 (New York) or 0596-61-61-77 (Martinique), www.martinique.org.

Guadeloupe

As with sister island Martinique, you will need a passport, but no visa, to visit this French island. It's shaped like a butterfly, with its wings separated by the sea, **La Rivière Salée**. The east side is called **Grande-Terre** and covers about 360 square miles. Its terrain is mostly flat and dry, but sugar cane thrives in the limestone soil on huge plantations. The west side is larger (528 square miles), wetter and more mountainous, but is called, inexplicably, **Basse-Terre**, low land. Here, the lush plantations grow bananas.

Take a walking tour of the capital, **Pointe-à-Pitre**, to see **Place de la Victoire**, the main

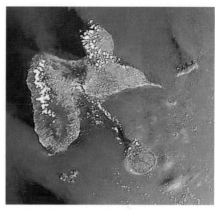
Guadeloupe from space

square surrounded by colonial-style buildings and facing the harbor, **La Darse**. Stop to observe the colorful activity at the **Darse Market**, then move on to **Museum Schoelcher**, a pink and white Colonial-style house that displays exhibits relating to Victor Schoelcher, a Frenchman who instigated the abolition of slavery in the 1800s. If you're literary-minded, stop at the **Museum Saint John Perse**, another lovely Colonial-style building devoted to the life and works of Alexis

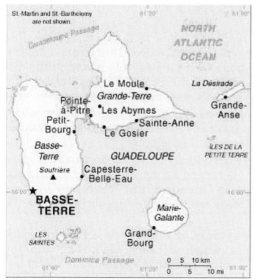
Guadeloupe

Saint-Léger, a poet and diplomat of the 19th century.

Don't miss the aromatic and bustling flower market on **Gourbeyre Square**, which is dominated by **Basilica Saint-Pierre et Saint-Paul**, a cathedral built in Latin-American style with leaded glass windows and a huge organ.

Day-Trips

Pointe-à-Pitre, Guadeloupe

Nearby, you'll find excellent shopping on Frébault, Nozières and Schoelcher streets.

When you're ready to tour more of the island, consider renting a car. Buses do not follow a schedule and taxis are expensive. If you're over 21, you'll need only a valid driver's license and a major credit card to rent a car for about $50 per day. Reserve in advance for the best rates. **Guadeloupe Car Hire** runs a rental quote system that allows you to compare rates (☎ 866-735-1715 in the US, http://guadeloupe.rentalcargroup.com), or call Budget once you're on the island, ☎ 590-21-14-39.

From Pointe-à-Pitre, take the "Riviera" road that leads to many of the hotels. Stop briefly at **Bas-du-Fort** to see **Fort Fleur d'Epée** and ogle the yachts docked at the nearby marina. A bit farther along the highway, look for the **Guadeloupe Aquarium**, which is the fourth-ranked aquarium in all of France and open 9 am-7 pm daily. Admission is about €8.50/$11.

The tourist town of St. François is home to several fine resorts, and just beyond is **Pointe des Châteaux**, a bizarre area of rocky formations with La Désirade island in the distance. The close-by towns of Ste. Anne, St. François and Le Moule have some of island's most beautiful beaches.

Le Moule is also the location for **Musée Edgar Clerc**, which is worth a visit if you have any interest in pre-Columbian civilizations that once lived on Guadeloupe.

Porte d'Enfer (Gate of Hell) is just to the north and offers a must-see view from its ragged shore. An equally worthwhile stop is **La Pointe de la Grande Vigie**, where you'll have a fabulous overlook of stark white cliffs rising abruptly from the ocean.

Get to **Basse-Terre** by crossing the Pont de la Gabare bridge over the Rivière Salée, which will take you directly into the National Park, which covers a fifth of Guadeloupe's total terrain. Don't bypass this park, with its rainforest, waterfalls,

Guadeloupe shoreline

walking paths and the **Parc Zoologique et Botanique**, a zoo and botanical garden.

Later, take the northern route along the butterfly wing to **Compagnie Fermière de Grosse Montagne**, a working sugar factory that has been refurbished into a work of art with oversized machines painted in vibrant colors. Another worthy stop is the **Musée du Rhum**, which has English signs explaining the island's rum-producing history and offers a tasting session.

As you round the island's tip and turn south, you'll pass miles of sandy beaches along the leeward coast. One of the best is **Grande Anse Beach**, but you may want to head for **Malendure Beach**, where you can catch a ride on a glass-bottom boat to **Pigeon Island** and **Cousteau Reserve**, considered one of the best dive spots in the world.

One of Guadeloupe's oldest churches is farther south in the village of Vieux-Habitants, but you may wish to bypass this and go directly to the capital city of Basse-Terre. History buffs will be interested in the 1643 fortification that was once called Fort St. Charles and is now known as **Fort Delgrès**, in memory of Louis Delgrès, an early hero in the movement for the abolition of slavery, who died in 1802. Visit the outdoor market to get a sense of the town, and take a quick look at the

Day-Trips

Colonial architecture of the **Prefecture, Conseil Général**, and **Palais de Justice**.

The dormant volcano, **La Soufrière**, is about seven miles away in the mountaintop suburb of Saint Claude. You can hike to the 4,813-foot summit, where fumaroles and sulfuric vapor create an eerie landscape. A small museum at the lookout point describes the arc of volcanoes that formed the Lesser Antilles.

Stop at the **Centre de Broderie** in Vieux-Fort, to watch lace in the making, on the way to **Trois Rivières** and the famous **Parc des Roches Gravées**, with rock engravings that date back to 300 AD. In the village of Bananier, to the south, notice the islands of Les Saintes just off shore, then turn west to the magnificent waterfalls of **Chutes du Carbet** (the Caribbean's highest) and the **Grand Etang** (Grand Pond).

Guadeloupe is so big and so diverse, you'll want to spend a few days exploring it, so plan to make reservations at one of the world-class resorts, private villas or small inns. Near Ste. Anne, **Club Med La Caravelle** (☎ 888-932-2582, www. clubmed.us) has a great seaside location, and **Hotel Rotabas**, (☎ 590-88-25-60, www.lerotabas.com) offers good rates in nice little bungalows. **French Caribbean International** books a variety of accommodations throughout the island (☎ 800-322-2223 in North America or 805-967-9850, www.frenchcaribbean.com). Also check the online information provided by **Antilles Info Tourisme** (www.antilles-info-tourisme.com/guadeloupe).

Being an authentic department of France, meals are excellent throughout Guadeloupe, even at the beach shacks. People dine late and slow, with a glass of wine in hand. Being a Caribbean island, the food is kicked up a notch with West Indies' spices, and rum plays a part in most pre-dinner happy hours and after-dinner entertainment. The town of St.-Francois has the best and most restaurants, but don't hesitate to order grilled fish at the sand-floored places near the water. In the evening, most of the major hotels serve delicious dishes. If you want a view, try **La Toubana**, on a cliff near Ste. Anne, ☎ 590-88-25-78. For a bit of romance, try **Café Iguana** (☎ 590-88-61-37) in St.-Francois.

For more information about Guadeloupe, contact the Office Départemental du Tourisme, ☎ 590-82-09-30, www.antilles-info-tourisme.com/guadeloupe.

Key Facts & Contacts

Airlines

Air Canada, ☎ 888-247-2262 (US & Canada), 758-454-6038, www.aircanada.ca.

Air Caraibes, ☎ 877-772-1005(US), 758-452-2463 or 758-453-0357, www.air-caraibes-charter.com.

Air Jamaica, ☎ 800-523-5585 (US), 0208-570-7999 (UK), 758-453-6611, www.airjamaica.com.

American, ☎ 800-433-7300 (US), 758-454-6777, www.aa.com.

American Eagle, ☎ 800-433-7300 (US), 758-452-1820, www.aa.com.

British Airways, ☎ 800-247-9297 (US), 0870-850-9850 (UK), 758-452-3951, www.britishairways.com.

Caribbean Airline, (BWIA) ☎ 800-920-4225 (North America), 845-362-4225 (UK), 800-744-2225 (St Lucia), 758-452-3778, www.caribbean-airlines.com.

Continental, ☎ 800-525-0280 (US & Canada), www.continental.com.

Caribbean Star, ☎ 800-744-7827 (Caribbean), 268-461-7827 (Antigua base), 758-452-5898.

Delta Air Lines, ☎ 800-221-1212 (US & Canada), 758-452-9683.

LIAT, ☎ 888-844-5428 (Caribbean), 268-462-0700 (US), 758-452-2348, www.flyliat.com.

Northwest, ☎ 800-225-2525 (US & Canada), www.nwa.com.

United ☎ 800-538-2929 (US & Canada), www.ual.com.

US Airways, ☎ 800-428-4322 (US & Canada), www. usairways.com.

Virgin Atlantic, ☎ 800-744-7477 (Caribbean), 800-821-5438 (US), 0870-380-2007 (UK), 758-454-3610, www.virgin-atlantic.com.

Airports

Hewanorra International Airport, ☎ 758-454-6355

George F. L. Charles (Vigie) Airport, ☎ 758-452-1156 (regional flights)

Anchorages

Customs and immigration can be cleared at Rodney Bay, Castries, Marigot Bay or Vieux Fort. A full-service marina is at Rodney Bay. At Marigot Bay, you must anchor in the harbor and dinghy to the customs office. Boats can also anchor off Reduit Beach, Pigeon Point, Anse Chastanet, Anse Cochon, and Soufrière Bay.

- **Rodney Bay Marina, ☎** 758-452-0324 or 758-452-0235, www.rodneybaymarina.com.
- **Port Castries, ☎** 758-468-4806.
- **Marigot Bay, ☎** 758-458-3318.
- **Soufrière, ☎** 758-459-5656.

Area

238 square miles (27 miles long and 14 miles wide).

ATM Machines

Cash machines are found in shopping centers, hotels, marinas and banks throughout the island.

Banking Hours

Banks open Monday through Thursday, 8 am to 2 pm, and Friday 8 am until 5 pm.

For general banking questions, phone the Bank of St. Lucia on Bridge Street in Castries, ☎ 758-456-6000.

Buses

Public transportation is by privately owned minivans that cover the main routes between the capital of Castries and Gros Islets (route 1A), Soufrière (route 3D), and Vieux Fort (route 2H). The main bus station is behind the Castries market on Jeremie Street.

Capital

Castries

Credit Cards

Visa, MasterCard, and American Express are widely accepted. However, most gas stations and many small restaurants and shops do not accept credit cards.

Currency

The official currency on St. Lucia is the Eastern Caribbean dollar, EC$. One US dollar exchanges for EC$2.67. Many businesses accept US dollars, but you should carry enough EC dollars to cover one day's expenses, especially if you will be traveling outside the main tourist areas.

Departure Tax

St. Lucia's departure tax is US$25/EC $68. Children under 12 are exempt. Plan to have the exact amount when you check in for your return flight, since change may not be available.

Drinking Water

Tap water is safe, but bottled water is readily available. It is not advisable to drink from streams and rivers, no matter how sparkling clean they appear.

Driving

Driving is British-style, on the left. There are paved roads to all the main towns and villages, except in the northeastern part of the island. A four-wheel-drive vehicle is necessary to reach remote areas. Coastal highways are narrow, winding and steep, but in good repair.

Drugs

There are stiff penalties for use, possession, or selling of narcotic drugs.

Electricity

St. Lucia's electricity is 220 volts AC, 50 cycles, with a square three-prong outlet, so you must use a converter and plug adapter for most US appliances. Many hotels have 110-volt outlets in the bathroom for shavers.

Emergency

Fire, police, and ambulance, ☎ 911.

Hospitals

- Victoria Hospital, Castries, ☎ 758-452-2421 (24-hour emergency room).
- St. Jude's, Vieux Fort, ☎ 758-454-6041 (24-hour emergency room).
- Soufrière Hospital, Soufrière, ☎ 758-459-7258.
- Dennery Hospital, Dennery, ☎ 758-453-3310.

Internet Access Locations

Pointe Seraphine in Castries (no phone).

Carib Travel Agency on Micoud Street in Castries, ☎ 758-452-2151, and on Clarke Street in Vieux Fort, ☎ 758-454-6450.

Computer Sales and Tech Service on Chaussée Road in Castries, ☎ 758-458-1908.

Data Dive Internet Café in the Linmore's Building on Coral Street in Castries, ☎ 758-451-8797.

Wegosite Travel and Tours at The Courtyard, Vieux Fort, ☎ 758-454-7722.

Language

The official language is English, but residents speak Creole, a French-based patois among themselves.

Location

St. Lucia is 21 miles south of Martinique and 26 miles north of St. Vincent in the eastern Caribbean. It is between 60° and 61° west longitude, 13° and 14° north latitude.

Political Status

St. Lucia is an independent state within the British Common-wealth. The monarchy is represented by an appointed governor-general, and a prime minister is the effective head of state.

Population

About 160,000 people live on the island, with approximately one-third of the population residing in or near the capital city. Most islanders are of African ancestry.

Shopping Centers

Gablewood Mall, Sunny Acres, Castries, ☎ 758-453-7752.

JQ Charles Mall, Rodney Bay, ☎ 758-458-0700.

La Place Carnage, Jeremie Street, Castries, ☎ 758-452-7318.

Pointe Seraphine, Castries (no phone).

Castries Market, Jeremie Street, Castries (no phone).

Rodney Bay Marina, ☎ 758-452-0324.

Taxes & Tips

An 8% government tax is added to hotel and restaurant bills. Most hotels and restaurants also levy a 10% service charge.

No taxes are charged on items bought in the shops.

Taxis

Taxi Service is abundant on the island. See *Getting Around* in the *Travel Information* section for a listing of taxi companies. Expect to pay about US$8 to go the short distance from Charles Airport to hotels in or near Castries, and approximately US$60 to go from Hewanorra Airport to Castries, a 40-mile, one-hour trip.

The license plate of a legitimate taxi is either blue or red, and contains the letters "TX."

Telephone

The area code for all of St. Lucia is 758. For local calls, dial only the last seven digits of the number. When calling the island from the US, dial 1 + 758 + seven-digit local number. To call the US from St. Lucia, dial 1 + area code + local number. To call the UK from St. Lucia dial 011 + 44 + local number.

Time

The island is on Atlantic Standard Time, which is one hour ahead of Eastern Standard Time and four hours behind Greenwich Mean Time. St. Lucia does not observe Daylight Savings Time. When it is noon in New York during the winter, it is 1 pm on St. Lucia. During the summer, St. Lucia is on the same time as the eastern United States and five hours behind GMT.

Tourist Board Office Locations

Pointe Seraphine and **La Place Carenage** in Castries, ☎ 758-452 7577.

Soufriere, across from the waterfront on the main road, ☎ 758-459-7419.

George F. L. Charles Airport, ☎ 758-452-2596.

Hewanorra International Airport, ☎ 758-454-6644.

In the US

The St. Lucia Tourist Board
800 Second Avenue
Fourth Floor
New York, NY 10017
☎ 800-456-3984, 212-697-9360, www.stlucia.org

In Canada

Tourist Board of St. Lucia
65 Overlea Boulevard, Suite
Toronto, Ontario M4H 1P1
☎ 800-869-0377, 416-362-4242, www.stlucia.org

In the UK

Tourist Board of St. Lucia
1 Collingham Garden
East Court, London SW5 OHW
☎ 207-370-7123

Index